LOVE CRUMBS

*To my family
Jonathan, Ruby and Poppy
for loving me as I am.
I'm so grateful for you.*

LOVE CRUMBS

NADINE INGRAM

With photography by
ALAN BENSON

A JULIE GIBBS BOOK
for

SIMON &
SCHUSTER

FOREWORD
7

INTRODUCTION
9

FOREST 10

BUSH 60

ORCHARD 104

MEADOW 160

SEA 208

TECHNIQUES & GLOSSARY
246

INDEX
265

ACKNOWLEDGEMENTS
270

FOREWORD

I cannot remember if I have ever sat and felt the tears run down my face while reading a cookbook. Tears of loss, tears of joy. Of longing, of lessons learnt. Of realising there is someone else out there who has seen the beauty of the ordinary, felt similar anguishes and slights, to know that through her eyes and words, we are not alone.

Baking is not a ritual that exists to appease oneself. Its nature is to create something that is to be shared, something that represents love, care and solidarity. *Love Crumbs* is something of a rarity in this cluttered world of recipe books. It breaks new ground, as Nadine's use of poetry and prose transform each and every recipe into a sensory experience that begins long before you assemble the ingredients and fossick around in your kitchen for a bowl and wooden spoon.

The recipes themselves speak of love and life. Flavour combinations that range from the familiar and comforting to new, exciting and innovative. The clever notations in many recipes to make cakes of differing sizes and shapes. The excellent glossary of ingredients and terms that have already answered some questions for me. And above all, the kindness with which she writes, noting that some things may be a step too far for some cooks and it's okay if you want to take an easier road.

Like all great books, this book exudes the skill of many. Nadine's work and words are brought to life by an incredibly talented team. The blending of illustration, perfectly styled photography and clever design create a book that you will want to come back to year after year.

As I return to Nadine's words over and again, I feel and know those same pre-dawn hours we have shared in our time in separate kitchens, where sometimes the questions seem bigger and harder than they ought to be. And know that when those challenges arise, to immerse oneself in the time-honoured rituals of creating beautiful things to share, that speak of love for others, can be all the salve one needs.

The true beauty of *Love Crumbs* is that even if you can't find the time to bake, simply by sitting and immersing yourself in Nadine's exquisite turn of phrase your life will be a richer, sweeter place.

ANNIE SMITHERS

INTRODUCTION

My journey through cake has really been an expression of my nature, to reveal to the world who I am. More recently I've started to explore the sensory parts of nature that spark my creativity and the way I bake. Perfume, spice and fruit are at the forefront of these adventures and it seems to me that these are also the things that attract us to one another. We so often marvel at the beauty of nature, yet we are becoming so disconnected from it.

Writing this book has given me an opportunity to rekindle my own experiences of life through the love crumbs of my creativity and has encouraged me to celebrate the nature of our humanity through the medium of cake. These are cakes that are steeped in nature and connected to the conversations we all face each day. Cakes that reflect the very real, courageous journeys we all make through life.

Each recipe is introduced through love letters, prayers, music, myths and fables to create a meaningful memoir of cake.

The chapters FOREST, BUSH, ORCHARD, MEADOW and SEA are inspired by where things grow and are a metaphor for our own nature. Each cake finds its own place through its story or ingredients, and some belong on thresholds in between. I wanted to honour the botanicals that are imbued into our spirit and stories throughout these pages. The forgotten fruits like quince and medlar, the Australian bush botanicals such as cinnamon myrtle that are so common but rarely get used, as well as the sacred fruits like quandong and yuzu that we should all worship at the altar of our cooking.

It's with the utmost integrity that I want to honour and document my journey in bringing sweetness into people's lives through the love crumbs of cake.

MR & MRS
Manjari chocolate. Hazelnuts. Blackberries.
15

FIRST DATE TIRAMISU
Coffee. Mascarpone. Chocolate sponge. Cocoa nibs.
21

WORKADAY MALT LOAF
Malt. Emmer wheat. Treacle.
25

CAKE FOR OUR WILDERNESS
Almonds. Cinnamon. Cocoa nibs. Vegan.
27

CHESTNUT TORTE
Chestnuts. Pine nuts. Chocolate.
31

ENCHANTED ALMOND TREE
Chocolate. Almonds. Amaretto.
35

CAKE FOR JANE & JEREMY STRODE
Walnuts. Maple. Rye.
41

GINGERBREAD HUG
Ginger. Fennel. Dill.
45

HANSEL & GRETEL
Brambles. Gingerbread. Brown butter breadcrumbs.
49

MY CHRISTMAS PUDDING
Mandarin. Dark chocolate. Pedro Ximénez.
52

THE FABLE OF THE WOLVES
Rhubarb. Oatmeal. Ginger.
57

FOREST

When night falls in the forest and the woodland silhouettes appear as etchings against the twilight, a chorus of starlings trill, inviting me into their orchestra. Gradually all the other creatures emerge, even the shy ones covered by rocks and the forest is ablaze with my tribe.

In complete and utter solidarity, the cakes in this chapter are here to tell you – you are not alone.

The botanicals I've chosen for these cakes and the stories entwined amongst them express my experience of marriage, friendships and community.

This chapter is peppered with all the love and loneliness of relationships and charts our voyage to bring meaning to our lives and those we choose to share them with.

The textures and flavours of these wanderings are founded in the bark of cocoa nibs, the smokiness of chestnuts and the fruit of chocolate, for heart opening and endurance.

Along the path there are thorny brambles and devilish berries, along with blackberries for good fortune and wisdom.

Enchanted almond tree hollows for us to rest.

Rhubarb baked into a Yorkshire parkin for my friend JC. In the Yorkshire triangle, rhubarb is harvested by candlelight so I thought it belonged in a cake traditionally eaten by firelight for Guy Fawkes night.

Wattle seeds to renew, cottages of gingerbread for refuge and a clearing in the wilderness for us all to gather and share in my forest of cakes.

MR & MRS
Manjari chocolate. Hazelnuts. Blackberries.

Forest wanderings amongst the textures of a marriage.
When you let someone see the real you and they love you for it.

(The day before)

BLACKBERRY COMPOTE

1. Place the berries, sugar and orange zest in a heatproof bowl, then toss to combine and cover tightly with plastic film. Place the bowl over a saucepan of barely simmering water for 20 minutes, so the blackberries can steam, then turn the heat off and allow the berries to cool in the syrup over the saucepan. The blackberries can be poached in advance and kept in the fridge for around 1 week.

HAZELNUT DACQUOISE

1. This cake has five layers of dacquoise, which are shaped free-form onto baking paper. Follow the 'how to shimmy with sponge' method on page 256 to shape the sponges, beginning by preparing the baking paper circles needed for the layers of dacquoise. You will need five 20 cm | 25cm circles and as many trays. Preheat the oven to 175°C.

2. Place the hazelnuts in a food processor and grind until you achieve a combination of fine crumbs mixed with more coarse pieces for crunch. This is best done using the pulse function, so the hazelnuts grind evenly and don't turn into a paste. Remove the hazelnut from the food processor and set aside.

3. Place the egg whites and salt in the bowl of an electric mixer fitted with the whisk attachment and whip on high speed until soft ribbons start to form, then reduce the speed to medium. Gradually add the icing sugar, 1 tablespoon at a time, waiting 5 seconds between each addition, until all the icing sugar is incorporated. Continue to whip until firm-peak stage when the meringue will be thick and glossy, then beat the meringue for a further 2 minutes to ensure it is stable. Remove the bowl from the mixer and gently fold through the hazelnuts and vanilla until they are nicely incorporated.

4. Divide the dacquoise evenly between the five circles you have prepared by following the shimmy method. You can use a scale to weigh each one, so you know they're all exactly the same, or just estimate, then use an offset palette knife to smooth and level each meringue layer. Bake the dacquoise for 25 minutes or until the top is crisp and golden, then remove from the oven and cool the layers on their tins.

CHOCOLATE MOUSSE

1. Place the chocolate and butter in a large heatproof bowl. Eventually all the ingredients for the mousse will be folded together in this bowl, so choose it accordingly. Place the bowl over a saucepan of barely simmering water. Once the chocolate and butter have melted, turn the heat off, allowing the bowl to remain on top of the saucepan to maintain the heat while you get on with making the whipped eggs and sugar (sabayon).

(cont.)

SIZE	20cm	25cm
SERVES	12-25	15-20
BLACKBERRY COMPOTE		
fresh or frozen blackberries	400g	480g
caster sugar	80g	100g
orange, zested	1	1
HAZELNUT DACQUOISE		
whole hazelnuts, blanched and peeled	250g	300g
egg whites	160g (approx 6 eggs)	190g (approx 7 eggs)
pinch of salt		
icing sugar, sifted	230g	280g
vanilla	1 tsp	1 tsp
CHOCOLATE MOUSSE		
Valrhona Manjari chocolate or dark chocolate (minimum 64% cocoa solids)	165g	220g
unsalted butter	25g	55g
eggs	3	4
caster sugar	130g	150g
water	40ml	45ml
double cream	165g	200g
pure cream	165g	200g
sea salt	¼ tsp	(pinch)
CHOCOLATE FOREST TEXTURES		
dark chocolate block (minimum 60% cocoa solids)	200g	250g
cocoa nibs	20g	30g
GANACHE		
dark chocolate (minimum 66% cocoa solids)	100g	120g
pure cream	100g	120g

2 Prepare for whipping the eggs by cracking them into the bowl of an electric mixer fitted with the whisk attachment, but don't start whipping until I give you the go ahead.

3 Have a sugar thermometer ready, then combine the sugar and water in a small saucepan over low heat, stirring until the sugar is dissolved. If you can see sugar crystals forming up the sides of the pan, dip a pastry brush in water and sweep it around the inside of the saucepan, so the crystals fall back into the syrup. This will prevent the sugar from crystallising. When the sugar comes to the boil, increase the heat to medium and, immediately after that, start whipping the eggs on high speed. It will only take a couple of minutes for the temperature of the sugar syrup to reach 120°C, once it does, remove the saucepan from the heat.

4 By this stage the eggs should be fluffy and tripled in volume. Reduce the speed to medium and trickle the syrup into the eggs at that space between the side of the bowl and the whisk. You might get a few splatters if the sugar meets with the whisk, but this is nothing to worry about. Once all the sugar has been added, continue to whip the sabayon for 5 minutes or until cool, then remove it from the mixer.

5 Using a hand whisk, whisk the creams together until they are softly whipped to the same consistency as the sabayon. It's important not to overwhip the cream, as this will make folding it through the softer ingredients more difficult – more folding means less air in the mousse and I know you want to avoid that! Remove the bowl of chocolate from the saucepan, then add the salt and give it a bit of a mix using a spatula. Fold one-third of the sabayon into the chocolate until you can't see any streaks, making sure you are scraping all the way to the bottom of the bowl with the spatula to incorporate any chocolate at the bottom into the mousse. Fold through the remaining sabayon, one-third at a time, then finally fold through the cream gently. Set the mousse aside at room temperature for now.

TO MOULD THE CAKE

1 Line a 20 cm | 25 cm round cake tin with baking paper. This tin will be what you use to set the layers of dacquoise and mousse in overnight. To make removing the cake from the tin easier the next day, I recommend cutting two 5 cm x 40 cm strips of baking paper to line the base of the tin. Lay them over one another to from a cross in the centre of the tin, then run the strips up the sides and let them fall over the rim. Then line the tin as you usually do. Alternatively, you could line the inside of the tin with plastic film, making sure the plastic is snugly pressed into the tin groove, so you have a sharp-looking cake.

2 Peel the baking paper from the dacquoise layers and place one layer into the base of the prepared cake tin. If the dacquoise layer doesn't quite fit, use a sharp paring knife or a pair of scissors to shave off a little from the circumference. Spoon one-quarter of the chocolate mousse over the dacquoise and spread it to the edges using a small offset palette knife.

3 Drain the juices from the blackberry compote, so you are left with just the whole fruit, then spoon one-quarter of the blackberries evenly over the mousse. Add another layer of dacquoise, then mousse and berries until you reach the top of the cake tin, finishing with a final layer of dacquoise. Cover the cake with some baking paper and place it in the fridge overnight to set.

(The day before)

CHOCOLATE FOREST TEXTURES

1. Grate 50 g off the side of the chocolate block using a microplane or the medium-coarse side of a box grater. You won't be able to achieve this with chocolate buttons or feves, because you'll probably grate your fingers. Admittedly, that hasn't stopped me from trying over the years! Refrigerate the grated chocolate for now.

2. To make the chocolate curls, it's best to temper the chocolate to give it better snap, shine and overall stability. You will need a digital thermometer for this and to know that it works before proceeding, as often the batteries go flat once you start melting the chocolate, putting you in a precarious position.

3. Chocolate tempering is nothing to get nervous about and it really takes very little time. Essentially, tempering is the same as any other union or relationship built within baking. In this case, it's the creation of a crystal structure within the chocolate by means of raising the temperature to collapse the six different kinds of crystals, then lowering the temperature to rebuild the structure of just one of those crystals (leaving the others behind). The method I like best for achieving this is called 'seeding'.

4. Prepare a baking tray by upturning it onto your bench or, if you have marble in your kitchen, clear a space to spread the chocolate over it. The marble will regulate (temper) the temperature of the chocolate quickly, ensuring it sets evenly. For either surface, make sure they are very clean and dry.

5. Roughly chop the remaining chocolate block that you used for grating and place two-thirds of it into a heatproof bowl over a pan of barely simmering water, making sure the water doesn't touch the bottom of the bowl. Keep the remaining one-third of the chocolate close by. Stir the chocolate every 30 seconds to distribute the heat and ensure you're not overheating it, until the temperature reaches 45°C, then remove it from the saucepan. At this stage, all the different crystals in the chocolate are collapsed in structure. The most desirable crystal (the one that gives the chocolate shine and snap) is called 'beta'. To make this crystal rise above all the others, you need to create a chain by lowering the chocolate's temperature. The chain is initiated by adding the final one-third of the chopped chocolate (the seed) to give the crystals something to grab onto in order to begin the links of the chain.

6. I like to have the remaining one-third of chocolate chopped a bit finer, which helps it to melt easier so you aren't left with unmelted bits of chocolate hindering the process. Now add the remaining chocolate, stirring constantly and agitating the chocolate to cool it until the temperature reaches 27°C. This is the stage where the beta crystals are most happy. The chocolate will be quite thick now and you will just need to warm it slightly over the water bath to 32°C to make it more workable. Do so by flashing the bowl over the heat for a short period of time until this temperature is reached, then remove the bowl from the heat. Use a tea towel to wipe the condensation from the bottom of the bowl quickly, so it doesn't splash into the chocolate or land on any surface you are just about to pour it onto. This would cause the chocolate to seize.

7. Pour the chocolate onto the prepared surface and use an offset palette knife to spread the chocolate out to 2 mm-thick. The chocolate should take between 3–5 minutes to set and, during this time, you should have a dough cutter, palette knife or sharp scraper ready to make the chocolate curls. The chocolate needs to be a little under-set to form the perfect curl. *(cont.)*

Before you begin, secure the tray so it doesn't slide along the bench. Test the edge of the chocolate by angling the scraper or knife at a 45-degree angle and pushing away from your body to form the curl. Make the curls all different shapes, as they would appear in nature, then keep them in the fridge in an airtight container until you are ready to use them.

GANACHE

1 Roughly chop the chocolate into small pieces and place in a bowl beside the stove. Pour the cream into a small saucepan and bring to the boil over medium heat, then pour the cream over the chocolate and stir to combine until smooth and all the chocolate has melted. Allow the ganache to cool at room temperature. Ideally, you want the ganache to set to a firm consistency that can be smoothed over the cake in a controlled fashion – like the consistency of soft butter – as opposed to being very runny and drizzly, which can result in the cake not being covered with a thick enough layer. Trust me when I say waiting until it reaches the right consistency will save you time masking and re-masking a thinly veiled cake.

TO ASSEMBLE

1 Remove the cake from the fridge and lever it out of the tin by pulling the strips of baking paper up and out. Peel away all the paper and place the cake onto the serving platter, then use a small offset palette knife to coat the top and sides of the cake with the ganache. While it's still wet, cover the surface with the grated chocolate and cocoa nibs, then arrange the curls as you wish. I always try to imagine this cake sitting on the forest floor. (*end*.)

> **NOTE.**
> If you want to be economical with your chocolate purchasing, make the chocolate forest textures first, then recycle leftover chocolate into the mousse and ganache. Tempering chocolate requires a minimum amount due to the seeding process, but everything that is left over can be used again. Alternatively, this cake is full of texture, so if you didn't want to temper chocolate, you could simply coat it with grated chocolate and cocoa nibs instead.

FIRST DATE TIRAMISU
Coffee. Mascarpone. Chocolate sponge. Cocoa nibs.

Heart, heart, do you remember when our eyes met across a pan of artichoke petals
Do you remember when you realised in that moment he was the one
Unfurling the layers of verdant leaves between our fingertips,
like the pages of a love story that had already been written.

Heart, heart, do you remember his tender invitation
Do you remember this first dawn of your last romance,
When the sun rose over our plates of velvety tiramisu
and the lifelong affair that came next?

SIZE	20cm	25cm
SERVES	12-25	15-20
PASTRY CREAM		
milk	250ml	280ml
egg yolks	3	4
caster sugar	50g	55g
plain flour	20g	25g
FRENCH FLOURLESS CHOCOLATE SPONGE		
egg yolks	3	4
icing sugar	170g	220g
egg whites	4	5
cocoa powder, sifted	70g	90g
SPONGE FINGERS		
eggs		3
caster sugar, plus extra 1 tbsp for sprinkling		100g
00 flour or plain flour		125g
icing sugar, for dusting		
MASCARPONE CUSTARD		
mascarpone	400g	500g
pure cream	200g	250g
1 x quantity pastry cream (from left)		
marsala	30ml	50ml
TO ASSEMBLE		
espresso, cooled	180ml	240ml
marsala	50ml	75ml
coffee liqueur (such as Tia Maria or Kahlua)	100ml	150ml
grated dark chocolate	60g	60g
cocoa nibs	30g	30g

PASTRY CREAM

1. You'll need to make the pastry cream at least 4 hours prior to using it, so it has time to cool. Pour the milk into a saucepan and bring to the boil over medium heat. Meanwhile, whisk the egg yolks and sugar until pale, then add the flour and whisk until well combined. When the milk comes to the boil, reduce the heat to low. Remove half the milk from the pan and pour it over the egg yolk mixture. This warms it a little in preparation for being added to the scalding milk. Give the yolk mixture a quick whisk, then pour it into the boiled milk (still over low heat), ensuring you scrape all the yolks from the bowl with a spatula. Stir with a wooden spoon or heatproof spatula for 2 minutes or until the cream starts to thicken. As soon as it does, swap your spoon for a whisk and continue to cook the pastry cream for a further 1 minute to ensure the flour is completely cooked. Remove from the heat and spread the cream out on a shallow tray. Cover with plastic film and refrigerate until cold.

FRENCH FLOURLESS CHOCOLATE SPONGE

1. Preheat the oven to 150°C. Prepare 2 x 20 cm | 2 x 25 cm round cake tins by lining the base only with baking paper.

2. Place the egg yolks and half the icing sugar in the bowl of an electric mixer fitted with the whisk attachment and whip on medium-high speed for 10 minutes or until they have doubled in volume and become pale and fluffy. Decant them into a medium bowl and thoroughly clean and dry the mixer bowl.

3. Add the egg whites to the clean mixer bowl and whip until soft peaks form, then gradually add the remaining icing sugar, little by little, continuing to whip until stiff peaks form. Gently fold one-third of the cocoa through the egg yolks, then fold through one-third of the whipped meringue. Continue to alternate the cocoa and meringue, folding carefully until the batter is smooth. A few streaks remaining is OK; it is preferable not to fold the batter too many times.

4. Divide the batter evenly between the prepared cake tins and gently level the top using a palette knife. Place the sponges in the oven without delay and bake for 12 minutes | 15 minutes or until the top is still soft but has a little resistance when pressed with your finger. Remove the sponges from the oven and leave to cool completely in the tins while you make the sponge fingers. (*cont.*)

SPONGE FINGERS

1. Preheat the oven to 170°C. Line 2 large baking trays with baking paper and fit a piping bag with a #11 plain nozzle.

2. Place the eggs and caster sugar in a heatproof bowl (preferably the bowl of an electric mixer) and give them an initial whisk with a hand whisk. Place the bowl over a saucepan of barely simmering water and continue to whisk the eggs every now and then until they become almost too hot to touch (50°C). It's not necessary to whisk them with any volume in mind, you just need to keep the heat circulating evenly so they don't scramble. Remove the eggs from the heat and place in the electric mixer fitted with the whisk attachment, then whip on high speed for 5 minutes or until pale, fluffy and cooled completely.

3. Remove the bowl from the mixer and sift the flour directly into the egg mixture (sabayon) in two batches, folding gently between each addition so as to preserve as much air as possible in the eggs. Fill the piping bag with the batter and pipe into 12 cm-long sponge fingers, spacing them 3 cm apart on the prepared trays. Dust the sponge fingers lightly with icing sugar, then once the icing sugar has dissolved into the sponge fingers, dust them again and allow the sugar to dissolve once more. Finally sprinkle each sponge finger with the extra caster sugar and bake for 12–15 minutes or until golden around the edges and crisp on top. Remove from the oven and allow to cool on the trays.

MASCARPONE CUSTARD

1. Whip the mascarpone and cream together using a whisk until it is very firm, pushing it to the point where it is about to over-whip, but stopping just before it does.

2. Place the pastry cream in a separate bowl and notice firstly that it has moulded into the shape of the tray you spread it onto when it was hot. Instead of mixing or whipping the pastry cream, use a spatula to gently press it to make it smooth. I can't emphasis enough how important it is that you don't start mixing it or whisking it, as this will soften the pastry cream, making it runny and the consistency of the cream will be lost. As you press the cream with your spatula it will start to become smooth; this is all that is needed. Add one-third of the whipped cream and press it through until smooth. Fold through the rest of the cream in two batches to preserve the thickness of the custard, then finally fold through the marsala gently until combined.

TO ASSEMBLE

1. Combine the coffee, marsala and liqueur in a flat dish with deep sides, ensuring the liquid is cold or the sponge fingers will become very soft and dissolve while you're handling them. Soak three sponge fingers at a time in the coffee, then arrange to cover the base of a large glass trifle dish or ceramic bowl. Cover the sponge fingers with one-third of the mascarpone custard, then place a layer of chocolate sponge on top. Brush the sponge with a little of the soaking liqueur then top with another one-third of the cream. Repeat the layers, finishing with a layer of cream. Grate chocolate over the top and sprinkle with cocoa nibs.

2. Refrigerate for a minimum of 2 hours or overnight to allow all the coffee layers to mingle. (*end*.)

> **NOTE.**
> This tiramisu has thin layers of chocolate sponge in it, which is non-negotiable in my mind. However, making the sponge fingers can be swapped for store-bought ones to save time.

WORKADAY MALT LOAF
Malt. Emmer wheat. Treacle.

For those whose work becomes a fortress.
A refuge from the loneliness between lost and found
and a disappearance through the graft
of building yourself into someone.

(The day before)

1. Take two small bowls, place the prunes and the sour cherries in one bowl, and the dates and raisins in the other. Pour 150 ml hot, strong black tea into each bowl and soak the fruit overnight.

(On the day)

1. Preheat the oven to 175°C. Line a 10 cm x 25 cm x 7 cm-deep loaf tin with baking paper. Place the prunes and sour cherries in a food processor together with any tea that hasn't been absorbed and purée, leaving a little texture so the mixture isn't completely smooth.

2. Place the dates, raisins and any tea that hasn't been absorbed in a small saucepan with the water and bring to the boil. Simmer for 1 minute, then add the bicarbonate of soda and mix well so that the mixture foams up momentarily. Turn off the heat and set the fruit aside to cool a little.

3. Combine the malt extract, treacle and sugars in a saucepan over medium heat and stir using a heatproof spatula to dissolve the sugar. This step can be ambiguous as the malt doesn't become transparent and the mixture remains quite opaque and grainy, but if you stir for 1 minute after the syrup starts to simmer this will be adequate. Turn off the heat and leave the syrup to cool for 15 minutes.

4. Sift the flour, salt and baking powder into a large bowl and return any salt flakes and bran back into the flour. This process is only to remove baking powder or flour lumps, so just press any of those through and carry on. Make a well in the centre of the flour and pour in all the malt syrup, making sure to scrape the bottom of the saucepan thoroughly with a spatula to remove all of it. Add the fruit and purée and crack the eggs in there, too. Whisk everything together gently to incorporate the mix into a sticky, thick batter that seems to stand upright, then pour it into the prepared loaf tin and smooth the top using a spoon or an offset palette knife.

5. Bake the loaf for 30 minutes, then reduce the oven temperature to 170°C and bake for a further 20 minutes. To test the loaf is ready, insert a skewer and look for a little bit of stickiness remaining. Remove from the oven and lift the loaf out of the tin to cool on a wire rack.

6. Serve slathered with cultured butter. You can wrap the loaf in baking paper and keep it at room temperature to mature over the coarse of the week, if it lasts that long! (*end.*)

LOAF TIN SIZE	10cm x 25cm x 7cm-deep
SERVES	12-15
prunes, pitted	100g
dried sour cherries	50g
fresh dates, pitted and roughly chopped	50g
raisins	100g
strong black tea	300ml
water	50ml
bicarbonate of soda	¼ tsp
malt extract	150g
treacle	50g
dark brown sugar	75g
Demerara sugar	25g
emmer wheat flour (*see glossary*) or plain flour	225g
sea salt	pinch
baking powder	1 tsp
eggs	3
cultured butter, to serve	

CAKE FOR OUR WILDERNESS
Almonds. Cinnamon. Cocoa nibs. Vegan.

There is a place where we all meet in our wilderness
amongst the tender roots of our belonging to one another.

Where our paths might cross now and then
and we walk a little while together.

The journey of friends through coppice, ravine and swamp
through the wilderness where we find ourselves in each other.

ALMOND AND COCOA NIB PRALINE CRUST

1. Firstly, prepare a baking tray for the praline by lining with baking paper and spraying or brushing the paper with oil. This will prevent your finished praline from sticking. To toast the almonds, scatter them evenly onto a baking tray and pop them in the oven at 150°C for 15 minutes to release their nutty aroma.

2. While the almonds are cooling, make the praline by combining the sugar and water in a small saucepan over low heat. Using a heatproof spatula, stir to dissolve the sugar and use a pastry brush dipped in water to brush any sugar crystals down from the sides of the pan. Removing these now will prevent the praline from crystallising. Once the sugar starts to boil, stop stirring and increase the heat to medium, then continue to boil the caramel for around 5 minutes or until the colour turns pale amber. Quickly add the 100 g toasted almonds to the caramel and use a wooden spoon to stir until the almonds are coated, then pour the praline into the prepared tray to cool completely.

3. Once the praline is cool, place in a food processor and blitz to form a fine crumb. Decant into a bowl, add the cocoa nibs and mix until well combined.

4. Use a pastry brush to generously grease the insides of the bundt tin with vegan margarine, taking care to reach any fine detail of the tin. Pour in the almond and cocoa nib praline and roll it around to ensure it sticks to the margarine and thoroughly coats the inside of the tin. Use your hands to coax the praline into any hard-to-reach places, then place the tin in the freezer (or if there's no space, the fridge).

(cont.)

BUNDT	25cm x 7cm
SERVES	10-12

ALMOND AND COCOA NIB PRALINE CRUST	
spray oil (recommended)	220g
natural almonds, toasted (SEE NOTE)	100g
caster sugar	120g
water	1 tbsp
cocoa nibs	120g
vegan margarine	100g

CAKE	
natural almonds, toasted (SEE NOTE)	200g
plain flour	200g
caster sugar	375g
cocoa powder	150g
cinnamon	1 tsp
baking powder	2 tsp
oat or almond milk	460ml
orange, zested	1

CAKE

1. Preheat the oven to 160°C. Place the almonds in a food processor and blitz to a fine crumb, similar to breadcrumbs. The pulse function may be needed here for an even consistency, although, a slight variation in texture is fine.

2. Place the flour, sugar, cocoa, cinnamon and baking powder in a large bowl and use a whisk to combine everything together. Make a well in the centre, add the oat or almond milk and orange zest, then whisk together until a smooth batter forms.

3. Remove the bundt tin from the freezer or fridge and give the inside a light spray with oil (if you have some). This is one final insurance policy against the cake sticking. Pour the batter into the tin and smooth the top using a spoon. Bake for 35 minutes, then reduce the oven temperature to 150°C and bake for a further 20 minutes. Test for readiness using the blade of a thin, sharp knife as this will allow you to see a larger test area than a skewer, since you want the cake to be slightly fudgy in the centre. When ready, remove the cake from the oven and allow to cool for only 10 minutes before inverting onto a cooling rack. Lift and remove the tin to reveal the glistening crust. If you leave it any longer, you risk the cake sticking as the praline and cocoa nib crust cools.

4. This cake needs no icing and keeps well at room temperature for 4–5 days. (*end.*)

> NOTE.
> There are two quantities of natural almonds in this recipe. These are the ones with the skin still on. It's worth noting, they can be toasted together and then separated later to save you toasting twice. Also, the almonds for the cake can be processed straight after the praline without having to wash the food processor in between.

CHESTNUT TORTE
Chestnuts. Pine nuts. Chocolate.

In London in winter, I would disappear into the basement kitchen of Le Gavroche before dawn. The pheasants hanging above the chopping block would be the first thing to greet me. In the morning and for the whole season, I would be captivated by the ingredients we would cook with.

I had never seen chestnuts before and remember watching like a wide-eyed child as they were roasted and shelled. Mainly, though, they remind me of a time in my life when the Christmas angel on Regent Street, and the chestnut vendor who stood in the shadow of her wingspan, were a guiding presence in the bleakness of a British winter.

Sometimes community can be just two people.

1. Preheat the oven to 140°C. Line a 20 cm | 25 cm cake tin with baking paper.
2. Place the chestnuts in the bowl of a food processor and blend until they resemble coarse breadcrumbs. Tip the chestnut crumbs into a bowl, then add the pine nuts to the food processor and blitz to the same size. Add the pine nut crumbs to the chestnut and give them a little mix with a spoon to distribute them evenly.
3. Melt the chocolate and butter in a large heatproof bowl over a saucepan of barely simmering water, ensuring that the base of the bowl doesn't touch the water. Meanwhile, place the egg whites in the bowl of an electric mixer fitted with the whisk attachment and whip on high speed until soft ribbons form. Reduce the speed to medium and gradually add the caster sugar, 1 tablespoon at a time, leaving 5 seconds between each addition. When the meringue is glossy with firm peaks, reduce the speed to low and trickle in the egg yolks, then mix for a further 5 seconds before removing the bowl from the stand.
4. Remove the chocolate from the heat, add the brown sugar and mix through using a spatula until it's dissolved, then add the nut crumbs and stir thoroughly to combine. Fold the whipped eggs gently through the chocolate mixture, one-third at a time, then fold in the marsala. When there are no streaks of either egg or chocolate remaining, pour the batter into the prepared cake tin and smooth the top using an offset palette knife. Sprinkle the top with cocoa nibs to completely cover the surface, adding the desired amount of smoked salt to finish.

(cont.)

SIZE	20cm	25cm
SERVES	10-12	12-15
chestnuts, cooked and peeled (SEE NOTE)	250g	300g
pine nuts, toasted	100g	120g
dark chocolate (minimum 66% cocoa solids)	170g	210g
unsalted butter	170g	210g
eggs, separated	4	5
caster sugar	80g	100g
brown sugar	70g	85g
marsala	30ml	40ml
cocoa nibs	60g	80g
smoked salt	¼ tsp	½ tsp
double cream, to serve (optional)		

5   Bake the cake for 45 minutes. Test for readiness by pressing the centre of the cake with your finger. A gentle bounce back is what you're looking for here, as it's good to leave the centre of the cake slightly undercooked. Turn the oven off and leave the cake to cool in the oven with the door slightly ajar for 30 minutes. If your oven door doesn't stay open on its own, just wedge a wooden spoon into the door to allow the heat to escape.

6   Remove the cake from the oven and allow it to cool for a further 30 minutes before releasing from the tin.

7   If you haven't used a springform tin, place a plate face-down on top of the cake and invert it onto the plate, then flip it back onto a serving platter. Lashings of double cream as an accompaniment is what's needed here. (*end.*)

> NOTE.
>
> If you are lucky enough to find fresh chestnuts and would like to roast them yourself, use a sharp paring knife to score an X on the bottom of each chestnut. This is so the nut can stretch out of the skin when it is roasting without exploding. Scatter the chestnuts onto a baking tray and roast in a 190°C oven for approximately 20 minutes or until the flesh appears to be emerging from the shells. Remove the nuts from the oven and wrap in a tea towel. Let them sit for a few minutes to allow the skins to steam a little, then massage the nuts through the tea towel to loosen the skins. Unwrap the chestnuts and peel the shells and skin away. The chestnuts are now ready to use.

ENCHANTED ALMOND TREE
Chocolate. Almonds. Amaretto.

Almond tree hollows that lure me to rest where the amaretto air is drunk.
Beckoned into a deep kind of silence to become reacquainted with myself.
Each breath closer to rekindling my creativity
through layers of toasted meringue and scorched nuts.

SIZE	20cm	25cm
SERVES	10-12	12-15

ALMOND PRALINE AND PASTE		
natural almonds, roasted	80g	100g
caster sugar	80g	150g

ALMOND CUSTARD		
egg yolks	3	4
caster sugar	60g	80g
double cream	125g	150g
pure cream	125g	150g
vanilla paste	1tsp	1tsp
almond paste (from above)	80g	100g
mascarpone	250g	300g

FRENCH FLOURLESS CHOCOLATE SPONGE		
egg yolks	6	7
icing sugar, sifted	220g	275g
egg whites	7	8
salt	pinch	pinch
cocoa powder, sifted	90g	110g

ALMOND ROCHER		
flaked almonds	200g	260g
egg whites	5	6
salt	pinch	pinch
icing sugar, sifted	200g	260g
vanilla paste	¾ tsp	1 tsp

CHOCOLATE GANACHE		
dark chocolate, roughly chopped, or buttons	100g	150g
pure cream	100g	150g

ALMOND PRALINE AND PASTE

1 Line a tray with baking paper and set it aside. Place the almonds and caster sugar in a frying pan or medium-based saucepan and toss together to combine, then place over medium heat, ensuring that if you are using gas, the flames aren't licking up the edges of the pan. Shake the almonds occasionally and when you start to see the sugar turn glassy and melt around the outside, use a wooden spoon to gently stir the nuts every so often to distribute the melting sugar. Eventually, the sugar will start to caramelise, sending little plumes of caramelised sugar into the air. If you feel it's happening too quickly, just remove the pan from the heat and stir the almonds off the heat, calmly returning back to the heat until all the sugar has dissolved and there is a golden caramelised coating on the almonds. Turn the heat off and scatter the almonds onto the prepared tray. If you can, separate the almonds by using the tip of your wooden spoon to flick them apart, so that you have individual almonds to decorate the top of the cake. Allow the praline to cool completely.

2 Once cooled, crush half the praline into a paste using a pestle and mortar or place it in a plastic bag and smash using a rolling pin until as fine as possible. For this application, choose the almonds that are clumped together and save the singular ones for the top decoration. The paste you make by crushing the almonds will be used to make the custard. The remaining almonds can be cut in half lengthways using a very sharp knife and set aside to decorate the cake later. (*cont.*)

ALMOND CUSTARD

1. Whisk the egg yolks and sugar together using a hand whisk until they are pale and thick.

2. Place the creams and vanilla in a saucepan over medium heat and bring to the boil, then reduce the heat to low, pour one-third of the cream over the top of the yolks and whisk until combined. This will temper the yolks in preparation for going back into the hot cream. Return the yolk mixture to the saucepan of cream and stir over low heat using a heatproof spatula or wooden spoon until the custard thickens. Do not use a whisk, as this will introduce too much air into the custard, which will cool it down and prevent it from setting. Just stir slowly and calmly, maintaining contact with the base of the saucepan to prevent the custard from catching. The custard will be ready when it coats the back of the spatula without running off. This process will take about 2–3 minutes, but if you feel it's all happening too fast and the custard is becoming too hot and starting to bubble, remove the saucepan from the heat and continue to stir off the heat. To achieve a really thick custard you can 'purge' the custard by moving it on and off the heat to continue the cooking process without boiling it. The difference between a thick and thinner custard will change the consistency of the overall filling of the cake. Both are lovely in their own way. Remove the custard from the heat and thoroughly whisk through the almond paste. Pour the custard into a bowl and cover with plastic film, pressing it directly onto the surface of the custard to prevent a skin from forming. Cool the custard in the fridge overnight or for a minimum of 4 hours.

FRENCH FLOURLESS CHOCOLATE SPONGE

1. Preheat the oven to 150°C. Line 2 x 20 cm | 2 x 25 cm cake tins with baking paper in the base only. The sides don't need lining.

2. Place the egg yolks and half the icing sugar in the bowl of an electric mixer fitted with the whisk attachment and whip until pale and thick. This method is called 'sabayon' in French, which is a term used to describe eggs and sugar whipped together. Historically, it comes from the Italian 'zabaglione' with the addition of wine.

3. Decant the sabayon into a larger bowl, so you can use the electric mixer bowl to whip the whites. Ensure the bowl is clean and dry and place the whites and salt in the bowl fitted with the whisk attachment, then whip on high speed until soft ribbons form. Reduce the speed to medium and gradually add the remaining icing sugar, 1 tablespoon at a time. Continue to whip the meringue until firm peaks form, but don't overbeat.

4. Using a spatula, fold the meringue into the sabayon one-third at a time, alternating with the cocoa, also one-third at a time. I like to sift the cocoa over the surface of the sabayon again as I fold it through to prevent any lumps finding their way into the sponge. Be gentle as you fold and don't be too obsessed with folding every last streak of meringue through in the first two additions. By the time you reach the final addition of meringue, you will have folded the batter so much that the initial two batches will be well combined. The most important thing here is that any meringue lumps are flattened out before you fold them through the sponge. These may start to form as the meringue sits dormant in the stand mixer bowl. To prevent this, use a spatula to first smooth them over the surface of the sponge before actually folding them through. Trying to remove a lump of meringue from the sponge after its folded through will result in over-working the batter. If you can see lumps, use a whisk in a folding motion to remove them.

5   Pour the sponge into the prepared cake tins and smooth the surface gently with an offset palette knife. Bake for 15–18 minutes. The sponge is ready when the middle bounces back when pressed with your finger. Remove the sponges from the oven and allow to cool in the tins.

ALMOND ROCHER

1   Preheat the oven to 160°C. Line the base and sides of 2 x 20 cm | 2 x 25 cm cake tins with baking paper. Scatter the almonds evenly onto a baking tray and toast for 15 minutes or until they are dark golden, checking halfway through and giving the pan a shake to ensure they colour evenly. Once you are happy all the almonds are coloured nicely, remove from the oven and set aside to cool while you prepare the meringue.

2   Place the egg whites and salt in the bowl of an electric mixer fitted with the whisk attachment and whip on high speed until soft ribbons form, then reduce the speed to medium and gradually add the icing sugar, 1 tablespoon at a time, allowing 5 seconds between each addition. Whisk the meringue for 5–7 minutes or until thick and glossy. There is a lot of sugar in the meringue and it will take time to dissolve it. Remove the bowl from the electric mixer. Roughly crush the toasted almonds using your hands then, using a spatula, fold through the meringue along with the vanilla paste until thoroughly combined. Divide the meringue between the prepared tins and bake for 35–40 minutes or until the top is crisp and golden. Remove the rocher from the oven and allow to cool in the tins.

CHOCOLATE GANACHE

1   Place the chocolate in a bowl and have a whisk at-the-ready. Place the cream in a saucepan over medium heat and bring to the boil, then pour the cream over the chocolate and whisk until smooth and glossy. Set the ganache aside at room temperature until you are ready to assemble the cake.   (*cont.*)

TO ASSEMBLE

1. Finish the almond custard first by whisking the mascarpone until firmly whipped. Using a spatula, fold the custard through the mascarpone in three batches. The first addition is to create an initial union between the custard and the mascarpone, so that their consistencies become closer to one another. The second and third additions create the marriage. To make it harmonious, fold gently and ensure that any lumps in the mascarpone are smoothed out before attempting to add more custard – this is best done with a spatula. The aim here is to retain the thickness you have whipped into the mascarpone by adding the custard slowly. Once you have finished, you should have a thick filling that holds up firmly and will be spread over the cakes, not poured over them. If the finished almond custard is not as thick as you had hoped, return the entire filling to the stand mixer and whisk on medium speed until firm.

2. Invert the sponges and tip them out of the cake tins, then peel off the baking paper. Place one sponge onto your serving platter and pour over half the ganache, then spread it evenly over the surface using an offset palette knife. Remove the rochers from the cake tins by pulling up the paper liners to lift them out. Place one of the layers on top of the ganache, then spoon over half the almond custard and spread it all the way to the edges. Sprinkle with half the sliced almond praline. Repeat the layers again: sponge, ganache, rocher and custard, finishing the cake by standing the remaining almond praline decoration upright. Any crushed praline resulting from the slicing process can be sprinkled on top for contrast.

3. The almond rocher really is best eaten on the day it's assembled, because the praline melts and the custard fades to a matt colour overnight. However, all the components of this cake can be made the day before in preparation for assembly the next day. Keep the sponges and rocher at room temperature overnight and the praline will need to be kept in an airtight container to avoid the humidity melting it away. The only thing I would leave to make on the day is the ganache. It's so quick and, if you make it the day before, it will need to be re-softened, anyway, which takes just as much time. (*end.*)

CAKE FOR JANE & JEREMY STRODE
Walnuts. Maple. Rye.

So people will keep saying his name.

This maple filling is a classic by Jane Strode that I started using in this tart when Flour and Stone was newly opened. Jane and I have been sharing ideas and values since we first met and worked together at MG Garage. We both revel in the relationships built within kitchens and consider ourselves lucky to have the medium of food to express ourselves and connect with people.

PASTRY

1. Place the butter and sugars in the bowl of an electric mixer fitted with the paddle attachment and cream on medium speed for 2–3 minutes or until combined. It doesn't need to be pale and fluffy at this stage, beating pastry butter for too long will add a lot of air to the dough and this will make the pastry fragile when baked. Once you are satisfied the butter and sugars are combined, continue beating as you add the egg yolks one at a time, ensuring each yolk is well combined before adding the next. Scrape down the sides of the bowl with a spatula to grab any butter that has made its way up.

2. Sift the rye flour, spelt flour and salt together, returning any coarse husks from the flour that get stuck in the sieve back into the mix. Add the flour and walnuts to the butter and beat on low speed until all the flour has been combined – this should take no longer than 30 seconds. If the flour is overworked at this stage the pastry will be tough and you will lose the delicate nature of the sable. Remove the bowl from the machine and fold the pastry a couple of times with a spatula to make sure any butter at the bottom has been incorporated into the dough.

3. Transfer the pastry to a large square of baking paper that's big enough to roll the pastry onto, then place another piece of baking paper on top of the pastry and flatten it. Roll the pastry out between the two sheets of paper to make a 30 cm | 35 cm round that is 7 mm-thick. Peel the paper off from either side occasionally to readjust it over the pastry, if needed, then place the pastry in the fridge to rest for 30 minutes.

4. Preheat the oven to 150°C. Grease a 25 cm | 30 cm tart tin with butter and dust with flour or give it a light spray with oil.

5. Remove the pastry from the fridge and test its pliability by bending it gently. The process of bringing the pastry to ideal temperature to line the tart tin usually takes around 15 minutes. Due to the high butter content of the pastry, it will probably crack when you mould it into the tin, but don't worry, it can be coaxed back into shape easily.

(cont.)

SIZE	25cm	30cm
SERVES	12-15	15-20
PASTRY		
unsalted butter, softened	175g	220g
icing sugar, sifted	80g	100g
Demerara sugar	40g	50g
egg yolks	2	3
rye flour	160g	200g
spelt flour	50g	65g
sea salt	¼ tsp	½ tsp
walnuts, toasted and finely ground	120g	150g
MAPLE FILLING		
maple syrup	200ml	250ml
honey	200g	250g
unsalted butter	160g	200g
brown sugar	200g	250g
eggs	2	3
rye or sourdough breadcrumbs	30g	40g
rye flour	1 tsp	1½ tbsp
sea salt	¼ tsp	¼ tsp
limes, juiced	3	4
walnuts, toasted	400g	500g

6 Remove the top sheet of paper and invert the pastry over the top of the tart tin, then peel off the bottom sheet of paper gently. Now use your hands to carefully tuck the pastry into the tart tin all the way around. Then go around again, this time focusing on setting the pastry more securely into the groove where the base of the tart tin meets the sides. Finally, on the third time around, press the pastry into the sides of the tart tin and create that beautiful right-angle relationship between the base and sides of the pastry case. Neaten up the rim of the pastry case using a pair of scissors, cutting it 5–7 mm above the rim of the tart case to create an even edge and give a bit more height for all the filling. Pop the pastry case in the freezer to set hard for 15 minutes.

7 Prepare a 30 cm | 35 cm round piece of baking paper and, once the tart case has rested, line the inside with the prepared paper, tucking it snugly into the base of the pastry. Fill the case with baking beads, ensuring that the paper is not hanging over the edge, which will place pressure on the fragile pastry as it bakes and may cause it to break, leaving you with a less than desirable height on your finished pastry case. Bake the pastry case for 30 minutes, then remove it from the oven and gently remove the baking beads and paper. Return the tart case to the oven for a further 10 minutes to finish cooking the centre of the pastry. Remove it from the oven and set aside.

MAPLE FILLING

1 Reduce the oven temperature to 140°C. Melt the maple syrup, honey and butter together in a medium saucepan without boiling, then turn off the heat and set aside for a moment.

2 Whisk the sugar and eggs together using a hand whisk without aerating the eggs too much. When the filling in this tart is baked, it's nice for it to be flat, but if there is too much air in the eggs it may souffle around the edges. Add the warm syrup mixture to the eggs and whisk together gently, then whisk through the breadcrumbs, flour, salt and lime juice to incorporate everything together well. Taste the filling and decide if a squeeze more lime juice might be in order. I often substitute part of the lime juice for lemon juice here, because limes can be expensive and unyielding when out of season and lemon juice will still give a delightful result.

3 Fill the tart case with the walnuts, scattering them evenly over the base. Give the maple filling one last whisk and pour it into a jug or receptacle that is easy to pour from, then return the tart case to the oven and fill to the rim to cover the walnuts. It's easier to do this while the tart case is safely in the oven, so you don't risk spilling the filling in transit. Bake the tart for 45 minutes or until the centre is set with a small amount of wobble remaining. Allow to cool for two hours, then use a serrated knife to cut the tart. Fine, pointed knives will tend to drag the walnuts through the filling. (*end.*)

GINGERBREAD HUG
Ginger. Fennel. Dill.

Snowflakes blanketed the limbs of pine trees
and a frosty moss clung to the walls of our stone cottage.

Those years, we filled the rooms with babies
as the smell of gingerbread baking floated through the forest.

We placed rows of pears in the window for all the loved ones far away,
then we danced and sang in the dreaming of our little family.

CAKE

1 Preheat the oven to 160°C. Prepare a bundt tin by buttering the inside thoroughly to stop the batter from sticking, ensuring that if you are using an ornate tin, you use a pastry brush to get the butter into all the nooks and crannies. Sprinkle the fennel seeds over the butter and dust the inside of the tin with caster sugar. Place the tin in your freezer while you prepare the cake batter. It's worth noting here that while most bundt tins say they are non-stick, they still require greasing as an extra precaution. I tend to use sugar to dust inside the tin when there is no glaze for the cake, as flour can leave a matt finish. Sugar, though, will impart a shine and sometimes a lovely caramelised nature to the outside of the cake.

2 Sift the self-raising flour, malt, bicarbonate of soda, salt and spices together twice and set them aside. You may see some malt flakes, bicarb lumps or salt in the sieve, so press through what you can with your fingertips then return the remainder back into the dry ingredients. The purpose of sifting is for aeration and spice distribution, so those bits can just be tossed back into the mix.

3 Grate the pears, skin and all, using the largest side of a box grater, rotating the pear and grating all the way down to the core to yield between 250 g and 300 g of flesh. Discard the core and set the pear to one side for now, don't worry about the browning.

4 Cream the butter, sugar and golden syrup in the bowl of an electric mixer fitted with the paddle attachment on medium speed until pale and fluffy or use a wooden spoon to cream them together in a mixing bowl. Use a fork to give the eggs a little whisk, then add the egg gradually (the equivalent of one egg at a time) to the creamed butter, allowing each addition to incorporate before adding the next. If the butter wasn't softened enough or the eggs were too cold the mixture may start to curdle. This can be rectified by popping the mixing bowl in the oven (providing the bowl is heatproof) for 10 seconds to warm the mixture a little, then returning it to beat and cream together. Once all the egg is combined, reduce the speed to low and add the dry ingredients in four batches, alternating with the buttermilk, also in four batches. *(cont.)*

BUNDT SIZE	22cm x 7cm-deep
SERVES	12-15
CAKE	
fennel seeds, toasted	1 tbsp
caster sugar, for dusting	100g
self-raising flour	300g
malt	50g
bicarbonate of soda	1½ tsp
sea salt	½ tsp
ground ginger	6 tsp
ground cinnamon	2 tsp
ground aniseed	2 tsp
ground cardamom	1 tsp
ground nutmeg	1 tsp
ground cloves	1 tsp
ground allspice	½ tsp
small pears	2 (about 400g)
unsalted butter, softened, plus extra for greasing	200 g
dark brown sugar	250g
golden syrup	100g
eggs, at room temperature	4
buttermilk	170ml
TO DECORATE	
caster sugar	150g
dill	1 bunch
fresh egg white or 50ml pasteurised egg white	1

5 Remove the bowl from the mixer and fold through the grated pear, then pour the batter into the prepared bundt tin and smooth the top using the back of a spoon. Pop the cake straight into the oven for 50 minutes. Check it's ready by inserting a skewer, if it comes out clean the cake is cooked. That being said, a little residual stickiness is great and will make the cake moist for another couple of days.

6 Once the cake comes out of the oven allow it to cool and rest for only 15 minutes before inverting it onto a wire cooling rack. Remove the tin straightaway, so that the sugar you have used to line the tin doesn't set the cake into the tin. The cake should then be cooled for approximately 30 minutes for optimum flavour.

TO DECORATE

1 Scatter the sugar onto a flat tray and set aside, then pick the dill fronds into small sprigs and place them on a separate tray lined with baking paper. Lightly whisk the eggwhite. Using a pastry brush, brush the sprigs liberally on both sides with the egg white. This will assist you in trying to separate the dill fronds by using the pastry brush bristles to make more defined pine trees. Transfer them to the tray with the caster sugar and gently pat each side into the sugar before returning them to their own tray. Spend a little time fanning out the fronds so they're not all clumped together, then allow the sprigs to dry in the open air for a few hours at room temperature.

2 Decorate the cooled cake with the dill sprigs like a Nordic pine forest in winter. (*end.*)

HANSEL & GRETEL
Brambles. Gingerbread. Brown butter breadcrumbs.

For Hansel and Gretel's homecoming,
through thickets of prickly brambles, buttery gingerbread lairs.
and a moonlit pathway back to forgiveness.

(The day before)

GINGER CRUMB

1. Preheat the oven to 150°C. Line the base and sides of a 25 cm cake tin with baking paper using the following instruction. This cake will be baked in a water bath, so you need to use a conventional tin, not a springform tin, to ensure it doesn't leak. On this occasion, you won't be tipping the cake upside down to get it out, instead, you will be levering it out with the aid of two paper strips lining the base of the tin. So before you line the tin, lay a couple of long baking paper strips approximately 5 cm-wide and 40 cm-long crossing over one another so they meet in the centre of the tin, then run the strips up the sides and let them fall over the rim. Now line the tin as you usually do and set it aside.

2. Ensure the sourdough is completely stale then place in a food processor and blitz into crumbs, leaving a few pebbly pieces (no bigger than a pea) for crunch. If the bread is not dry enough it will tend to lodge itself in the blade and bring the whole process to a halt. If this happens, the bread can be dried out in the oven on a low temperature (120°C) for 20 minutes to make it easier to crumb.

3. Transfer the breadcrumbs to a bowl and repeat the process with the ginger biscuits. But this time blitz them to a fine crumb, as they will contribute the cakey element to the base. Add the biscuit crumbs to the sourdough crumbs then add the brown sugar and mix together using a wooden spoon.

4. To make the brown butter, melt the butter in a small saucepan over medium heat, watching carefully as it turns a nut-brown colour, then remove it from the heat and pour over the crumb mixture. If the butter is on the heat for too long, it will become what is called 'noir', black like the night. It will be dark and bitter and cannot be saved, so keep an eye on it.

5. Mix the butter through the crumbs until very well combined, then scatter the crumb evenly into the base of the prepared cake tin, using the back of a tablespoon to press it down and remove any air pockets. I always feel as though I can hear Hansel and Gretel walking through the forest floor at this stage, trampling all the twigs and leaves along their path.

6. Bake the base for 15 minutes or until golden, then remove it and reduce the oven temperature to 120°C. Place the cake tin into a larger, deep-sided baking tray that can be used as a water bath. This method of baking creates a slow heat, which will enable the cake to cook evenly throughout, avoiding cracking and a souffle top. (*cont.*)

SIZE	25cm
SERVES	12-15

GINGER CRUMB	
stale sourdough bread	100g
ginger biscuits	100g
soft brown sugar	30g
unsalted butter	80g

CAKE	
Valrhona Orelys chocolate or white chocolate, feves or roughly chopped	120g
smoked sea salt	1 tsp
eggs	5
caster sugar	140g
cream cheese (preferably Neufchatel), softened	300g
mascarpone	200g
fresh ricotta, drained	280g
vanilla bean, split and seeds scraped / vanilla extract	1 / 1 tsp
lemon, zested	1
brambles, blackberries, blackcurrants or mulberries	400g

CAKE

1. Melt the chocolate in a stainless-steel bowl over a saucepan of barely simmering water, making sure the bottom of the bowl doesn't touch the water or the chocolate will seize. Remove the bowl from the heat, then stir through the smoked salt and set aside. Separate the eggs, placing the yolks into a small bowl and the whites into the bowl of an electric mixer fitted with the whisk attachment. But wait until I give you the go ahead to start whisking.

2. Weigh the sugar, reserving 50 g for the egg whites and place this next to the mixer in preparation for later. Place the remaining 90 g sugar, cream cheese, mascarpone and ricotta into the bowl of a food processor and blend everything together until smooth. Scrape down the sides of the bowl using a spatula and blend again to ensure there is no residual cream cheese lumps in the mixture. When adding the vanilla, if you are using a vanilla bean, use a sharp paring knife to slice the bean lengthways down the centre and scrape out the seeds onto a chopping board using the blade of the knife. Add the vanilla seeds, the melted chocolate and lemon zest to the cheeses and blend again to combine. (SEE NOTE on vanilla sugar, page 261).

3. Pour the cake filling into a bowl large enough to accommodate the whipped egg whites. Now begin whisking the egg whites on high speed until you see soft ribbons starting to form. Reduce the speed to medium and gradually add the sugar until firm peaks start to form. Be careful not to overwhip the whites. Remove the bowl from the mixer and use a spatula to fold the meringue through the cake filling in two batches, pressing out any lumps formed in the meringue before folding it through, then pour the cake filling over the crumb base.

4. Place the baking tray containing the cake tin in the oven and use a jug to pour water into the baking tray until it comes two-thirds of the way up the sides of the cake tin. Close the oven door and bake the cheesecake for 1 hour, then open the oven door and press the brambles into the surface of the cake. Bake the cake for a further 30 minutes or until the centre springs back when pressed with your finger. If you feel the cheesecake is not giving you this news, just leave it in the oven for another 10 minutes to be sure.

5. Take the baking tray out of the oven and remove the cake from the water bath. Chill in the fridge overnight.

(On the day)

1. To leverage the cake out of the tin, gently pull the strips of baking paper up, a little at a time, until you can feel the base has released from the tin. Place the cake tin on a 45-degree angle and slip the cake out onto a plate, then remove the collar from the outside and slide the strips from underneath. If you don't want the paper base left under the cake, you will need to do a tricky inversion onto another plate and then flip it back the right way up. If you decide to do this, make sure you place a piece of baking paper on top of the cake first, so the crust formed on top of the cake doesn't get stuck to the plate you are using to flip it with.

2. The best way to cut this cake is with a hot knife that has been run under hot water in between each slice. Or by dipping the knife into a large jug of boiling water from the kettle. (*end.*)

MY CHRISTMAS PUDDING
Mandarin. Dark chocolate. Pedro Ximénez.

Creaming butter and sugar in a ceramic bowl awakens a sense of nostalgia in me. The chime of the wood against the porcelain, the gritty sound of the sugar as I encourage it to mingle with the butter and the smell of faux vanilla mixed in amongst it all. I'm entranced as I chase a lump of butter that is always much too small for the bowl and much less softened than I'm trying to convince myself it is. You might not be familiar with this joy but I promise, if you use a wooden spoon, you will be transported to a simpler place in time.

CERAMIC PUDDING BOWL SIZE	900g
SERVES	10-12
dried fruit (SEE NOTES)	375g
candied clementines, finely sliced	75g
Pedro Ximénez sherry or brandy	80ml
dark chocolate (minimum 55% cocoa solids), finely chopped	100g
mandarin jam or marmalade, roughly chopped	75g
green or red apple, coarsely grated	1
orange, zested	1
lemon, zested	1
natural almonds, toasted and finely chopped (optional)	55g
unsalted butter, softened, plus extra 1 tbsp for greasing	65g
brown sugar	25g
caster sugar, plus extra 1 tbsp for dusting	25g
eggs	2
ground allspice	¼ tsp
ground cloves	¼ tsp
ground nutmeg	½ tsp
ground cinnamon	1 tsp
gluten-free flour	55g
TO SERVE	
crème Anglaise (SEE RECIPE, page 147)	

(The day before)

1 The day before you intend to make and steam the pudding, you will need to rehydrate all the dried fruit except for the candied clementines. Dried fruit is improved immeasurably by first covering the fruit with boiling water from the kettle and letting it rehydrate for 30 minutes. Drain the water off the fruit and pour over the sherry. This will help the fruit to soak up the alcohol and will create more moisture in the final pudding. Set the fruit aside on the bench overnight.

(On the day)

1 Butter the pudding basin using a pastry brush, then coat the butter with sugar and tap out any excess. I like to use sugar because it gives the pudding a lovely, glossy shine, whereas flour can dull the finish of the pudding when it is turned out. Set the basin to one side for now.

2 Half-fill a large saucepan (that you have a lid for) with water and place over medium heat while you get on with making the pudding.

3 Place the chocolate in a food processor and chop as fine as possible; this is so it distributes well through the pudding crumb. Having the chocolate chilled in the freezer overnight will help make the crumb finer. Combine the chocolate, fruit soak, mandarin jam, apple, orange zest, lemon zest and almond (if using) in a large bowl, then mix together and set to one side.

4 Combine the butter and sugars in a medium mixing bowl and use a wooden spoon to whip them together until smooth and creamy. If you ensure the butter is super-soft, this step will be a breeze as it's not necessary to aerate the butter too much, you just want to create a smooth cohesion with the sugars.

5 Add the creamed butter to the large bowl of fruit and use a wooden spoon or your hands to fold the butter through the pudding until it is fully combined.

6 Crack the eggs into a separate small bowl and whisk them a little with a fork, then gradually trickle them into the fruit mixture until they are fully incorporated. Now, sift all the spices and the flour into the pudding mixture and fold them through. Make a wish into the batter and ask a loved one nearby to stir the pudding and make a wish, too, then pour the batter into the buttered pudding bowl and smooth the top with a palette knife or a spoon.

7 To prepare the pudding for steaming, place a buttered square of baking paper on top to cover the whole surface of the pudding, then cover the pudding with a large sheet of foil that reaches all the way down the sides of the basin. Use some cooking twine to wrap around the rim of the pudding twice and secure the foil in place with a double knot to prevent any water from entering during the steaming process.

8 Place the pudding in the saucepan of boiling water, making sure the water reaches at least halfway up the sides of the pudding basin. Set the heat to simmer now (just ticking over) and put the lid on to steam for 3 hours 30 minutes. It will be necessary to continue topping up the water level (preferably with boiling water from the kettle) during the coarse of the cooking time to ensure the pudding steams evenly. Afterwards, turn the heat off and remove the pudding from the water, taking care as the basin will be very hot.

9 Allow the pudding to set outside of the saucepan for a minimum of 20 minutes, then snip off the string, remove the foil and paper and invert it onto a serving plate. Flame with more sherry, if you wish (*see notes*). Accompany the pudding with crème Anglaise (*see recipe*, page 147) or brandy butter.

10 If you are steaming the pudding in advance and reheating on Christmas day, this can be done by tying a fresh piece of foil over the basin and returning the pudding to a covered saucepan of simmering water for 45 minutes. The pudding can also be reheated in the microwave on medium heat for 12–15 minutes, but be sure to replace the foil with plastic film or an upturned plate. (*end.*)

NOTES.

Choose any dried fruit that takes your fancy for this recipe. I like currants, sultanas, raisins, prunes, figs and sour cherries. Just bear in mind that some fruit will need to be roughly chopped. Dried figs, for instance, are actually quite lovely just cut into quarters.

You can steam the pudding up to two months in advance of reheating it. Store it in a cool, dry place until Christmas day.

To flame the pudding, arrange the pudding in situ at the table where you are entertaining your loved ones and place a lighter nearby. Then return to the kitchen and heat the sherry in a small saucepan until it is piping-hot, but not boiling, as this will evaporate the alcohol, which is what makes it flame. Once the sherry is hot, take it to the table and tilt the saucepan at a 45-degree angle, then hold a flame from the lighter near the surface of the sherry. You will hopefully see the alcohol set alight straight away with a red-blue glow that hovers over the pan, then immediately pour the sherry over the top of the pudding. The glow from the lit sherry in the saucepan can be subtle, but once you pour the alcohol over the pudding it will become brighter.

THE FABLE OF THE WOLVES
Rhubarb. Oatmeal. Ginger.

When wolves move through the woods in their packs it's the old and sick who walk in front, to set the pace so they don't get left behind. The wolves in the middle are the youngest, they are flanked either side by the strongest and the best in case there is an attack. The last one is the leader who ensures that no one is left behind, keeping the pack unified and on the same path.

This cake is for my departed friend JC. He loved baking Yorkshire parkin with his mam and became a guardian to many. We shared many a philosophy, recipe and fable – this was one of his favourites. I believe he was one of the great leaders, always proud to walk at the back of the pack.

DISH SIZE	20cm x 30cm x 3cm
SERVES	10-12
BAKED RHUBARB	
stalks rhubarb	5
vanilla bean	1
caster sugar	200g
orange, peeled into strips and juiced	1
YORKSHIRE PARKIN	
treacle	150g
golden syrup	150g
unsalted butter	95g
brown sugar	110g
oatmeal	150g
plain flour	110g
baking powder	1¼ tsp
bicarbonate of soda	¾ tsp
ground cinnamon	2 tsp
ground cloves	½ tsp
ground nutmeg	½ tsp
ground allspice	¼ tsp
ground ginger	2 tbsp
eggs	3
buttermilk	150ml
pieces stem ginger, finely chopped (optional)	2

BAKED RHUBARB

1 Preheat the oven to 160°C. Cut the rhubarb stalks lengthways down the middle then cut into 25 cm-long batons. Arrange, in rows, in a baking dish. Split the vanilla bean lengthways down the middle and scrape the seeds out onto your chopping board. Sprinkle the seeds with 1 tablespoon caster sugar and use an offset palette knife to rub the sugar through the seeds. The friction from the sugar will disperse the tiny seeds evenly through the sugar and break up any clumps. Sprinkle the vanilla sugar and remaining caster sugar over the rhubarb, then add the orange peel and juice over the top of the fruit. Bake for 20–25 minutes or until the rhubarb is softened. Bear in mind that once the rhubarb goes into the parkin it will not cook any further, so baking the rhubarb to the point where it will be tender within the crumb of the cake is important here. Test the stalks by pressing them with your finger; you're looking for them to 'squash' under the pressure of your touch. Remove from the oven and set aside, keeping the oven on. *(cont.)*

YORKSHIRE PARKIN

1. Line the base and sides of a 20 cm x 30 cm x 3 cm baking dish with baking paper. Place the treacle, golden syrup, butter and brown sugar in a small saucepan and bring the mixture almost to the boil, then remove the saucepan from the stove and allow to cool for 15 minutes.

2. Sift all the dry ingredients together into a medium bowl. You will find there will be coarser parts of the oatmeal remaining in the sieve, so just return the husks back to the bowl along with the dry ingredients. The purpose of this step is to aerate and distribute the spices through the flour, you will definitely appreciate the texture of those coarse oats as they will preserve the moisture in the cake.

3. Make a well in the centre of the dry ingredients and pour in the warm treacle mixture along with the eggs and buttermilk. Whisk everything together until well incorporated. The stem ginger can be added last and I highly recommend this addition; it provides pleasant spikes of ginger as you eat this deliciously warming cake.

4. Pour the batter into the prepared baking dish and smooth the top using an offset palette knife. Bake for 25 minutes or until a crust starts to form on the top of the cake. Remove the cake briefly from the oven at this stage and arrange the rhubarb batons across the top in rows, pressing them ever so slightly into the surface. Return the cake to the oven and reduce the temperature to 150°C for a further 15–20 minutes. To test the cake is ready, use the sharp point of a small knife. The crumb of this cake should be left slightly sticky, so when you remove the knife, you should feel a little resistance. Rest assured, traces of raw batter will be obvious and, if this is the case, just return the cake to the oven in 5-minute increments to avoid overcooking.

5. Eat beside the fire with a strong pot of Yorkshire tea. (*end.*)

TREE OF LIFE
Apples. Rosella wheat. Cultured cream.
65

HOME
Tomato. Passionfruit. Strawberry. Sunflower seeds. Pepper.
69

NETTLE RICOTTA CAKE
Nettle. Basil. White peach.
73

AUTUMN QUINCE & AMARO TART
Quince. Emmer wheat. Cinnamon myrtle. Native amaro.
77

MOTHERHOOD
Davidson plum. Strawberry. Champagne.
82

A BLESSING FOR THE SEEDS
Coffee. Wattleseed. Hazelnuts.
87

LITTLE QUEENIE
Strawberries. Hibiscus. Mint. Pink pepper. Cardamom.
91

TRUTH-SEEKER
Yuzu. Macadamia.
95

UNDER THE QUANDONG TREE
Quandong. Bush honey. Lemon verbena. Almonds.
101

BUSH

The bush is my home from home and where I feel most myself.

All the botanicals in this chapter are from that place and express the kinship I feel with the bush. Its muted shades of sage and cinnamon myrtle touch the quiet in me. I feel as if I'm still walking across the streams and rocks of those fields. All those botanicals have imbued my life with such meaning.

Across the creek, in one of the paddocks of my childhood farm there was a deep water well that had been boarded up. Every time us kids went on adventures to our hideaway under the fig tree, the elders would warn us not to go near the well.

There was a circle of stinging nettles that grew, forming a perfect moat around the well so none of us could get near it anyway. I believe nature knew to grow them to stop us from falling in. Curiosity would get the better of us though. We would crane our necks and peer into the blackness between the cracks of rotting wood covering the well. This has become a lifelong obsession of mine – to seek where I am told not to go.

Yuzu fruit is the truth-seeker in me, paired with native macadamias in the lightness of a chiffon, because carrying the truth isn't always easy.

The nettles became woven into a cake, a reflection on looking inwards and searching for the scent of ripening peaches from the orchards nearby.

I discovered the scent of eucalyptus in mint, cardamom and pepper.

Hibiscus for feminine power and Davidson plums for patience in mothering.

Ancient botanicals of quince and grains of emmer to honour my ancestors and the richness they have imparted into my life through living theirs.

With sacred fruits of quandong to acknowledge the country we grow and cook from.

TREE OF LIFE
Apples. Rosella wheat. Cultured cream.

We are etched by time
Like trees scarred by fire,
Black staining heartwood.

Yet we have grown through sun and rain
with lines of laughter
and mornings of birdsong.

Our weathering is a gift of growing old
to learn by heart,
what any tree can teach you.

PIE DISH SIZE	20cm	25cm
SERVES	10-12	12-15
PASTRY		
unsalted butter, softened, plus extra for greasing	170g	240g
Demerara sugar, plus extra for sprinkling	55g	80g
caster sugar	90g	130g
vanilla paste	½ tsp	1 tsp
eggs, plus 1 extra beaten egg for glazing	1	2
egg yolk(s)	1	2
rosella wheat flour (SEE GLOSSARY), plus extra for dusting	210g	300g
baking powder	¾ tsp	1 scant tsp
sea salt	¼ tsp	½ tsp
almond meal	60g	90g
orange, zested	½	1
lemon, zested	½	1
milk, for glazing	1 tsp	1 tsp
APPLE FILLING		
large Granny Smith apples, peeled and cored	5	7
unsalted butter	100g	150g
crème fraîche	70g	100g
dark brown sugar	35g	50g
TO SERVE		
vanilla ice-cream or pouring cream (optional)		

PASTRY

1 Place the butter, Demerara sugar, caster sugar and vanilla paste in the bowl of an electric mixer fitted with the paddle attachment and cream together on medium speed. It is important not to over-aerate the butter too much, as this will make the pastry crumbly and unworkable. A light beat to dissolve the sugars and create a little air is sufficient in this instance.

2 Beat the eggs and additional yolk/s together in a bowl, then a little at a time, add this mixture to the butter, incorporating well between each addition and scraping down the sides of the bowl using a spatula. Sift the flour, baking powder, salt and almond meal together in a large bowl, returning any coarse almonds or salt that become stuck in the sieve back into the mix. Add the dry ingredients and orange and lemon zests to the butter mixture and mix on low speed until just incorporated, no longer. Remove the bowl from the machine and make a couple of folds by hand using a spatula to completely incorporate the pastry. Due to the high butter content of this pastry it will be rolled out between two sheets of baking paper, so it can be manoeuvred into the pie dish more easily.

3 Divide the pastry into two pieces; approximately two-thirds of the pastry will be used for the pie base and one-third for the pie top. Cut two large squares of baking paper and place each piece of pastry into the centre of each square. Top the pastry with another piece of baking paper and press to flatten the dough. Using a rolling pin, roll the pastry base out to a 25 cm | 30 cm round that is 5 mm-thick. Then roll the pie top out to a 20 cm | 25 cm round that is a 5 mm-thick. Place both the top and base into the fridge to rest for 1 hour while you get on with making the pie filling.

(cont.)

APPLE FILLING

1. Cut the apples into approximately 1 cm cubes. Melt half the butter in a large saucepan over low heat, add half the apples and cook, stirring occasionally to stop them from colouring, for 10–15 minutes or until softened. Add the remaining butter and apples and cook for a further 15 minutes or until they are softened. Thereby creating a couple of different textures as, by now, the first apples will be falling apart. Set the cooked apples aside and when cooled fold through the crème fraîche and brown sugar.

татоо ASSEMBLE

1. Prepare a 20 cm | 25 cm diameter pie dish by buttering the base and dusting it with flour, tapping out any surplus flour. Remove only the pastry base from the fridge and start by lining the bottom of the pie dish with the base. The pastry will be quite rigid at this point, so give it a moment to become more malleable so you can mould it into the base. To prepare, peel the top sheet of paper away then replace it temporarily, flip over the pastry and release the bottom piece of paper. Lift the pastry off the paper and align it over the centre of the pie dish. Tuck the edges neatly into the dish. If the pastry starts to tear, don't worry, just use the warmth of your fingertips to mould it back together. Press out any pockets of air between the pastry and the pie dish and trim around the edge of the dish with a paring knife to remove any surplus pastry. This pastry is very forgiving, so don't worry if it cracks as you're lining the base, just use your fingertips to press it back together.

2. Fill the pastry base with the cooled apples and flatten them down evenly. Remove the pie top from the fridge and release it from the baking paper as you did with the base. Align it over the centre of the pie and use your fingertips to seal the pie top to the base. Even though the edges will look quite rough at this point, now is a good time to refrigerate the pie so the pastry can set. This will take 15 minutes, during which time you can preheat the oven to 165°C.

3. After the pie has rested, remove it from the fridge and trim round the rim of the pie dish using a sharp paring knife. If you try and do this before resting the pastry it may tear due to the sticky nature of the dough. Use a fork to create a decorative edge around the pie and brush the top with the beaten egg mixed with the milk. Score the top by sweeping a fork over the surface to create concentric circles, then sprinkle the top with Demerara sugar.

4. Bake the pie for 40 minutes | 50 minutes or until the top is golden brown. Remove from the oven and allow to rest for 20 minutes before cutting.

5. I love to serve this pie with vanilla ice-cream or thick pouring cream. (*end.*)

HOME
Tomato. Passionfruit. Strawberry. Sunflower seeds. Pepper.

We carry home with us wherever we go.
This sense of place that travels with me arrives as the fuzzy scent of a tomato vine.
The pepper tree falling like green rain over the passionfruit vine.
Rows of burnished sunflower faces cowering in the sun.
An old fig tree resting on the slope of the mountain and the secrets told under its branches.
All of these memories coming to rest inside me like a mist in a hidden gully.

(The day before)

TOMATO AND PASSIONFRUIT JAM

1. Remove the cores from the tomatoes and cut them in half. Slice the halves into thin slices and place in a large bowl. Add the sugar to the tomatoes and toss together to coat the fruit, then place a plate upside down over the tomatoes to weigh them down and set aside at room temperature overnight.

(On the day)

2. The next day, you will notice the sugar has dissolved and the tomatoes look shrivelled and dehydrated. This process is used in jam-making when the shape of the fruit needs to be maintained. Had you put the sugar over them on the same day, they would cook down to more of a purée and lose their texture.

3. Pop a small plate in your freezer, which you'll later use to test the jam's setting point. Place the tomatoes and the passionfruit pulp in a large, heavy-based saucepan or jam pan over medium heat. Be sure to use a spatula to scrape all the sugar from the bottom of the tomato bowl into the pan, then add the zest and juice of the lemons and bring to the boil. To retain the colour of the fruit, it's best to cook the jam quickly and rapidly, so don't walk too far away from the pan. Once boiling, increase the heat a little to medium-high to achieve a rapid boil.

4. Use a heatproof spatula or wooden spoon to sweep across the base of the saucepan every now and then to ensure the jam doesn't stick, but try not to stir as this can cause the jam to be cloudy.

5. Once you start to feel the jam sticking to the base of the pan, this is usually a sign the jam is almost ready. Reduce the heat to low momentarily, then scoop out 1 tablespoon of the jam and place on the frozen plate. Wait 10 seconds before running your finger through the jam. Does the line join back together quickly? Or does it stay parted? *(cont.)*

PIE DISH/PLATE SIZE	25cm	28cm
SERVES	10-12	12-15

TOMATO AND PASSIONFRUIT JAM		
vine-ripened red tomatoes	500g	
granulated sugar	330g	
fresh passionfruit pulp	225g	
lemons, 1 zested, both juiced	2	

SUNFLOWER SEED CRUST		
sunflower seeds	60g	75g
icing sugar	50g	60g
rosella wheat or spelt flour, plus extra for dusting	220g	265g
sea salt	pinch	¼ tsp
unsalted butter, slightly softened, plus extra for greasing	170g	200g

STRAWBERRY FILLING		
fresh strawberries, hulls removed	600g	800g
unsalted butter, well-softened	2 tsp	3 tsp
caster or granulated sugar	50g	75g

PEPPER PRALINE CREAM		
pink peppercorns	3 tsp	3 tsp
caster sugar	3 tbsp	3 tbsp
pure cream	180g	220g
double cream or mascarpone	180g	220g

6 The jam will be set when the latter occurs, so if it runs back together, return the jam to medium heat and boil for as long as necessary until the jam remains parted when you test it. Another clue it's ready is if the jam wrinkles when you push it with your finger. This being said, I always favour preserving the flavour of the fruit above achieving setting point. Most jam recipes have a 100 per cent sugar to fruit ratio, whereas mine has 66 per cent. This is a big factor in giving the flavour of the fruit a chance to sing, but it does mean you need to wait a little longer for the setting point to be reached or just don't worry about it being so set. It's always better for the jam to taste of the fruit you made it with, rather than being perfectly set.

7 Once the jam is set to your liking, turn off the heat and allow it to cool in the saucepan. Pour it into jars or a suitable container to store in your fridge.

SUNFLOWER SEED CRUST

1 Preheat the oven to 150°C. Grease a 25 cm | 28 cm pie dish or plate with butter and dust with flour then tap out the surplus flour.

2 Toast the sunflower seeds in a small frying pan for 1 minute or until the aromas are released. Place in a food processor or pestle and mortar and finely crush. You will end up with some powdery crumbs and some slightly coarser pieces for texture, both are lovely.

3 Sift the icing sugar, flour and salt together into a bowl and return any coarse husks from the flour that have been trapped by the sieve back into the mix, then add the crushed sunflower seeds and toss them through. Cut the butter into small cubes and, using your fingertips, rub it into the flour mixture to form a coarse breadcrumb-like texture. Depending on the temperature of your butter, the pastry may start to feel a little sticky before you are able to rub the butter in finely enough. Don't panic, just keep rubbing in the butter. If it turns into more of a paste, that's fine. Shape the pastry into a ball and flatten down to 3 cm-thick, then wrap in plastic film and refrigerate for approximately 1–2 hours or until pastry is hard.

4 Remove the pastry from the fridge and, using the largest side of a box grater, grate the pastry evenly over the surface of your pie dish or plate, pushing it up the sides as necessary. Now press it into the dish using your fingertips, so the base is an even 7 mm-thick all over once you have pressed it down. Use your sense of touch to locate uneven pockets and grate in more pastry as needed then crimp the pastry around the outside or use a fork to score the edges. Place the pastry in the fridge to rest for 15 minutes. Bake the pastry for 30 minutes or until lightly coloured, then remove from the oven. No baking beads are needed here.

STRAWBERRY FILLING

1 Spread the jam in a 7 mm-thick layer over the base of the pie crust, leaving a 1 cm border around the edge. Arrange the strawberries upright on top of the jam, squeezing in as many as possible. Brush the strawberries lightly with butter and sprinkle over the sugar. Return the pie to the oven for 45 minutes. The strawberries will become shiny with the butter and sugar, and their juices will meld with the tomato jam. Remove the pie from the oven and allow to rest for 30 minutes before cutting.

2 This pastry is quite fragile, so choosing a shallow pie dish is wise. That way, you won't lose the edges of your pastry when you cut it. The best dish to use for this is just an ovenproof dinner plate, so that you can leverage under the crust and remove the slices easily.

PEPPER PRALINE CREAM

1. Prepare a flat tray lined with lightly oiled baking paper and set it beside the stove.

2. Toast the peppercorns in a small frying pan over medium heat, tossing for 30–45 seconds to release their flavour, then pour them into a small bowl momentarily. Sprinkle the caster sugar evenly over the base of the same frying pan, then swivel the pan over medium heat until the sugar melts and you can see clearly to the bottom of the pan. Remove the pan from the heat and stir through the peppercorns using a heatproof spatula.

3. Pour the praline immediately onto the prepared tray to seize it from colouring any further and allow it to set until cool and brittle.

4. Crush the praline in a pestle and mortar or pop it into a durable plastic bag (I use a disposable piping bag) and smash it up finely using a rolling pin. Whip the creams together using a hand whisk until very softly whipped, then fold through the praline. This cream is really best made just before you serve the tart, although the praline can be made in advance. Serve the praline cream alongside the tart. (*end.*)

NOTE.
This recipe for the jam makes two jars. You will only use half a jar for the pie, regardless of the size you make, so the rest is for your toast another day. You could halve the jam recipe, but it's a lot of work for one jar of jam and it's always good to have ingredients in the pantry for later. You can keep the jam for up to three months in the refrigerator or for one year in sterilised jars.

NETTLE RICOTTA CAKE
Nettle. Basil. White peach.

Amongst the amber bracken turning with emerald tinge,
the nettles emerge in spring,
weaving their moat around the well of my unravelling.
Stinging at my ankles
I beat a path to light-heartedness,
where peach skins tickle my nose
and the juices run down my chin.

NETTLE AND BASIL PURÉE

1. Ensure you handle the nettles with thick, rubber gloves as regular disposable gloves will not be thick enough to protect you from the stings. Prepare a large bowl of iced water ready to refresh the nettles in after they've been cooked – this is so they retain their colour.

2. Bring a large saucepan of water to the boil and, meanwhile, remove any stems from the nettles. Plunge the nettles and the basil into the water and simmer for 4 minutes. Drain in a colander over the sink, then immediately submerge them in the iced water for 2 minutes to arrest the cooking process. Remove from the water and, using your hands, squeeze to extract as much water as possible. Blend the nettles and basil using a stick blender or a high-performance blender, as most regular blenders won't have blades sharp enough to purée the nettles smoothly. The purée will retain a little texture, so don't worry about it being completely smooth. Store the purée in the fridge until needed. Nettle purée can also be frozen, so you may want to prepare a few batches in advance and freeze in 120 g | 150 g blocks.

CAKE

1. Preheat the oven to 150°C. Line a 20 cm | 25 cm cake tin with baking paper. When lining the cake tin for this cake, use a whole sheet of baking paper, as opposed to a base piece and a collar, as you will need some way of pulling the cake out of the tin once it's baked. This cake is soft when cooked and very difficult to invert to remove from the tin. Alternatively, you could use a springform tin.

2. Toast the pine nuts in a small frying pan over medium heat, tossing constantly to ensure they colour evenly, then scatter them onto a tray to cool completely. Place the cooled pine nuts in a food processor and chop as finely as possible. Because pine nuts are high in oil they will remain fairly coarse, so to combat this, add the almond meal to the blender at the end and continue blending to absorb the oils and create a finer crumb.

(cont.)

SIZE	20cm	25cm
SERVES	10-12	12-15
NETTLE AND BASIL PURÉE		
fresh stinging nettles (*SEE NOTE*)	150g	200g
basil leaves	30g	50g
CAKE		
pine nuts	90g	110g
almond meal	90g	110g
unsalted butter, softened	95g	120g
caster sugar	180g	220g
fresh ricotta, drained	160g	200g
nettle purée (from above)	120g	150g
eggs, separated	3	4
lemons, juiced	1	2
orange, zested	½	1
sea salt	pinch	pinch
ripe peaches, thinly sliced	3	4
a few basil leaves		
nasturtium flowers and leaves		

3   Cream the butter and only 100 g | 120 g of the sugar in the bowl of an electric mixer fitted with the paddle attachment on medium speed, using a spatula to scrape down the sides of the bowl regularly, for 5–7 minutes or until pale and fluffy. Add the drained ricotta and nettle purée to the butter and whip again on medium speed to incorporate, then add the egg yolks, one at a time, and whip until fully combined.

4   Decant the batter into a larger bowl and fold through the lemon juice and orange zest. Place the egg whites and salt in the electric mixer fitted with the whisk attachment and whisk on high speed until soft ribbons form. Reduce the speed to medium and gradually add the remaining sugar until the egg whites are thick and glossy.

5   Using a spatula, gently fold the meringue through the nettle batter one-third at a time until there are no streaks remaining. Pour the batter into the prepared cake tin and smooth the top using an offset palette knife. Arrange the peach slices, basil leaves and nasturtiums over the top as you wish, ensuring that the peaches are thinly sliced, otherwise, they may sink to the bottom of the cake. Alternatively, cut the peaches in half and set them into the batter where they will hopefully sit just above the surface, peeking through.

6   Place the cake in the centre of the oven directly on the oven rack without a tray underneath, if possible, as this cake needs a little more heat underneath to bake the bottom. Bake for 20 minutes. After the initial 20 minutes, reduce the temperature to 140°C and bake for a further 30–35 minutes. This cake is very light and mousse-y, so can't be tested with a skewer, but if you press your finger in the centre of the cake it will bounce back when it's cooked. Turn the oven off and leave the cake in the oven with the door ajar to cool for a further 20 minutes. If your oven door doesn't stay open, just wedge a wooden spoon in the door to keep it ajar. Remove the cake from the oven and allow it to cool completely in the tin, then lift it out of the tin by pulling up the paper. (*end.*)

NOTE.
Nettles can be found at local farmers' markets, but are usually not advertised. They are seasonal to spring and summer and, if you want to grow them yourself, they only take six weeks. Strike up a conversation with the growers at the markets. It's amazing the stories that can come out of these interactions. Leftover nettle purée can also be folded through risotto or made into a pesto for pasta.

AUTUMN QUINCE & AMARO TART

Quince. Emmer wheat. Cinnamon myrtle. Native amaro.

Chartreuse-perfumed quince emerges as nature prepares to fall away.
Ghostly gums shimmer with their painterly silver streaks
and cinnamon myrtle blossoms hang like garlands of stars
to light our path amongst the tawny amber colours of autumn.
Our reflections fall upon a slow-moving stream as we float
on a raft of all the stories and songs imbued
by ancient fruit, botanicals and grain.

TART TIN SIZE	26cm
SERVES	12-15

POACHED QUINCE

quinces	5
water	1.5 litres
caster sugar	800g
vanilla bean, split and seeds scraped	1
fresh bay leaf	1
lemon, thinly sliced	1

CINNAMON MYRTLE CUSTARD

double cream	200g
pure cream, plus extra to serve	400g
vanilla bean, split and seeds scraped	1
dried cinnamon myrtle leaves	3 tsp
cinnamon quill	½
lemon myrtle leaves / dried lemon myrtle	5 / 2 tsp
orange, zested	½
egg yolks	8
caster sugar	120g

HAZELNUT AND EMMER SABLE

unsalted butter, softened, plus extra for greasing	175g
icing sugar, sifted	70g
Demerara sugar	50g
egg yolks	2
emmer or spelt flour (SEE GLOSSARY)	200g
whole hazelnuts, peeled and finely ground	80g
sea salt	¼ tsp

AMARO JELLY

titanium-strength gelatine leaves	2
quince poaching syrup (from above)	200ml
amaro	100ml

(The day before)

POACHED QUINCE

1. Peel and core the quinces, then place the core, seeds and peel into a piece of calico or muslin and tie it off with cooking twine or string. The seeds and peel will help the quince develop a ruby colour while poaching, although it's not absolutely essential to use them.

2. Combine the water, sugar and vanilla bean and seeds in a large saucepan. Add the bay leaf, lemon and bag of quince seeds and cores (if using) and bring everything to the boil. Reduce the heat to a simmer and cook for a further 10 minutes so all the aromatics infuse into the syrup. Drop the quinces into the syrup, ensuring they are covered by the liquid, then place a round of baking paper over the top. Return to the boil, then reduce the heat so that the syrup is just ticking over. Poach the quince for 3 hours, then remove the pan from the heat and allow the quinces to cool in the syrup overnight.

(On the day)

CINNAMON MYRTLE CUSTARD

1. Pour the creams into a medium saucepan and add the vanilla bean and seeds, cinnamon myrtle, cinnamon quill, lemon myrtle and orange zest. Bring everything to the boil, then turn the heat off and allow the saucepan to stand at room temperature for 1 hour. This is so all the flavours infuse into the cream. This step can be done the day before and kept in the fridge overnight, which allows the flavours to really permeate through the cream.

2. After the cream has infused, return the saucepan to medium heat and bring to the boil. Meanwhile, using a hand whisk, whisk together the egg yolks and sugar until pale. Once the cream is boiling, pour it over the egg yolk mixture and whisk again to thoroughly combine into a smooth custard. It is not necessary to return the custard to the heat, just strain the custard through a mesh sieve to remove all the aromatics, then set to one side.

HAZELNUT AND EMMER SABLE

1. Place the butter and sugars in the bowl of an electric mixer fitted with the paddle attachment and cream together on low speed for no more than 2 minutes. They should be pale, but not too fluffy. This step can also be done with a wooden spoon since it is not essential to aerate the butter. In fact, this is detrimental, as overbeating the butter may make the sable very crumbly and too fragile once baked. Remember, you are not making a cake here, you are making pastry.

2. Scrape down the sides of the bowl using a spatula (if using an electric mixer) to ensure the butter is being creamed evenly with the sugar. Add the egg yolks one at a time to the butter, waiting until each one combines before adding the next, then remove the bowl from the stand mixer. Sift the flour directly into the bowl with the butter, add the hazelnuts and salt and fold the dry ingredients through using a spatula. When making sable, this step is always done by hand so as not to overwork the gluten in the flour, which will toughen the pastry. Once the dry ingredients have been added to the butter the texture will seem more like a paste, this is due to the high butter-to-flour ratio. Ensure there are no remaining streaks of butter by scraping all the way to the bottom of the bowl with your spatula.

3   Place a large piece of baking paper on your bench and scoop the pastry into the centre. This pastry is going to be rolled out between two sheets of paper, because it is too sticky to roll with a rolling pin, so bear in mind the piece of paper will need to be at least 32 cm-square to enable you to roll it big enough to fit the tart tin. If your paper is not that wide, just use two sheets side-by-side. Top the pastry with another sheet of paper and, using your hands, pat the pastry into a round disc to create the beginnings of the shape you need to line the tart tin. Take your rolling pin and roll the pastry out evenly between the two sheets, rotating it 90 degrees as you go, to achieve a round sheet of pastry that is 5 mm-thick and 32 cm in diameter. Place the pastry in the fridge for 30 minutes to rest and set.

ROLLING, LINING AND BAKING THE PASTRY CASE

1   Lightly grease a 26 cm-round tart tin with butter and dust with flour or give it a light spray with oil. Remove the pastry from the fridge and test the pliability of the sheet by bending it gently. The process of bringing the pastry to ideal temperature to line the tart tin can be ambiguous given variable factors, such as room temperature and the amount of air you have incorporated into the pastry, so a little intuition is required here. Usually 15 minutes out of the fridge is an optimum length of time to attempt the lining process. In any case, remember this pastry is high in butter, so don't worry, it can be coaxed into shape easily with a little persuasion by you!

2   Remove the top sheet of paper, then invert the pastry over the top of the tart tin. Peel off the bottom sheet of paper gently. Now use your hands to carefully tuck the pastry into the tart tin all the way around; this is a preliminary effort to stop the surplus pastry from tearing over the rim. Then go around again, this time focusing on setting the pastry more securely into the groove where the base of the tart tin meets the sides. Finally, on the third time around, press the pastry into the sides of the tart tin to create that beautiful right-angle between the base and sides of the pastry case. Neaten up the rim of the pastry using a pair of scissors, cutting it 5–7 mm above the rim of the tart tin to create an even edge. The idea here is to give a bit more height for all the filling that will be baked into the tart and a favourable proportion of custard, pastry, fruit and jelly. Pop the pastry case in the freezer to set hard for 15 minutes.

3   Meanwhile, preheat the oven to 150°C. Prepare a 30 cm-round sheet of baking paper or foil to set inside the tart tin for blind baking. Remove the pastry case from the freezer and while still frozen line the inside with the prepared circle, tucking it tightly into the right-angle you've created. Fill the case with baking beads. Ensure the paper or foil is not hanging over the edge or it will place pressure on the fragile pastry as it bakes, which may cause it to break, leaving you with less height on your finished pastry case. Bake the pastry case for 45 minutes, then remove it from the oven and allow the pastry to set for 15 minutes. Gently remove the baking beads and paper from the pastry case.

4   Reduce oven temperature to 120°C. Drain the poached quince from the syrup, being sure to reserve all the syrup. Halve the quinces and place evenly into the baked tart case. Pour the custard over the quince, leaving 7 mm at the top for the jelly later, then return the tart to the oven. If you feel more confident filling the tart case with the custard while it's in the oven, this can save you the fear of spilling the custard in transit to the oven. Bake the tart for 45 minutes or until the top of the tart is not wobbly and the custard is set, then remove it from the oven and allow to cool for 30 minutes. The tart will need to be chilled further in the fridge to allow the jelly to set on top, but an initial cooling on the bench (*cont.*)

is advisable for the happiness of your fridge and the safety of any ingredients in there that don't appreciate temperature fluctuations. Chill in the fridge for a minimum of 1 hour before adding the jelly.

AMARO JELLY

1. Cover the gelatine leaves in very cold water and leave them to soak and soften while you make the jelly. Place the quince syrup and amaro in a small saucepan and bring to the boil, then remove the pan from the heat. Squeeze out the surplus water from the gelatine leaves and add them to the syrup and amaro, stirring gently to dissolve the gelatine completely. Strain the jelly through a fine sieve into a bowl to remove any minuscule amounts of undissolved gelatine or debris from the quince cooking liquid. Cool the jelly at room temperature until you can see it starting to thicken around the edges. This will become apparent as the jelly begins to set on the sides of the bowl and will usually take the hour the quince tart is cooling in the fridge.

2. Remove the tart from the fridge and pour the jelly evenly over the tart all the way to the rim. Don't worry if pieces of the quince are still peeping through the jelly, as this is how it would exist in nature. Set the jelly for another 30 minutes in the fridge, making sure it sits flat on the shelf. Remove the tart any time after that to serve.

3. This tart is best served with extra pure cream trickled over the top. (*end.*)

MOTHERHOOD
Davidson plum. Strawberry. Champagne.

Motherhood has been a chance for me to make my own family that I may nurture and be nourished by. A calling to create a gang that could see one another through thick and thin. The core of motherhood is unconditional love, but then heartbreak shows up to teach you that you're not as selfless as you thought. The person you've spent all this time constructing needs to be abandoned if you're going to succeed at this new motherhood job description. This role arrives on your threshold by force of nature, surrounded by stars and light, and makes you feel invincible. Then, that strength shoots straight to your heart and buries itself there forever. This seed remains as a soothing balm of your own brilliance and courage in bringing another life into the world. This can explain that fearless glow around any mother that only grows brighter through the relentless nature of motherhood and the overwhelming gifts that it bestows along the way.

PLUM COMPOTE

1. Add the vanilla bean and seeds to a medium saucepan with the Davidson plums and sugar. Place on the stove over medium heat and stir with a wooden spoon to distribute the sugar. Once the fruit comes to the boil, reduce the heat to low and simmer until the plums are tender. Add the strawberries and cook the compote for a further 2 minutes, then turn off the heat and leave the compote at room temperature to cool.

BUTTER CAKE WITH MERINGUE

1. Preheat the oven to 160°C. Line 2 x 25 cm | 2 x 30 cm round cake tins with baking paper and set aside. Using an electric mixer fitted with the paddle attachment, cream the very soft butter together with the sugar and vanilla on medium speed for about 3 minutes or until pale and fluffy. Give the eggs a light whisk with a fork, then gradually add them to the butter, a little at a time, waiting for each addition to be incorporated before adding the next. Scrape down the sides of the bowl and under the paddle regularly and continue to beat for another 2–3 minutes once all the eggs have been added.

2. Sift the flours and baking powder together twice, then reduce the mixer to the lowest speed. Add the dry ingredients to the bowl in three batches, alternating with the milk, also in three batches. Being careful not to overwork the flour. Don't worry if it seems the flour is all over the sides of the bowl and paddle. Once you have added the last batch of milk, turn the machine off and scrape down the sides of the bowl and paddle, then turn the machine to high speed for 2 seconds to give it a final blast. This aerates the batter, activates the baking powder and incorporates the last of the flour, which makes for a fluffier cake. Remove the bowl from the mixer and decant the batter into a large bowl. Wash and dry the electric mixer bowl in preparation for the meringue.

3. Add the egg whites and salt to the electric mixer fitted with the whisk attachment and whip on high speed until soft ribbons start to form. Reduce the speed to medium and add the sugar, 1 tablespoon at a time, leaving 5 seconds between each addition. Once all the sugar has been added, continue to beat until firm peaks form then remove the bowl from the mixer and use a spatula to gently fold half the meringue through the butter cake batter. Once combined, fold through the remaining meringue. Divide the cake batter evenly between the two prepared cake tins and smooth the tops with an offset palette knife. Bake the cakes for 20 minutes | 25 minutes, then reduce oven temperature to 150°C for a further 20 minutes | 35 minutes. Test the cakes for readiness by gently pressing your finger in the centre of the cake. If it bounces back slightly, it's cooked. Remove cakes from the oven and allow to cool completely in the tins.

ZABAGLIONE

1. Half-fill a medium saucepan with water and bring to the boil over high heat. Place the egg yolks into a large, heatproof bowl, add the sugar and whisk until pale and creamy. Add the Champagne or wine and whisk everything together briefly to combine. Reduce the heat under the saucepan so it's just simmering and sit the bowl on top, then continue to whisk the yolks until thick and pale. When you're making a zabaglione, it's important the yolks don't get too hot or (*cont.*)

SIZE	25cm	30cm
SERVES	15-20	20-30
PLUM COMPOTE		
vanilla bean, split and seeds scraped	½	1
Davidson plums or queen garnet blood plums	250g	500g
caster sugar	50g	100g
strawberries, hulled	250g	500g
BUTTER CAKE WITH MERINGUE		
unsalted butter, well-softened	250g	500g
caster sugar	250g	500g
vanilla bean, split and seeded scraped	½	1
eggs	4	8
self-raising flour	200g	400g
cornflour	50g	100g
baking powder	1 tsp	2 tsp
full-cream milk	125ml	250ml
egg whites	4	8
salt	½ tsp	1 tsp
caster sugar	90g	180g
ZABAGLIONE		
egg yolks	4	8
caster sugar	50g	100g
Champagne or sparkling wine	125ml	250ml
mascarpone	125g	250g
pure cream	125g	250g
TO DECORATE		
Davidson plum powder	10g	20g
icing sugar	1 tbsp	1 tbsp

they will scramble. I usually remove the bowl from the saucepan every now and then, whisking both on and off the heat for a total of about 10 minutes. This ensures the zabaglione doesn't cook too fast, allowing you to incorporate lots of air into it. As the zabaglione gets closer to being completely cooked the foamy bubbles around the outside will gradually start to disappear and the consistency will resemble a thick custard. To tell if it's ready, draw your whisk through the mixture and let it fall onto the surface to see if it forms a ribbon. If the ribbon disappears quickly back into the mixture, you need to keep whisking over the heat. If it sits proud on the surface for a few seconds, it's ready. Set the zabaglione aside at room temperature to cool.

2   While the zabaglione is cooling, place the mascarpone and cream in a bowl and use a hand whisk to whip until thick but not over-whipped. Once the zabaglione has completely cooled, fold one-third of the zabaglione at a time into the cream until it is all incorporated and you have a deliciously thick custard to fill your butter cake with.

TO ASSEMBLE

1   Remove the cakes from their tins by inverting them onto separate cake racks. Using a serrated knife, trim the dark crust off the base of one of the sponges. Turn the other sponge the right way up and trim the top off this one. Now you should have one sponge without a top crust (this is the base of your cake) and one sponge without a base crust (this is the top layer of your cake).

2   Place the base cake, trimmed-side up, onto a serving platter and, using an offset palette knife, spread the surface with the zabaglione. Spread evenly with the plum compote, allowing some of the syrup to trickle down the sides. Manoeuvre the other cake layer into place on top of the compote, then dust the top of the cake with Davidson plum powder. Position your template, if using one, on top and dust with icing sugar, then gently lift the template to reveal the design. This template was made using a piece of acetate, however, I have created so many over the years using a plastic bucket lid or even a piece of cardboard.

3   For a more economical version, the top can be dusted with icing sugar first with the stencil design in Davidson plum powder. Alternatively, crushed freeze-dried strawberry powder would also be lovely here. (*end*.)

> NOTE.
> If you would like to make a stencil for decorating the top of the cake, create your own using a scalpel or craft knife, a piece of cardboard or thin plastic and a cutting mat or non-slip chopping board.

A BLESSING FOR THE SEEDS
Coffee. Wattleseed. Hazelnuts.

A blessing for the seeds that crave human touch to bloom. Beyond the farmer and all the things the soil imagines for them, they realise a new awakening when they are infused and invigorated into budding through someone's caress.

SIZE	20cm	25cm
SERVES	10-15	15-20

HAZELNUT PRALINE		
hazelnuts, toasted and skins removed	100g	
caster sugar	100g	
wattleseeds	½ tsp	

COFFEE PASTRY CREAM		
wattleseeds	4 tsp	5 tsp
instant coffee granules	4 tsp	5 tsp
espresso	20ml	25ml
full-cream milk	300ml	400ml
egg yolks	4	5
caster sugar	60g	80g
plain flour	20g	25g
hazelnut praline paste (store-bought)	50g	65g

SPONGE		
unsalted butter	80g	105g
espresso (1 shot)	20ml	25ml
eggs	6	8
caster sugar	200g	265g
wattleseeds	4 tsp	5 tsp
instant coffee granules	4 tsp	5 tsp
sea salt flakes	½ tsp	½ tsp
Japanese cake flour or 140g plain flour plus 25g cornflour	165g	220g
hazelnut meal or toasted hazelnuts (skins removed and finely ground)	50g	65g

COFFEE CREAM		
pure cream	200g	250g
double cream or mascarpone	150g	190g
quantity coffee pastry cream (from above)	1	1

HAZELNUT PRALINE

1. Line a tray with baking paper and set aside. Place the hazelnuts and caster sugar in a frying pan or medium-based saucepan and toss to combine, then place over medium heat, ensuring that if you are using gas, the flames aren't licking up the edges of the pan. Shake the hazelnuts occasionally and when you see the sugar turn glassy and melt round the outside, use a wooden spoon to gently stir the nuts every so often to distribute the melting sugar. Eventually, the sugar will start to caramelise, sending little plumes of caramelised sugar into the air. If you feel it is all happening too quickly, just remove the pan from the heat and stir the hazelnuts off the heat, calmly returning to the heat until all the sugar has dissolved and there is a golden, caramelised coating covering the hazelnuts. Turn the heat off and scatter the hazelnuts onto the prepared tray. If you can, separate them by using the tip of your wooden spoon to flick them apart so you have individual hazelnuts for decorating the top of the cake. Sprinkle the nuts evenly with the wattleseeds and allow the praline to cool completely. Once cooled, keep half of the hazelnut praline whole and crush the remainder in a pestle and mortar or place in a plastic bag and smash roughly using a rolling pin. This praline amount is ample for both recipe sizes.

COFFEE PASTRY CREAM

1. Place the wattleseeds and coffee granules in a pestle and mortar and grind until they are very fine. Place in a medium saucepan with the espresso shot and milk over medium heat and bring to the boil, then turn off the heat and allow to infuse for 15 minutes.

2. Meanwhile, place the egg yolks and caster sugar in a medium bowl and whisk with a hand whisk until pale, then add the flour and whisk this through. Return the milk to the boil, then reduce the heat to low and pour one-third of the milk infusion over the egg yolk mixture, whisking it well to incorporate. This process tempers the yolks in preparation for being added to the scalding milk. Return the tempered egg yolk mixture to the milk and whisk gently until the cream starts to thicken; whisk a little quicker to ward off any lumps from forming. Initially, using a whisk is the best tool to avoid lumps forming and then you can swap to a heatproof spatula, which allows you to get into the corners of the pan as you continue to cook the custard over very low heat for 2 minutes. Remove the pan from the heat and strain the pastry cream through a fine *(cont.)*

sieve, pressing with a spatula to remove the coarser parts of the wattleseeds. Whisk through the hazelnut praline paste thoroughly and pour the cream into a container. Cover the surface directly with plastic film to prevent a skin from forming, then pop in the fridge to cool completely.

3 I love the texture of wattleseeds and I have put them in the sponge also, but straining the coarser parts out will result in a more finessed cream and finished cake overall.

SPONGE

1 Preheat the oven to 170°C. Lightly grease 2 x 20 cm | 2 x 25 cm cake tins with butter and pop in a base liner of baking paper to make removing the sponges easier. No need to flour the tins.

2 Melt the butter in a small saucepan, turning off the heat before it starts to boil. Add the espresso to the butter and let them sit together to mingle.

3 This sponge is an old-fashioned Genoese base and so the eggs and sugar are heated first over simmering water before being removed from the heat and whisked until cooled and triple in volume. Choose a heatproof bowl (preferably the bowl from an electric mixer) and crack the eggs into the bowl, then roughly whisk through the sugar using a hand whisk. Place the eggs and sugar over a saucepan of barely simmering water, ensuring that the bowl is not touching the water, and whisk constantly so they don't sit idle and scramble. It is not necessary to engage any fierce whisking action here as the electric mixer or beaters will do that later, you just need to keep the eggs and sugar moving as they are warming. Once the mixture is slightly hot to touch (50°C on a thermometer) remove from the heat and place the bowl onto an electric mixer fitted with the whisk attachment. Beat the eggs on high speed for 5 minutes or until completely cool.

4 Meanwhile, grind the wattleseeds, coffee granules and salt together in a pestle and mortar or a spice grinder until they are fine. Sift them with the flour and hazelnut meal twice to aerate and wake up the flour and distribute everything together. Press any coarse pieces of nut or wattleseed through the sieve as best you can, then discard the very coarse bits.

5 By now the eggs will be cool and have tripled in volume, so remove the bowl from the mixer. Sift one-third of the flour onto the surface of the eggs and gently fold it through using a spatula or metal spoon. Repeat with the next two-thirds. Once all the flour is combined, add 3 tablespoons of the sponge mixture to the melted coffee butter and fold it through to lighten the liquid, then fold this back through the sponge. This will prime the liquid to make it thicker and, in turn, cause less deflation in the finished sponge.

6 Pour the batter into the prepared cake tins and gently smooth the tops using an offset palette knife or a spoon. Pop the cakes into the oven for 20 minutes | 25 minutes. The sponges are ready when the middle of the cake bounces back slightly when pressed with your finger. Remove the sponges from the oven and allow to set in the tins for 2 minutes, only then remove them by tilting the tins at a 45-degree angle and slipping them out onto a cooling rack using your fingertips. Cool the sponges completely before assembling the cake.

COFFEE CREAM

1 Whisk the pure cream and double cream or mascarpone together until firmly whipped. Remove the pastry cream from the fridge and scoop it into a medium bowl, then use a spatula to 'press' the pastry cream into the bowl, flattening it to smooth it out. It's important that you don't start whisking it or stirring it with force, as this will turn it runny again. Fold half the whipped cream mixture through the pastry cream using the same flattening motion, followed by the remaining half until there are no streaks of uneven colour remaining and the filling has maintained a firm consistency for smoothing over the cake.

TO ASSEMBLE

1 To create a finished cake that has the appearance of being fully formed in one tin, I like to slice the top off one of the sponges and the bottom off the other. This forms a gentle serrated line, as it would if the cake had been one and then sliced into two. It fools the eye and creates an authenticity through cheating. There aren't a lot of tricks like that in life that you can get away with.

2 The cake you cut the top off will become the bottom layer, while the second cake will need to be inverted and have the bottom sliced off to form the top of the cake. Go ahead and use a sharp, serrated bread knife to cut just 2 mm off each sponge, then dust away any crumbs and clean down your work surface. If all of this sounds like too much hard work, skip the trimming part and be proud of the amazing sponges sitting on top of each other as they are.

3 Place the bottom sponge onto your chosen cake platter and use an offset palette knife to spread half the coffee cream over the top of the cake all the way to the edges. Sprinkle over most of the crushed praline (reserving a little for the top), then top with the second sponge and spread the remaining coffee cream over the top of the cake, embellishing with a few swirls. Dot the whole hazelnuts and remaining crushed praline over the top to finish the cake.

4 This cake is best eaten on the day it is baked, although the pastry cream and the praline can be made the day before. (*end.*)

LITTLE QUEENIE
Strawberries. Hibiscus. Mint. Pink pepper. Cardamom.

A love letter to a queen. A little prayer of cake to replenish the feminine power that duty may have stripped from her. A whisper in her ear as soft as a last breath, in gratitude for walking her life in the service of others.

SIZE	20cm	25cm
SERVES	10-12	12-15
BUTTERMILK SPONGE		
eggs, separated	6	8
caster sugar	180g	240g
cream of tartar	¼ tsp	½ tsp
plain flour (SEE NOTE)	150g	200g
cornflour (SEE NOTE)	30g	40g
baking powder	1 tsp	1½ tsp
unsalted butter	25g	35g
buttermilk	100ml	130ml
vanilla paste	1 tsp	1 tsp
STRAWBERRY COMPOTE		
dried mint	1 tbsp	1½ tbsp
pink peppercorns, crushed	½ tsp	1 tsp
cardamom pods, cracked	6	8
caster sugar	100g	120g
lemons, zested	1	2
dried hibiscus petals	4	6
vanilla bean, split and seeds scraped	1	1
ripe strawberries, hulled	400g	500g
MASCARPONE FILLING		
cream cheese	75g	100g
mascarpone	150g	200g
crème fraîche (or use 250g pure cream and 125g yoghurt)	225g	300g
caster sugar	60g	80g
vanilla paste	1 tsp	1½ tsp
TO DECORATE		
fresh egg white or 50ml pasteurised egg white	1	1
mint sprigs, picked	8	12
caster sugar	50g	50g
cardamom, crushed	1 tbsp	1 tbsp
strawberries, hulled	125g	125g
pink peppercorns, cracked	1 tsp	1 tsp
dried hibiscus petals	6	10

BUTTERMILK SPONGE

1. Preheat the oven to 170°C. Grease and line 2 x 20 cm | 2 x 25 cm cake tins with baking paper and set them aside. I prepare all the ingredients before I start whipping the eggs for the sponge, that way, folding the sponge can happen swiftly and there is no delay in putting the sponge in the oven.

2. Place the egg whites in the bowl of an electric mixer fitted with the whisk attachment, but don't start whipping just yet. The egg yolks can be set to one side in a small bowl next to the stand mixer, just give them a little whisk with a fork for now. Combine the caster sugar with the cream of tartar in a small bowl and set beside the mixer. Sift the flours and baking powder together twice then set them to one side, being sure to leave the sieve nearby also.

3. Melt the butter in a medium saucepan (I know this size seems excessive, but bear with me), then turn off the heat. Add the buttermilk and vanilla paste, allowing them to warm slightly in the residual heat of the pan.

4. Now you can whip the egg whites. Begin on high speed to create volume until you see soft ribbons starting to form, then reduce the speed to medium. Gradually add the sugar mixture to the meringue, 1 tablespoon at a time, leaving 10 seconds between each addition until all the sugar has been incorporated. Beat the meringue for a further 1 minute to allow the sugar to dissolve fully and create a more stable meringue base for the sponge. This will ultimately contribute to the height and fluffiness of the finished sponge, so be patient here.

5. Reduce the mixer speed to low and, while still beating, trickle the egg yolks directly into the bowl, scraping the last of the egg yolk out using a spatula. Increase the speed to medium until you can see that all the egg yolk has combined with the meringue. This will take no longer than 10 seconds. Remove the bowl from the mixer and, using a spatula, make a couple of folds through the meringue, scraping all the way to the bottom of the bowl to ensure the eggs are fully incorporated.

(*cont.*)

6   Sift half the flour evenly over the top of the sponge and fold through gently until all the flour is combined, then sift in the remaining flour and fold it through. Add approximately 1 cup of sponge batter to the saucepan with the buttermilk mixture, then gently fold them together using a spatula. This will create a fluffy cloud of buttermilk. Then fold the buttermilk cloud back through the sponge until everything is well combined and hopefully still lovely and fluffy.

7   Divide the sponge between the prepared tins and smooth the tops ever so slightly with a palette knife. Place the tins immediately into the centre of the oven and bake for 18 minutes. Check the sponges at 15 minutes; they will be ready when the middle springs back slightly when pressed with your finger. Remove the tins from the oven and allow them to sit for only 2 minutes before slipping the sponges out onto wire cooling racks. This step prevents the sponges from shrinking around the edges.

STRAWBERRY COMPOTE

1   Reduce the oven temperature to 160°C and locate a deep baking tray in preparation for roasting the strawberries. While the sponges are cooling, combine the mint, peppercorns and cardamom together in a bowl. I find the most effective way to do this is in a spice grinder, but you could also use a pestle and mortar. Add this to the sugar along with the lemon zest, hibiscus petals and the seeds from the vanilla bean. Toss the strawberries in a large bowl with the sugar mixture and spread evenly over the base of the baking tray. Add the scraped vanilla bean and roast in the oven for 20 minutes, giving the tray a little shake halfway through to distribute the syrup. Remove the strawberries from the oven and allow to cool in the tray.

MASCARPONE FILLING

1   Soften the cream cheese by cutting it into large cubes and either microwaving it or popping it in the oven for a few minutes on 120°C. Once softened, place in the bowl of an electric mixer fitted with the paddle attachment and beat until smooth. Swap the attachment to the whisk and add the remaining ingredients to the bowl. Beat everything together to combine. Using a spatula, scrape down to the bottom of the bowl to check that all the cream cheese has been incorporated, then give one final whip until the cream is thick and fluffy. Remove the bowl from the mixer and set to one side.

TO DECORATE

1   Preheat the oven to 50°C. Line a baking tray with baking paper. Alternatively, if you have a dehydrator, the fruit can be dried easier and it will retain its colour better. You can also substitute whole freeze-dried strawberries, which you can slice thinly with a paring knife, but these can be costly and hard to find.

2   Lightly whisk the egg white, then brush the mint sprigs with a little egg white on both sides. Toss the leaves in the caster sugar and sprinkle with ground cardamom, then place onto the prepared tray or dehydrator shelf. Slice the strawberries into 2 mm-thick slices and place them on the tray with the mint, then sprinkle on both sides with cracked pink peppercorns. Place the tray in the oven for 4–6 hours or in the dehydrator on 60°C for 10 hours. If having the oven on for that long isn't practical for you, the mint will dry on its own overnight in the open air. The strawberries can't really be dried any other way, so you will need to omit them from the recipe.

TO ASSEMBLE

1. Place one sponge onto your chosen serving platter, then spread half the mascarpone filling evenly over the top of the sponge all the way to the edges, or use a piping bag fitted with a #11 plain nozzle. Press half the strawberries from the compote into the surface of the filling, bearing in mind that when you put the other sponge on top, the strawberries shouldn't protrude too high and prevent the sponge from sitting flat. Spoon some of the roasting syrup over the strawberries and trickle a little over the sides. Place the second sponge on top, then spread the sponge with the remaining mascarpone filling and remaining strawberries. Add the dried strawberries, hibiscus petals and mint, then finish with a few twists of cracked pink peppercorns, if you haven't dried your own strawberries.

2. This sponge, as with all sponges, should be eaten on the day it is baked. The filling and the strawberries can be prepared the day before, but the sponge must be baked the same day you are celebrating. There is no journey so arduous that a sponge should suffer being baked yesterday for. (*end.*)

> **NOTES.**
> Dried hibiscus is readily available from many delis.
>
> To make this gluten-free, substitute plain flour for gluten-free flour and use maize cornflour instead.

TRUTH-SEEKER
Yuzu. Macadamia.

Yuzu is the truth-seeker amongst the wilderness of our hearts.
A gift to know ourselves with kindness and untrammelled expression.
It gives us the freedom to choose our own uninhibited path,
and the courage to invite those who we meet along the way
to share that journey.

(The day before)

YUZU MARMALADE

1. Place a small plate in the freezer for testing the jam's setting point later on. Place the whole yuzu and the water in a large saucepan and bring to the boil over high heat. Once the fruit starts to boil, reduce the heat to medium so that it's simmering. Continue to cook the fruit for 1 hour–1 hour 30 minutes or until softened, then turn off the heat and allow the fruit to cool in the water. When the yuzu is cool enough to handle, remove it from the liquid, but keep the cooking liquid for now. Cut the yuzu in half and scoop out the flesh. Press the yuzu flesh over a sieve into a bowl to extract as much juice as possible, then measure the juice and add the reserved cooking liquid from the saucepan to make the total up to 1 litre. Discard the remaining cooking liquid.

2. Slice the yuzu skin into thin strips and return to the saucepan along with the 1 litre of yuzu liquid, the sugar and the lemon juice. Bring everything to the boil over high heat and continue to cook the yuzu mixture rapidly, stirring occasionally to ensure it doesn't catch on the base of the pan, until setting point is reached. A thermometer is the best instrument for testing the setting point of marmalade, which is 105°C. However, because of the high pectin content in yuzu, you can take it to 104°C, instead, to preserve the flavour of the fruit that could be compromised during that final 1°C. If you don't have a thermometer, you will be relying on your intuition and sight. Watch carefully and when it begins to stick more furiously to the base of the pan and the simmering bubbles become smaller and more consistently sized (less variable) in shape, the marmalade is nearing setting point. If you're still uncertain, remove the frozen plate from the freezer and spoon a tablespoon of marmalade onto the plate. Leave it for 10 seconds before running your finger through it. If it wrinkles and creates a pathway that doesn't join back together, it's set. If not, continue to cook and stir the marmalade until it does, then remove it from the heat. Pour the yuzu marmalade into sterilised glass jars for storage. I like to boil the jars back up again in a pot of water for 10 minutes to ensure a reliable seal. You will only use around 200 g of the marmalade for this recipe, but you can store the rest for up to one year.

(cont.)

CHIFFON TIN SIZE	25cm
SERVES	10-15

YUZU MARMALADE	
yuzu, stems removed	1kg
water	2.5 litres
granulated sugar	900g
lemons, juiced	4 (200ml)

MACADAMIA PRALINE PASTE	
whole macadamias	250g
caster sugar	250g
water	60ml

CHIFFON	
eggs, separated	9
brown sugar	40g
salt	pinch
macadamia paste (from above)	120g
water	70g
macadamia oil	70g
caster sugar	180g
cornflour	40g
plain flour	140g
macadamias, toasted and roughly chopped	50g

FROSTING	
cream cheese (preferably Neufchatel), softened	350g
icing sugar, sifted	50g
crème fraîche	100g
praline, finely chopped (from above)	100g
yuzu marmalade (from above), thick cut	100g

(On the day)

MACADAMIA PRALINE PASTE

1. Preheat the oven to 160°C. Scatter the macadamias for both the praline and the chiffon onto a tray lined with baking paper and toast in the oven for 20 minutes or until golden. Remove from the oven and separate 50 g, leaving the remainder on the tray. Chop the 50 g and set them aside to fold through the chiffon later.

2. Weigh the sugar and water and place in a medium saucepan, then stir together using a heatproof spatula and place over low heat. Have a little cup of water beside the stove and use a pastry brush dipped in the water to brush any sugar crystals from sides of the saucepan down into the sugar. This will stop the caramel from crystallising. Stir the sugar and water until the sugar crystals dissolve, but stop stirring once it starts to boil. Increase the heat to medium and continue to brush the sides of the pan if you see any crystals forming.

3. Once the caramel starts to change colour around the edges, swirl the pan in a circular motion to distribute the colour. Allow the caramel to reach a dark amber colour before turning off the heat completely. Working quickly, now tip the toasted macadamias from the tray into the caramel by gathering up the baking paper and using it as a funnel to transfer the nuts to the pan. Return the baking paper to the tray in preparation for pouring the nuts onto it, then use a spatula to stir the nuts into the caramel. Pour the praline evenly over the baking paper and allow it to cool for 30 minutes until it sets hard.

4. Place the praline in a blender and pulse until it is finely chopped, being careful not to blitz it into a paste. Remove 100 g of the praline from the blender to use for the frosting, then continue to blitz the remaining praline until it forms a paste. You may need to scrape down the inside of the blender with a spatula to ensure the blade catches all the praline and the paste becomes smooth. The paste will take around 10 minutes to form and will look like chunky peanut butter, depending on how sharp your blender blade is. Decant into a small bowl and set aside.

CHIFFON

1. Preheat the oven to 160°C. Have a 23 cm chiffon pan ready, tube inserted and ready to go, so that once you've made the chiffon batter it can be poured into the pan and swiftly placed in the oven. Make sure that you have adjusted your oven racks to fit the chiffon pan, ensuring a 5 cm clearance for rising, as scraping cake from the roof of the oven is no fun.

2. Place the egg yolks into a large mixing bowl with the brown sugar and whisk together well using a hand whisk. Add the egg whites and salt to the bowl of an electric mixer fitted with the whisk attachment, but don't start whipping until I give you the go ahead. You will need to have all your ingredients weighed, measured and ready to go before any whipping happens.

3. Firstly, weigh the macadamia praline paste, water and macadamia oil together in a small bowl and set them aside. Secondly, weigh the caster sugar and 20 g cornflour together in a separate small bowl and set it beside the electric mixer with a tablespoon in the bowl. Finally weigh the plain flour and remaining 20 g cornflour and place together in a medium bowl with a sieve nearby.

4. Pour the macadamia praline paste into the egg yolks and whisk everything together thoroughly. Sift the flour and cornflour mixture directly into the yolk mixture and gently whisk together to form a smooth paste. While the flours

have relatively low gluten, it is always best practice not to whisk the flour too much or it will toughen the sponge. The objective is to whisk just enough to obliterate the lumps and distribute the flour evenly.

5 Now you can begin whisking the egg whites at medium-high speed. Use the tablespoon in the small bowl of sugar to stir the cornflour through evenly and when soft ribbons start to form in the egg whites, begin adding the sugar mixture, 1 tablespoon at a time, sprinkling it evenly and gradually over the surface of the meringue. Continue adding the sugar 1 tablespoon at a time, leaving 5 seconds between each addition, until it is all incorporated, then continue whisking the meringue for 1 minute or until firm peaks form. Be careful not to over-whisk the meringue.

6 When the meringue is thick and glossy remove the bowl from the electric mixer and, one-third at a time, fold the meringue through the egg yolk batter. The first third of the meringue paves the way for the next two-thirds by smoothing the base and creating a consistency that more closely resembles the whites. You can be slightly less gentle with the first addition, but fold in the remaining egg whites as gently as possible to preserve the lightness of the chiffon. Lastly, fold through the 50 g chopped macadamias, checking that there are no lumps or streaks of meringue in the final batter.

7 Pour the batter into the chiffon tin and smooth the top with the back of a tablespoon. Ensure the batter touches the circumference of the tin, as this will make a connection and reinforce the eventual height of the cake. If you leave the batter domed, the cake will rise in this shape and you will end up cutting this off anyway and losing precious cake. At this stage, I used to tap the chiffon gently on the bench to release any air pockets, but more recently I have been dragging a skewer through the chiffon in a circular motion, starting at the outside of the tin and working my way into the centre, to settle the batter evenly into the tin. Either method will do the trick.

8 Place the cake in the oven, checking again that you have a 5 cm clearance for the cake to rise, then quickly but gently shut the door and bake for 50 minutes. Test the cake by pressing the centre to see if it bounces back, then remove from the oven. If the cake has risen above the three little feet on the tin, you will need to trim the crust. Use a serrated knife to slice off the top until it is just beneath those feet (no more), then invert the tin immediately so that the chiffon can hang upside down to cool for at least 4 hours.

9 To remove the cake from the tin you will need to use a knife with a thin, pointy blade or a large palette knife. Insert the blade between the cake and the tin and run it round the outside to release the cake. You will need to repeat this step with the inner tube, but for this I find a skewer or a paring knife more effective. Gently press the base of the tin inwards and the cake will fall from the tin. Use a serrated knife to trim the cake base level and then back to the pointy, large knife to release the cake from the inner tube at the top. Brush away any crumbs using your hands or a pastry brush and invert the cake onto a platter. Clean down the area around the cake so it is completely crumb-free.   (*cont.*)

FROSTING

1. Place the softened cream cheese in the bowl of an electric mixer fitted with the paddle attachment and beat on medium speed until smooth and fluffy. Using a spatula, scrape down the sides of the bowl and tip the machine hood back so you can scrape under the paddle all the way to the base of the bowl. Cream cheese lumps can be hiding under there! Continue beating for a further 1 minute and when you are certain you have obliterated any lumps, add the icing sugar and beat for another 1 minute. Swap the attachment for the whisk, add the crème fraîche and beat on relatively high speed for around 2 minutes to create a thick frosting.

2. Remove the bowl from the mixer and fold the reserved 100 g praline through the frosting. Now, gently fold through 1 tablespoon of the yuzu marmalade. Don't stir it too vigorously as this will thin the frosting and you'll find it difficult to ice the cake.

3. Ordinarily to ice a chiffon, due to the crumby nature of the sides, I would apply a crumb coating first, then refrigerate until it sets before applying the second coating. This traps the crumb in the inner frosting, allowing you to avoid the crumbs on the outer layer. In this case, though, the cream cheese will not set firmly enough to do this, so the frosting needs to be applied all in one go. Spoon half the frosting onto the top of the chiffon and use an offset palette knife to spread the cream to the edge. Using a circular motion and only going in one direction will decrease the likelihood of getting crumbs in the frosting. Keep pushing the frosting to the edge and eventually it will fall over the sides. Keep applying frosting only to the top but push it over the edges and down the sides. When it's halfway down the sides, start sweeping the icing around the outside. This method prevents crumbs sticking in the frosting because it's not being agitated too much. Once the chiffon is completely covered, whip around and create swirls as you wish, then spoon the remaining marmalade on top and swirl it into the surface, integrating it into the frosting.

4. This chiffon can be iced the night before and kept refrigerated – just cover loosely with plastic film or an upside-down plastic container to avoid it drying out. Cut the chiffon with a large, sharp serrated knife. (*end.*)

UNDER THE QUANDONG TREE
Quandong. Bush honey. Lemon verbena. Almonds.

The quandong tree is a sacred tree, where much Indigenous lore and teachings are passed down from old women to young women as the fruit is prepared under the shade of its branches. The fruit is taken for drying and the nuts gathered for making adornments.

TRAY SIZE	30cm x 40cm x 3cm
SERVES	10-12

QUANDONG COMPOTE	
frozen quandongs or plums, halved and stones removed	500g / 12
water	1 litre
orange, zested and juiced	1
star anise	1
caster sugar	80g

LEMON VERBENA CUSTARD	
double cream	150g
pure cream	300g
whole dried lemon verbena leaves, plus a few to decorate	6
lemon, zested	1
vanilla paste	1 tsp
wild honey	30g
egg yolks	5
caster sugar	150g
mascarpone	150g

SPONGE	
natural almonds, toasted	160g
plain flour	60g
cornflour	40g
ground cinnamon	1 tsp
icing sugar, sifted, plus a little to decorate	150g
bush or wild honey	90g
eggs, separated	5
vanilla paste	1 tsp
salt	pinch
lemon, zested	1
smoked salt (optional)	pinch

QUANDONG COMPOTE

1. If you are using quandongs, place the quandongs, water, orange zest and juice, and star anise in a medium saucepan over medium heat and bring to the boil. Reduce heat to low and simmer slowly for 1 hour or until the quandongs are tender. By not allowing the water to boil too ferociously, you'll maintain the shape of the fruit. As all quandongs are different sizes, you may need to simmer them for up to 20 minutes longer. The water will evaporate as the fruit cooks and, by the time they are tender, there will be barely any liquid left in the saucepan. If you feel they're not cooked but there is no liquid left in the pan, just add another 250 ml of boiling water and continue to cook until soft. Once the quandongs are tender, remove the star anise and add the sugar to the saucepan. Stir the sugar through the fruit using a wooden spoon until the sugar has dissolved. Continue to simmer the fruit for a further 20 minutes or until the syrup thickens slightly, then turn off the heat and cool the quandongs completely either at room temperature or in the fridge.

2. If you are using plums, preheat the oven to 150°C. Arrange the plums cut-side up on a baking tray with the star anise cracked over them. Squeeze the orange juice over the top of each plum half and sprinkle with the zest and caster sugar. Omit the water completely, then place the tray into the oven to bake the plums for 15 minutes. Remove the tray from the oven, turn the halves so that they are cut-side down and sitting in the juices, and return the tray to the oven for a further 5 minutes. The plums should be very tender when cooked, because eventually they will be rolled into the sponge and you will need to cut through them easily when you slice the cake. Remove the plums from the oven and cool in the juices.

(cont.)

LEMON VERBENA CUSTARD

1. Place the double cream, 150 g pure cream, verbena, lemon zest, vanilla and honey in a small saucepan over low heat and bring to the boil. Turn off the heat and allow the aromatics to infuse in the cream for at least 30 minutes. Meanwhile, pop the egg yolks and caster sugar into a medium-size bowl and, using a hand whisk, whisk together until pale and fluffy. Place a sieve over the bowl in preparation for the next step. Return the cream to the boil and then pour it through the sieve and over the egg yolks. Discard the aromatics and whisk the yolks and cream together until well combined. Return the custard to the saucepan over the lowest heat and stir slowly and constantly for approximately 2 minutes or until the custard thickens. If you see the edges of the custard curdling before this stage, remove it from the heat and give it a little whisk to cool it down and emulsify it back together, then return it to the heat to continue thickening. The important thing when making custard is not to rush it and make sure that, as you stir, you are scraping along the base of the saucepan to prevent the custard from sticking. To test if the custard is ready, lift your wooden spoon or spatula out of the custard and hold it vertically over the saucepan, then using your finger, draw a line across the back of the spoon through the custard. If the line doesn't join back together, the custard is ready. Remove the saucepan from the heat and pour the custard immediately onto a plate or flat tray to help it cool down quickly. Cover the surface with plastic film to avoid it forming a skin on top, then place it in the fridge to cool for at least 2 hours.

SPONGE

1. Preheat the oven to 160°C. Line a 30 cm x 40 cm x 3 cm baking tray with baking paper, ensuring the paper is neatly tucked into the corners and sits slightly above the rim of the tray. Before you begin whipping the sponge, prepare all the ingredients first, so that everything can be assembled calmly and baked with no last-minute stress.

2. Prepare the almonds first by thinly slicing 100 g for decorating the outside of the roulade. I like to slice them lengthways using the heel of a of a very sharp cook's knife, so that the shape of the almond kernel is maintained. If you don't feel like doing this or you don't have the knife to achieve it, the world isn't going to end – just slice them as you wish. Crush the remaining 60 g of almonds using a pestle and mortar or in a food processor until they form a fine powder, almost like conventional almond meal. Set aside for now.

3. Sift the flours and cinnamon together twice, then sift the icing sugar and divide it into two portions. Warm the honey in a small saucepan until it is runny and easy to fold through the sponge. Separate the eggs and place the yolks and half the icing sugar into the bowl of an electric mixer fitted with the whisk attachment and beat on medium speed for 3 minutes or until pale and fluffy. Decant the mixture into a larger bowl and fold through the vanilla, then clean and dry the bowl of the electric mixer.

4. Now whisk the egg whites in the electric mixer with a pinch of salt. When you see soft ribbons forming, reduce the speed to medium and gradually add the remaining icing sugar until the meringue is thick and glossy, taking care not to overwhip, then remove the bowl from the machine.

5. Fold the whipped egg whites gently through the egg yolks, one-third at a time, being sure to eliminate any lumps of egg white by flattening them with your spatula before folding them through. This will ensure you don't have any pockets of egg white through the sponge. Once the yolks and whites are combined, fold through the flours, one-third at a time, sifting them directly over

the eggs onto the surface of the sponge. Gently fold through, then fold through the ground almonds. Remember to scrape thoroughly all the way to the bottom of the bowl to incorporate all of the egg whites. Remove 1 tablespoon of the sponge mixture and fold it through the honey to create a consistency closer to the sponge. Fold this emulsion back into the sponge. This is a way of priming any liquid added to a sponge that would usually knock a lot of the aeration out due to the amount of folding required to combine it.

6   Pour the sponge into the prepared tray and use an offset palette knife to smooth the surface, being sure to push the sponge into the corners. Sprinkle half the sliced almonds evenly over the top, then bake the sponge for 12 minutes.

7   While the sponge is baking, prepare for rolling the roulade by placing a clean tea towel flat on your bench. Place a large sheet of baking paper, the same size as the sponge, on top of the tea towel. Scatter the paper with the remaining sliced almonds and sprinkle half the lemon zest evenly over the top. Check the sponge is cooked at the 12-minute mark by pressing the centre with your finger, if it bounces back, it's ready. If it doesn't, return the sponge to the oven for a further 2–3 minutes, then remove it and carefully invert onto the baking paper, so the dark, topside of the sponge is now facing down, then remove the tray. Allow the sponge to rest for 30 seconds before carefully peeling the baking paper away to reveal the pale side. Turn the sponge so that the shortest side is parallel to your body, then roll it up together with the paper, rolling it away from you. Leave the tea towel flat on the bench, then once the sponge and paper have formed a cocoon, you can roll them in the tea towel. This will create a preliminary bend in the sponge as it cools and should only be rolled loosely. Rolling it too tightly may result in tears in the sponge later. Cool the sponge for 30 minutes only.

TO ASSEMBLE

1   While the sponge is cooling, whisk the mascarpone and remaining pure cream together until very firmly whipped. Mascarpone has a tendency to overwhip to butter very quickly, so if you're whipping in an electric mixer, keep an eye on it. Fold the verbena custard gently through the whipped cream in two batches. The purpose of the cream here is to give the filling more structure, so that it doesn't run out of the roulade.

2   Unroll the sponge. The centre of the roll will remain a little curled, so don't force it or it may break. Using an offset palette knife, spread two-thirds of the verbena custard over the inside of the roulade, not forgetting the part of the sponge that is still curled – this is the centre of the roulade. Leave a 2 cm gap at the other end of the roll, then scatter evenly with three-quarters of the quandong compote or plums. Starting at the curled end and rolling a little tighter this time, roll the roulade back up without the paper. The cream will spread a little, so as you reach the 2 cm gap it will be covered. The almond slices on the outside will have pressed themselves into the outside of the sponge and this texture will now be revealed. Sit the roulade seam-side down so its weight reinforces the seam. Dust the roulade with a little icing sugar, then manoeuvre it onto a platter. Decorate the top with the remaining verbena custard and verbena leaves, and more quandongs or plums. Sprinkle with the remaining lemon zest and a small amount of smoked salt, if you wish. (*end.*)

ORCH

AGRARIAN APRICOTS
Apricots. Thyme. Almonds.
109

EVE
Figs. Tonka bean. Pine nuts.
113

APPLE AND MEDLAR CHARLOTTE
Apples. Medlars
117

BALLYMALOE TRIFLE
Peach. Rose geranium. Blackberries.
123

CITRUS MACADAMIA TORTE
Pink grapefruit. Macadamia. Cedro.
126

EXPLORING THE LANDSCAPE
OF MY HEART
Blackcurrants. Pear. Gianduja.
131

LUCKY
Kumquat. Tangerine. Macadamia. Calendula petals for healing.
137

MARIÚ
Grapes. Rosemary. Lemon.
143

SAVARIN
Clementines. Toffee. Crème Anglaise.
145

TAKUMI
Hōjicha. Dulce de leche. Cinnamon. Plums.
149

THE WALTZING ORANGE TREE
Blood orange. Cardamom. Orange blossom.
153

SAKURA
Cherry. Almonds. Japanese whisky.
157

ORCHARD

There is an orchard of stone fruit trees growing in the furrows of my heart. They were planted there as a child and I still run in between the trees and sit under the branches plucking ripe fruit from the laden boughs.

Plots of apples, apricots and peaches perfectly stitched like patchwork fields.

The apple trees have been there since the beginning, they have heard everything and will listen to all the old stories we tell ourselves. A vintage Charlotte to celebrate the journey and calendula petals sprinkled in for healing.

I've lived an intrepid life and my love for England took me down the green and shaded lanes of blackcurrants and rambling heirloom pears where I left behind a piece of my heart.

These explorations have tethered my spirit to an eternal love of learning and instilled gratitude for I've learned that life is short. Like the way cherry blossoms bloom and then fall so quickly in my sakura cake.

The citrus trees of grapefruit, kumquats, mandarins and oranges are pure luckiness. Blessings and good fortune during a life that began from the clay beneath those orchards.

This chapter is about being thankful through the creativity and layers of cake. It is my gift that I flourish in their making.

AGRARIAN APRICOTS
Apricots. Thyme. Almonds.

If we were formed from the clay then we must carry with us all the memories of the earth since ancient times. There are people I've met who naturally inhabit the clay they were formed from by listening and dancing to their own rhythm.

My grandfather, who was an agrarian man, was tethered to the earth and farmed with the moon in the palm of his hand. He would stand in the doorway after being in the field and his silhouette would take up the whole space within the frame, solid like the trunk of a big oak tree. He always seemed reluctant to step foot inside because I think he knew he would wither a little.

He drank his scotch on the veranda every evening looking beyond an orchard of stone fruit to a horizon that inspired many of his dreams and musings, pondering all the promises he had vowed to keep that day and making more again for tomorrow.

SIZE	25cm	30cm
SERVES	10-12	12-15

ALMOND SABLE		
unsalted butter, softened	190g	350g
icing sugar, sifted	80g	130g
Demerara sugar	55g	100g
egg yolks	2	3
spelt flour	125g	200g
emmer wheat flour	125g	200g
sea salt	¼ tsp	½ tsp
whole blanched almonds, toasted and finely ground	90g	160g

THYME CUSTARD FILLING		
double cream	425g	570g
pure cream	250g	375g
vanilla bean, split and seeds scraped or vanilla paste	1/2 tsp	1/2 tsp
thyme sprigs	5	7
egg yolks	8	10
caster sugar	100g	150g
fresh apricots / preserved apricot halves, drained	8/12	16/24
thyme sprigs, ½ picked into petals	5	7
icing sugar, for sprinkling		

ALMOND SABLE

1. Combine the butter and sugars in the bowl of an electric mixer fitted with the paddle attachment and cream together on low speed for no more than 2 minutes. They should be pale, but not too fluffy. Overbeating the butter may make the sable very crumbly and too fragile once baked.

2. Scrape down the sides of the bowl using a spatula (if using the mixer) to ensure the butter is being creamed evenly with the sugar. Beat in the egg yolks one at a time, then remove the bowl from the mixer as soon as the last one is incorporated. Sift the flours directly into the bowl, then add the salt and almond and fold through using a spatula. When making sable, this step is always done by hand so as not to overwork the gluten in the flour, which will toughen the pastry. Once the dry ingredients have been added to the butter the texture will seem more like a paste, this is due to the high butter-to-flour ratio. Ensure there are no remaining streaks of butter by scraping all the way to the bottom of the bowl with your spatula, then place a large piece of baking paper onto your bench and scoop the pastry onto the paper. This pastry is going to be rolled out between two sheets of paper because it is too sticky to roll with a rolling pin, so bear in mind the piece of paper will need to be at least 30 cm | 36 cm square to enable you to roll it big enough to fit the tart tin. If your paper is not that wide just use two sheets side-by-side, then top the pastry with another sheet of paper. Using your hands, pat the pastry into a round disc then roll the pastry evenly between the sheets, rotating it 90 degrees as you go to achieve a round sheet of pastry that is 5 mm-thick and 32 cm | 35 cm in diameter. Place the pastry in the fridge for 30 minutes to rest and set. *(cont.)*

LINING AND BAKING THE PASTRY CASE

1. Lightly grease a 25 cm | 30 cm round tart tin with butter and dust with flour or give it a light spray with oil.

2. Remove the pastry from the fridge and test its pliability by bending it gently. Usually 10 minutes out of the fridge is an optimum length of time to attempt the lining process. In any case, remember this pastry is high in butter, so it can be coaxed into shape easily with a little persuasion by you.

3. Remove the top paper, then invert the pastry sheet over the top of the tart tin. Peel the bottom sheet off and use your hands to gently tuck the pastry into the tart tin all the way around, as a preliminary effort to stop the surplus pastry from tearing over the rim. Then go around again, this time focusing on setting the pastry more securely into the groove where the base of the tart tin meets the sides. Finally, the third time around, press the pastry into the sides of the tart tin. Neaten up the rim of the pastry case using a pair of scissors, cutting it 5–7 mm above the rim of the tart tin to create an even edge, then pop the pastry case in the freezer to set hard for 15 minutes.

4. Meanwhile, preheat the oven to 150°C. Prepare a round piece of baking paper or foil 30 cm | 36 cm in diameter to set inside the tart case for baking blind. Remove the pastry case from the freezer and line the inside with the prepared circle, tucking it tightly into the right-angle you've created, then fill the case with baking beads. Ensure the paper or foil is not hanging over the edge, which will place pressure on the fragile pastry when baking and may cause it to break. Bake for 35 minutes then remove from the oven and allow the pastry to set for 15 minutes. Gently remove the baking beads and paper from the pastry case.

THYME CUSTARD FILLING

1. Place the creams, vanilla bean and seeds, and thyme in a medium saucepan and bring to the boil, then turn off the heat and allow the cream to sit and infuse for 30 minutes.

2. Meanwhile, whip the egg yolks and the sugar together using a hand whisk until pale and fluffy, then return the cream to the boil and pour it over the yolks. Whisk everything together thoroughly, then strain the custard through a fine sieve to remove the aromatics. It is not necessary to return the custard to the stove here, as it will finish cooking in the oven. Pour the custard into a jug ready for pouring into the case.

FILLING AND BAKING THE TART

1. Preheat the oven to 120°C. Place the baked tart shell on a flat baking tray then manoeuvre it into the oven and pour the custard into the case until it reaches 1 cm from the rim of the pastry. This is a task best done while the tart is in the oven to avoid any spillages.

2. Bake the custard for 35 minutes, then open the oven door and place the fresh or preserved apricots on the surface of the custard while the tart is still in the oven. It may be necessary to gently slide out the oven rack and dot the apricots into the custard, then slide it back in. Top the tart with the sprigs and petals of thyme and bake for a further 30 minutes or until the custard no longer wobbles. Press the middle of the custard with your finger to double-check the tart is firm, then remove it from the oven and cool the tart in the tin for 2 hours. Remove the tart from the tin and slice using a sharp, pointed knife.

3. Sprinkle with icing sugar to serve. This tart can be baked the night before and the leftovers (if there are any) keep reasonably well in the fridge for up to 2 days. (*end.*)

EVE
Figs. Tonka bean. Pine nuts.

Eve lives at the threshold between our inner landscape and
the outside world. When our natural expression takes flight
she is in the ether of our unique gifts.

That lifeforce forges a tangled pathway to the surface
through constant betrayals of the heart,
but when it reaches the light, we are set free.

PINE NUT CRUST

1. Preheat the oven to 160°C. Grease and line a 20 cm | 25 cm pie dish in preparation. Scatter the pine nuts onto a baking tray and toast in the oven for 15 minutes or until golden, then remove from the oven. Leave the oven on for the cake crust, then cool the pine nuts completely on the tray. Once cooled, grind the pine nuts in a food processor or pound them using a pestle and mortar until a fine crumb forms. Pine nuts contain quite a lot of oil, so if you are using a blender you will need to use the pulse function to avoid them ending up as paste.

2. Sift the icing sugar, almond meal and cornflour together into a bowl so they can get to know one another. Press any stubborn lumps of icing sugar through the sieve and return any coarse parts of almond to the bowl for texture. Cut the butter into small dice and scatter over the dry ingredients in the bowl, then use your fingertips to rub the butter into the flours until the mixture resembles breadcrumbs. Add the ground pine nuts and the salt. The mixture will start to become sticky and resemble a paste.

3. Scoop the paste into the base of the prepared pie dish and use your fingertips to push it up the sides, pressing the crumb into an even thickness to cover the base and sides of the dish. Don't waste time creating fancy trims and embellishments with the rim of the crust, because once the crumb of the pie has been baked any ornate finishing will disappear due to the high butter content.

4. Place the crust in the fridge to rest for 15 minutes then reduce the oven temperature to 150°C. Remove the pie dish from the fridge and bake for 30 minutes or until it is dark-golden all over. A darker crumb will be lovely here, as it enhances the nutty flavour of the pine nuts and with the large amount of butter in the crumb, it tastes like beurre noisette. Once you are happy with the colour, remove the crust from the oven while you prepare the rice pudding. Turn the oven off for a little rest for now.

(cont.)

PIE DISH SIZE	20cm	25cm
SERVES	10-12	12-15
PINE NUT CRUST		
pine nuts	80g	100g
icing sugar	30g	40g
almond meal	80g	100g
cornflour	45g	55g
unsalted butter, softened	85g	100g
salt	pinch	pinch
TONKA BEAN RICE PUDDING		
short grain rice (SEE NOTE)	180g	250g
milk	650ml	900ml
vanilla bean(s), split and seeds scraped	1	2
orange, zested	½	1
lemon, zested	½	1
tonka beans	2	3
caster sugar, plus 50g/75g for torching (optional)	75g	100g
fresh ripe figs	5	7
unsalted butter	30g	40g
egg(s)	1	2
egg yolks	2	3
pure cream	100ml	140ml
fig liqueur or Armagnac	30ml	40ml

TONKA BEAN RICE PUDDING

1. Place the rice in a medium saucepan and cover with cold water, then use your fingertips to swirl the rice around a few times. Drain the water then repeat the rice-washing twice more to remove some of the starch. You will notice the water becomes clearer each time. Cover the drained rice with the milk then add the vanilla bean and seeds and the orange and lemon zests. Finally, grate the tonka beans into the milk using a microplane or the finest side of a box grater.

2. Place the saucepan on your stovetop, choosing the hob that will give you an option for the lowest heat. Begin by bringing the rice and milk to the boil over medium heat, stirring occasionally using a heatproof spatula or wooden spoon. Then add only 75 g | 100 g of the sugar and stir again to dissolve. Now reduce the heat to the lowest setting and let the pudding simmer for 15 minutes, stirring every 3 minutes or so to prevent the rice from sticking and allowing it to cook evenly. Test the rice to see if it is cooked. By this time, the milk will be nearly all absorbed, so if you need to cook it for longer you will need to add another 100 ml milk to ensure it doesn't boil dry.

3. It's important the rice is cooked and not al dente. However, if it's mushy and overcooked, this may result in the pudding being claggy. Test the pudding every few minutes to make sure it is perfectly cooked, then turn off the heat and allow it to cool for 15 minutes, stirring occasionally to release the heat further. After this time, the oven can be preheated to 140°C.

4. At this stage, you should assess the figs for ripeness by cutting them in half. The pudding is only in the oven for a further 30 minutes on low heat, so if the figs aren't ripe they will not meld into the pudding. If they're a little firm or under ripe they can be softened by placing in a shallow frying pan with the orange juice and 2 tablespoons caster sugar. To do this, squeeze the orange juice from the zested orange (used above) into the frying pan then add the sugar and place over medium heat until syrupy. Place the figs face-down in the syrup and continue to swill the pan for further 1 minute to release the sugars from the figs, then remove them from the heat and set aside. This all being said, if the figs are ripe and juicy there will be no need to cook them at all.

5. To finish the pudding, add the butter to the rice pudding and mix it through using a wooden spoon. Whisk the egg, yolks and cream together using a fork then stir it through the rice pudding along with your chosen liqueur until it is well combined. Pour the rice pudding into the pie dish, leaving a little room for the figs, then pop the fruit, facing up, into the rice pudding, pressing to submerge into the rice. Bake the pie for 30 minutes until the centre of the pudding is firm when pressed with your finger. The pudding will continue to cook further once it is removed from the oven and so leaving it a little softer in the centre at this point is absolutely fine. Allow the pie to cool for 20 minutes before torching.

TO TORCH THE PIE

1 Sprinkle a small section on top of the pie with caster sugar then use a kitchen blowtorch to burn the sugar. Be careful not to allow the blowtorch to singe the pastry, so make sure to stand 'behind' the crust, pointing the blowtorch into the centre of the pie as you caramelise the sugar. Continue sprinkling the sugar in small sections at a time until you have burnt the entire top of the pie.

2 Cool the pie for 10 minutes before slicing into pieces. This pie really needs no other accompaniment, although, I would never say no to a little thick pouring cream trickled on top. (*end*.)

NOTE.

This pie was inspired by one I ate in Florence, where it is traditionally eaten for breakfast. In Florence, they would use arborio rice for the pudding. Far be it from me to school the Italians on what rice is best, but my preference is a traditional short grain rice whose personality isn't to be left al dente, as it is with arborio. For this pie I used a short grain Japanese rice, as it can be cooked gently all the way through while still retaining its shape. It's becoming increasingly difficult to find short grain rice in Australia, so Japanese rice has an advantage for this reason alone.

APPLE & MEDLAR CHARLOTTE
Apples. Medlars.

We tell our stories to the apple trees,
for they are the long-lived witnesses to our days.

We embellish our tales, layering details with each iteration
perhaps to rekindle what we didn't feel the first time.

The apple trees will listen to our fictions as we refine them.
They know each version has its own truth.

LOAF TIN SIZE	25cm x 10cm
PUDDING BASIN OR BUNDT TIN SIZE	20cm
BRIOCHE	
fresh yeast / dried yeast	15g / 7g
warm milk, plus a splash for glaze	60ml
caster sugar	1 tbsp
strong bakers flour	350g
salt, plus extra for glaze	1 tsp
eggs, plus 1 extra egg for glaze	4
unsalted butter, softened and roughly chopped	165g
MEDLAR PURÉE	
ripe, bletted medlars (SEE NOTES)	800g
lemons, zested and juiced	3
white sugar	approx. 100 g
APPLE AND MEDLAR FILLING	
Bramley or Granny Smith apples, peeled and cored	7
unsalted butter	100g
vanilla paste	2 tsp
water	300ml
cooked medlar purée (from above)	300g
CLARIFIED BUTTER	
unsalted butter	280g

BRIOCHE

1. Place the yeast, warm milk and 1 teaspoon of the sugar in a small bowl and mix everything together to dissolve the yeast.

2. Place the flour, salt and remaining sugar in the bowl of an electric mixer fitted with the dough hook and mix on low speed to combine. Meanwhile, give the eggs a little whisk with a fork to break them up, then turn the mixer off and add the eggs and yeast mixture to the well that has been formed by the hook. Beat on low speed until you can't see any loose flour remaining at the bottom of the bowl, then increase the speed to medium and beat for a further 10 minutes or until the dough is glossy and elastic. Scrape down the bottom and sides of the bowl using a spatula, then continue mixing on medium speed as you gradually add the butter, little by little, allowing each addition to be almost fully incorporated before adding the next. Once all the butter has been added, beat the dough for a further 5 minutes to develop its structure. Remove the dough from the mixer and transfer it to a large, lightly oiled bowl then cover with a cloth and place it somewhere warm to prove for 1 hour. Once it has doubled in volume, use your hands to fold the dough over itself twice, like a piece of paper. Cover the dough with the cloth again and repeat the proving process once more until it has doubled in volume.

3. Grease a 25 cm x 10 cm loaf tin with butter and dust with flour, then set aside. Tip the dough out onto a work surface lightly dusted with flour, then flatten it into a 30 cm x 25 cm rectangle. Starting from one of the short sides, roll up the dough into a tight cylinder and place it in the prepared tin. It should fit snugly in the tin, but if it doesn't, just use your fingers to press it outwards from the centre along the length of the dough to even out the surface. Cover the loaf with a tea towel and prove in a warm place for 2 hours or until the dough has doubled in volume and sits 2 cm above the rim of the tin. Don't be tempted to let the dough rise any more than this, otherwise it will spill over during baking and mess up the shape.

(*cont.*)

4 Preheat the oven to 180°C. Beat the extra egg, a pinch of salt and a splash of milk together with a fork and gently brush the egg wash over the brioche, using even strokes from one end of the loaf to the other. Bake for 30 minutes, then reduce the temperature to 170°C and bake for a further 20 minutes until a skewer insert into the centre comes out clean. Remove the brioche from the oven and tip it out onto a wire rack to cool completely.

MEDLAR PURÉE

1 Wash the ripe and bletted medlars and place them in a large jam pan or heavy-based saucepan with the lemon zest and juice, then cover well with water. Bring the fruit to the boil over high heat then reduce to a simmer for 10 minutes or until soft. Remove the pan from the heat and drain into a colander, then purée the fruit in a food processor until it is smooth. Press the purée through a fine sieve using the back of a spatula to remove the medlar skins and roughage. You will now likely be left with 50 per cent of the fruit that you started with. Weigh the strained purée and combine it in a smaller saucepan with 25 per cent of its own weight in sugar. Place the pan over medium heat and bring it to the boil, stirring the sugar until it has dissolved, then simmer for 5 minutes. Remove the purée from the stove and set aside at room temperature while you get on with making the apple and medlar filling.

APPLE AND MEDLAR FILLING

1 Cut the apples into a rough 1 cm dice. Combine half the butter and all the vanilla in a large saucepan over medium heat and heat until butter is melted. Add one-third of the apple and cook for a few minutes to soften without colouring. Add one-third of the water to steam and break the apple down further – this will take a few more minutes. Then add another one-third of the apple with half the remaining butter and another one-third of the water and cook the apples for 15 minutes or until softened and partly puréed. Finally add the remaining apple, butter and water and reduce the heat to low. Cook for 15 minutes then remove the pan from the heat and fold through the medlar purée. Set the filling to one side for now.

CLARIFIED BUTTER

1 This recipe calls for clarified butter, so that when the Charlotte goes into the oven to bake, the brioche doesn't burn due to the fat having been removed from the butter. Place the butter in a small saucepan over low heat until it comes to a gentle boil, then allow it to simmer so that foam forms on top. Gently skim the foam from the top, then turn off the heat and let the butter sit for a few minutes. Skim any remaining foam off the top and discard it. The next layer is the clarified butter, which you need to either skim off using a ladle or carefully pour into a jar and, by doing so, you will leave behind any milk solids that have settled on the bottom of the pan. Set the clarified butter aside and discard any solids. Ultimately, the clarified butter is best used after it is slightly set, since this will give you a better ratio of butter on each slice of brioche. Using it while it's in liquid form will mean there is less butter and less crispness in the finished Charlotte.

TO ASSEMBLE

1. You can wait until the brioche is day-old or even stale, although, I find it better using it fresh because it will more easily mould into the cooking vessel, especially when using an ornate one like I have.

2. Slice the crusts off the brioche and freeze them to use later, then cut off one-quarter of the loaf and tear it into rough pieces. Place the pieces in a food processor and process to form a fine crumb. Slice the remaining loaf lengthways into 7 mm slices in order to take advantage of the length of the loaf, which will become the height of the Charlotte.

3. Using a pastry brush, brush the inside of your pudding basin or bundt tin generously with clarified butter, then add the crumbs to and roll in a circular motion so the crumbs coat the butter. Using crumbs is a good way of filling in any details of the mould and also helps to hide the joins of the overlapped brioche. Using a pastry brush, butter both sides of the brioche slices with clarified butter and arrange them slightly overlapping in the mould, reserving some for the top. Reinforce them by using your hands to press the brioche slices into the sides of the mould.

4. Fill the mould with the apple and medlar filling, making sure to add in any juices that have separated out of the fruit, then press down using a spoon so the fruit is tightly packed. Cover with a final top of buttered brioche then cover the Charlotte with a piece of baking paper and place a heavy weight on top to ensure the juices soak into the brioche. This helps the structure of the pudding become more stable when it is turned out. I press mine overnight, but really, a couple of hours with a solid, heavy weight is sufficient.

5. Preheat the oven to 170°C. Remove the weight from the Charlotte and place it in a deep-sided dish (this is to protect your oven floor from the dripping butter) and bake for 45 minutes or until golden. Allow the Charlotte to rest for 30 minutes, then turn it out onto a serving plate alongside a big jug of pouring cream. (*end.*)

NOTES.

Dividing the apples for the filling into thirds creates three different textures in the Charlotte, which will in turn hold up the sides of the brioche. I add water to the apples because they don't really release enough juice to cook down to a soft consistency. Generally, the apples remain dry and then they colour, which will affect the flavour of the filling.

Medlars are a forgotten fruit from Victorian times and, while very rare, I always feel it's a great privilege to be able to use them because all the old ancient fruit has disappeared. Medlars are inedible until they are soft and turn brown. They will look like they're rotting, but this process is what makes them custard-y and delicious. This process is called bletting and can take weeks after they are picked. I leave them on the branches during this time and enjoy them as an arrangement in my home.

If you can't find medlars, you can simply omit the medlar purée from the recipe and fill the Charlotte with apple filling.

BALLYMALOE TRIFLE
Peach. Rose geranium. Blackberries.

'Let's go and pick some peaches from the garden,' he said, leading me down the path and through the arched gateway into the ancient walls of the orchard at Ballymaloe. The peaches grew along the stoic walls, branching off at many junctions like rail tracks reaching into the limestone. A gentle squeeze at first, before tweaking the ripe fruit from branches as we made our way along the row to gather just enough to make a torte.

Treading amongst alliums, asparagus gone to seed, and heirloom pears running rampant and gnarly. Bunnies scampering with the vibrations of our footfall and rouge tomatoes peering at us from their glasshouse windows.

He always plucks the leaves of the peaches last and lays them over the fruit in the basket for his journey back to the kitchen, for the appreciation of those he may pass along the way and for his own love of beauty.

JELLY MOULD SIZE	1500ml
SERVES	12-15

POACHED PEACHES	
yellow or white peaches	6
moscato or sweet wine	750ml
granulated sugar	375g
vanilla bean, split and seeds scraped	1
orange, finely zested	1
lemon, finely zested	1
large bunch of rose geranium, leaves picked	1

JELLY	
titanium-strength gelatine leaves	2.5
peach poaching syrup (from above)	300ml

PANNA COTTA	
titanium-strength gelatine leaves	2
pure cream	600g
caster sugar	50g
vanilla bean, split and seeds scraped	1
grappa, white rum or limoncello	30ml
blackberries, mulberries or raspberries	2

SPONGE	
eggs	4
sugar	100g
self-raising flour, sifted twice	130g
unsalted butter, melted	20g

A BIT OF MATHS.
If you don't know the capacity of your jelly mould, fill it with water then measure the water to see how it compares to this recipe. To downsize or upscale this recipe, use percentages to do the maths by first figuring out what percentage difference your mould is to mine and then just adjust each component of the recipe in equal measure.

(The day before)

POACHED PEACHES

1. If the peaches are slipstone, cut them in half and remove the stones as this will make slicing them later much easier. If they are clingstone peaches, just leave them whole as the stone will be easier to remove after they are poached.

2. Combine all the ingredients except for the peaches (and reserving some geranium leaves to serve) in a large saucepan over high heat and bring to the boil, then reduce the heat to medium and simmer for 5 minutes for the flavours to infuse into the syrup. Add the peaches to the syrup and return to a simmer to poach gently for 15 minutes if using whole peaches or 10 minutes for peach halves, then turn off the heat and allow the peaches to cool in the syrup.

JELLY

3. Prepare the jelly mould by ensuring it is clean and dry, no need to line or grease. Soak the gelatine leaves in iced water to soften them. Decant 300 ml of the syrup from the poached peaches and return it to the boil in a small saucepan. Remove the gelatine from the water and give it a light squeeze to remove any excess liquid, then add it to the hot syrup and turn off the heat immediately. Stir the jelly well to dissolve the gelatine completely, then pour the jelly through a sieve to remove any zests or impurities and allow to cool at room temperature for 30 minutes. Pour the jelly into the mould and clear a space in your fridge where the jelly mould can sit flat. As with a lot of these moulds, it is crucial to the design that all the layers sit flat as they set.

PANNA COTTA

1. Soak the gelatine leaves in iced water to soften. Meanwhile, combine the cream, sugar and vanilla bean and seeds in a medium saucepan over low heat. Stir the cream initially to ensure the sugar doesn't stick to the bottom of the pan and burn, then increase the heat to medium and bring to just below the boil. This will prevent the fat from separating from the cream and will ensure the panna cotta remains white. Remove the pan from the heat, then squeeze the gelatine leaves to remove any excess water and add them to the cream. Whisk the gelatine gently into the cream until it has all dissolved, then add the grappa and stir through to combine. Set the mixture aside to cool completely, after which time you will need to remove the vanilla bean and strain the panna cotta through a fine sieve.

SPONGE

1. Most jelly moulds are tapered and so the sponge layers in this mould are going to vary in diameter. This is great for people who don't have uniform-sized cake tins. I have used 3 x 20 cm round cake tins to form these layers, but you could just pour the sponge into a lamington or slice tray (40 cm x 30 cm or equivalent volume) and then cut the shapes from the sheet of sponge. It's also not essential that the sponge is perfectly cut because it won't be seen in the mould. Either way, the first task is to decide what tins you are going to use for the three layers, then line them with baking paper. Preheat the oven to 170°C.

2   Place the eggs and sugar in the bowl of an electric mixer fitted with the whisk attachment and whip on high speed until thick and doubled in volume. This will take about 5 minutes. Remove the bowl from the machine and use a spatula to gently fold through the sifted flour in three batches, being careful not to knock out any of that lovely air in the sponge. Just before the last remnants of flour have disappeared, trickle the butter evenly over the surface of the batter and fold it through until there are no streaks of butter remaining.

3   Pour the batter into the prepared tins and smooth the tops gently with a spoon or a palette knife, making sure the batter goes all the way to the corners/edges of the tins. Bake for 15 minutes, then check if the sponges are ready by pressing the middle with your finger to see if it bounces back slightly. Remove the sponges from the oven and leave to cool completely in the tins.

TO ASSEMBLE

1   Remove the jelly mould from the fridge and arrange the berries on the surface, then pour one-third of the panna cotta on top of the fruit to just cover it. Trim a piece of sponge for the first layer, making it 1 cm smaller than the mould all the way round, then settle it on top of the panna cotta, pressing it into the cream. I think it looks better if you don't see the sponge until you cut the layers, like a surprise. Arrange 4 peach halves on top of the sponge, then pour over another one-third of the panna cotta. Repeat this layering by adding another disc of trimmed sponge followed by 6 peach halves as the mould starts to widen. Finally, pour over the final third of the panna cotta and finish with a neatly trimmed piece of sponge that fits snugly (all the way to the edge) in the mould to form the foot of your trifle, then return it to the fridge to set overnight.

(On the day)

2   To remove the trifle from the mould, sit the mould in a basin of hot (not boiling) water for 1 minute or run under a hot tap until it turns really hot, then turn the mould on a 45-degree angle under the tap, turning it around under the hot water. Invert the trifle onto your serving platter and leave it to sit upside down for 5 minutes, by which time it should naturally fall out. If it needs a little more convincing, you will need to pick up the platter and the mould (gripping the two together) and give it a few encouraging shakes. Be warned, I have tipped one of these out and the jelly was still stuck in the mould perfectly. I just repeated the same process to remove the jelly separately and placed it on top of the cake. Decorate the top with reserved geranium leaves and serve immediately.

3   This trifle can be kept unmoulded in the fridge ahead of serving to avoid any last-minute stress. (*end.*)

NOTE.
If you are worried about taking a risk on a jelly mould, I would suggest just moulding the cake in a conventional springform tin that you have lined with plastic film.

CITRUS MACADAMIA TORTE
Pink grapefruit. Macadamia. Cedro.

I believe that the intentions of the baker become infused
into the cake and that the best cakes are made from love
and a lightness of spirit.

It seems reasonable that through all the mixing and folding our
emotions should find their way into the crumbs. There really is very
little embellishment needed for a cake made from the heart.

SIZE	20cm	25cm
SERVES	10-12	12-15
GRAPEFRUIT CONFIT		
ruby grapefruit	1	2
caster sugar	300g	400g
RICOTTA CAKE		
macadamias, lightly toasted	90g	110g
almond meal	60g	75g
unsalted butter, well-softened	95g	115g
caster sugar	180g	220g
eggs, separated	3	4
fresh ricotta	160g	200g
ruby grapefruit, zested and juiced	1 (100ml)	1½ (150ml)
salt		pinch
TO DECORATE		
ruby grapefruit, zested	1	
icing sugar	50g	
freeze-dried mandarin powder (optional)		
grapefruit confit (from above)		
candied cedro (*SEE GLOSSARY*)		

GRAPEFRUIT CONFIT

1 Slice the grapefruit in half vertically and squeeze out the juice. Cut each half into quarters, then place in a medium saucepan and cover well with cold water. Bring to the boil, then drain the water off into the sink. This is called blanching and it releases the bitterness from the peel and needs to be repeated a minimum of three times. If you were to continue boiling the water without draining it off, the bitterness would just cook back into the peel. Once you have blanched the grapefruit segments three (or four times, for good measure), drain off the water and return the grapefruit to the saucepan with the caster sugar over low heat. The sugar will start to dissolve and there will be quite a lot of liquid in the pan. Continue to boil, stirring only occasionally with a heatproof spatula, as too much agitation may cause the sugar to crystallise. Giving the pan a little shake is actually preferred to stirring, although eventually as the sugar starts to really coat the fruit, it will be necessary to put your spatula in there and turn the fruit to prevent it from catching on the base of the pan. Heat can vary, as can the grapefruit segment sizes, so it is difficult to pinpoint how long the confit will take, but a rough guide of 40 minutes would be fair. The fruit will become a beautiful, transparent ruby colour and once this stage is reached, regardless of how much sugar is remaining, I usually turn off the heat to reserve the flavour of the fruit. It's possible to keep cooking to evaporate all the sugar, but this may caramelise the fruit and detract from its flavour. Use a pair of tongs or a fork to remove the grapefruit from the pan and arrange them on a cooling rack to cool.

RICOTTA CAKE

1 Preheat the oven to 150°C. Grease and line a 20 cm | 25 cm cake tin.

2 The texture of the macadamias is really important here, since the aim is to achieve a nice, fine crumb with minimal pieces of coarse nuts. Alas, since macadamias have a very high oil content, blending them in a food processor can mean you

end up with a paste very quickly and so the temptation is often to just leave them coarse. To avoid this happening, after you've toasted them to a pale-golden colour, allow them to cool completely. If they are still warm those oils will turn them into a paste even quicker. The second tip is to only use the pulse function on the food processor, as blending them intermittently will reduce the risk of a paste forming. Finally, when you feel you have blended them quite finely without turning them into a paste, add the ground almonds and continue to pulse for a further 30 seconds or so. The almonds will soak up the oils and allow you to blend the macadamias as finely as possible.

3 Place the butter and the half the sugar in the bowl of an electric mixer fitted with the paddle attachment and whip on medium speed until pale and creamy, remembering to scrape down the sides of the bowl regularly using a spatula to ensure the paddle is catching all the butter. Once you are satisfied the butter is fluffy, add the egg yolks one at a time, ensuring each yolk is incorporated before adding the next, then scrape the down sides of the bowl again. Add the ricotta to the bowl and beat on medium speed until the batter is more voluminous and creamier, then add the macadamia mixture and beat briefly on low speed just to incorporate. Remove the bowl from the mixer, fold through the grapefruit juice and zest then decant the batter into a large bowl. Thoroughly clean and dry the mixer bowl.

4 Add the egg whites and salt to the clean mixer bowl and whip on high speed using the whisk attachment until soft ribbons form, then reduce the speed to medium and gradually add the remaining sugar a little at a time. Whip the egg whites to firm peaks then fold the egg whites through the cake batter one-third at a time. The first third can be mixed a little more vigorously, this is to loosen the batter and form a union between two components that are very different consistencies. The next two-thirds should be added more gently until there are no egg white streaks remaining. Pour the mixture into the prepared cake tin and bake for 20 minutes | 25 minutes, then reduce the temperature to 140°C and bake for a further 20 minutes | 25 minutes. Test the cake by pressing the centre with your finger, if it bounces back, it's cooked. This cake may need a further 5–10 minutes cooking time, depending on your oven. Remove it from the oven and cool in the tin

TO DECORATE

1 Slip the cake from the tin by inverting it onto a plate, then flipping it back the right way up onto your serving plate. Rub the grapefruit zest into the icing sugar using your fingertips then, using a sieve, dust the icing sugar over the top of the cake. Dust with a layer of mandarin powder, if using.

2 Use a peeler or super-sharp knife to slice wafer-thin slivers of the grapefruit confit and cedro, then arrange them on top of the cake as though they are floating. The grapefruit and cedro are hard to cut through while portioning the cake, so bear that in mind when arranging the fruit, making sure your knife can slip easily between the pieces.

3 This cake keeps for a few days in the fridge and is best enjoyed after being brought up to room temperature. (*end.*)

EXPLORING THE LANDSCAPE OF MY HEART
Blackcurrants. Pear. Gianduja.

Exploring the landscape of my heart, I listen to the rhythms and harmony
so I can belong with great integrity to the life I want to live.

Shining light into all the hideaway places,
leaving no stone unturned in the pursuit of that person.

One day, quite by surprise, I saw that luminosity reflected back
at me in waves of hazelnut dacquoise. Then I knew I had found her
and all the abundance it has taken me so long to embrace.

SIZE	20cm	25cm
SERVES	10-15	12-15

BLACKCURRANT COMPOTE		
blackcurrants (fresh or frozen)	300g	400g
caster sugar	50g	65g
orange, zested and juiced	1	1

BAKED PEARS		
pears (bosc are the best)	3	4
vanilla bean, split and seeds scraped	½	½
brown sugar	75g	100g
oranges, zested and juiced	1	1½

HAZELNUT DACQUOISE		
hazelnuts, toasted and peeled	375g	465g
unsalted butter, softened	90g	110g
egg whites	8 (240g)	10 (300g)
caster sugar	250g	310g

WHIPPED RICOTTA		
fresh ricotta, drained overnight	300g	400g
vanilla bean, split and seeds scraped	½	½
caster sugar	1 tbsp	1 tbsp
orange, zested	1	1

GIANDUJA GANACHE	
hazelnuts, toasted and peeled	100g
icing sugar	60g
good-quality milk chocolate (minimum 40% cocoa solids)	160g
crème fraîche	135g

TO ASSEMBLE	
icing sugar	1 tbsp

BLACKCURRANT COMPOTE

1. Place the blackcurrants, sugar and orange zest and juice in a medium saucepan over low heat and cook, stirring the fruit so that the sugar evenly coats the berries. Once the sugar is dissolved, increase the heat to medium and simmer the compote for 10–15 minutes or until the syrup thickens. Even if you're using frozen blackcurrants there shouldn't be much liquid coming out of the fruit and the syrup should glaze the fruit perfectly. Turn off the heat and allow the compote to cool completely in the saucepan. The compote can be made up to 4 days in advance and kept in the fridge.

BAKED PEARS

2. Preheat the oven to 160°C. Begin by peeling the pears, taking care to remove all the skin, even the little crown around the stem. Cut the pears in half and use a Parisienne scoop or melon baller to remove the core and the fibrous stem leading from the seeds to the stem, being careful to preserve as much of the pear flesh as possible. The stem should also come off but, again, try to maintain the integrity of the pear's shape by taking it off carefully.

3. Scrape the vanilla seeds from half the bean using a sharp paring knife and while the seeds are still stuck to the blade spread them evenly onto each pear half, then place the pears cut-side up in a flat baking dish. Sprinkle the pears with the sugar and zest, then squeeze over the orange juice and bake for 20 minutes. Remove from the oven, flip the pears over and return them to the oven for a further 15 minutes or until they are tender. The ripeness of the pears will determine the cooking time, so test them after the first 20 minutes by piercing them with the tip of a paring knife to check their tenderness. A little bite can be a lovely thing, so no need for them to be absolutely soft. Use your judgement to decide when they should be removed from the oven, then allow them to cool completely in the baking dish. The pears can be baked up to 4 days in advance and kept in the fridge.

HAZELNUT DACQUOISE

1. Preheat the oven to 175°C. After the hazelnut skins have been removed, crush the nuts finely either using a food processor or a pestle and mortar. It's fine to have a few coarser pieces for texture, although, the majority of the crumb should be fine like breadcrumbs.

2. Line the base only of 3 x 20 cm | 3 x 25 cm cake tins with baking paper and butter the sides of the tins with the softened butter. Remove 100 g | 120 g from the hazelnut crumbs and roll them around the inside of the tins, pressing them into the sides of the tins to embed into the butter. This will give the dacquoise a rustic edge when the cakes are removed from the tins. Don't worry if you also get crumbs on the base of the tin.

3. Separate and weigh the egg whites and place them into the bowl of an electric mixer fitted with the whisk attachment. Add a pinch of salt and whip the whites on high speed until soft ribbons start to form, then gradually add half the sugar, 1 tablespoon at a time, until the meringue is thick and glossy. Remove the bowl from the mixer and add the remaining crushed hazelnuts and the remaining sugar, then fold through thoroughly. Divide the dacquoise between the tins and use an offset palette knife to smooth the tops. Bake for 20 minutes or until golden and crisp. Remove the dacquoise from the oven, leaving them to cool for only 5 minutes, before slipping them out of the tins onto a cooling rack. As the dacquoise cools the meringue becomes chewy and a little sticky, so if you leave them in the tins for longer they may stick to the bottom.

4   The dacquoise layers will sink and form a crater in the middle, this is completely normal and will give you a place to fill with all the fruit and ricotta.

WHIPPED RICOTTA

1   The ricotta for this recipe is fresh, so it will need to be well-drained for 24 hours in advance. I wouldn't recommend using an Italian-style ricotta as it may not whip, instead, head to the deli section for the best ricotta, which is usually sold in the basket it was made in. Be sure to remove it from the plastic the night before as sometimes it sits in the whey and doesn't drain.

2   Scrape the seeds from the remaining vanilla bean and place them on a chopping board, then sprinkle with the sugar and use a knife or offset palette knife to rub the sugar into the seeds. This is the best way to distribute vanilla seeds through a mixture to infuse the flavour. (Read more about this technique on page 262.)

3   Combine the ricotta, zest and vanilla sugar in the bowl of an electric mixer fitted with the whisk attachment and whip everything together on high speed for 5 minutes, using a spatula to scrape down the sides of the bowl every now and then to incorporate any wayward ricotta lumps. This filling falls like soft clouds onto the cake layers and while it will start to form thick ribbons around the whisk as you whip it, the consistency will never be firmly whipped. It only has a very small amount of sugar because I want to retain the pure quality of the ricotta.

4   Use a spatula to remove the ricotta from the mixing bowl, then cover and place in the fridge until you're ready to assemble the cake.

GIANDUJA GANACHE

1   Technically, gianduja is a mix of milk chocolate and hazelnuts from Piedmont in Italy, so if you want to make a ganache that is strictly gianduja, you would need to source it from there. There are companies selling it all over the world – I make mine with Valrhona Jivara chocolate (40%) and local hazelnuts. Ensure the hazelnuts have been toasted to golden, as sometimes, if pre-peeled hazelnuts are sourced, they can be quite beige and the resulting flavour is not as good.

2   Place the hazelnuts and icing sugar in the bowl of a food processor or a blender and blitz together until a smooth paste forms. Use a spatula to scrape down the sides of the bowl regularly in order to achieve a consistent, smooth texture and engage the pulse function (if you have one) to return the nuts to the middle of the bowl. Once you are happy the paste is smooth, turn off and leave the paste in the food processor bowl.

3   Melt the milk chocolate in a medium heatproof bowl over a saucepan of barely simmering water, ensuring the water doesn't touch the bottom of the bowl. Stir the chocolate occasionally to distribute the heat and try not to heat the chocolate higher than 50°C. Pour the chocolate into the bowl of the food processor with the paste and blend until very smooth, again scraping down the sides of the bowl to create a cohesive mixture. Turn off the machine again. What you have in the food processor now is the components of gianduja. The addition of the crème fraîche below turns it into a ganache.

4   Bring the crème fraîche to the boil in a small saucepan over medium heat, then pour it into the food processor with the gianduja and continue to blend until shiny and silky. Pour the ganache into a bowl then cover it and leave at room temperature to cool until ready to use. (*cont.*)

5 This recipe will make more than enough for both cake sizes here, since a minimum amount of 100 g of hazelnuts in a domestic blender is needed to create a smooth paste. Rest assured, excess ganache can be kept in the fridge then melted and poured over ice-cream when comfort is needed.

TO ASSEMBLE

1 Position a dacquoise layer on your platter. Pour approximately ¼ cup | ½ cup of the gianduja ganache into the centre and spread to the outside of the cake using an offset palette knife, trickling a little over the edges. Arrange half the pears evenly over the surface of the chocolate, then spoon over half the whipped ricotta and gently push to the edges. Spoon one-third of the blackcurrant compote over the ricotta and top with the second layer of dacquoise. Repeat this layering, finishing with the third layer of dacquoise. Dust the top with icing sugar and scatter with the remaining blackcurrant compote.

2 Due to the fragile nature of the ricotta filling, this cake is best assembled very last-minute and eaten on the same day. All the components can be made ahead of time, however. The dacquoise can be made the day before. (*end.*)

LUCKY

Kumquat. Tangerine. Macadamia. Calendula petals for healing.

For light in the heart space.
This cake is for all those who have suffered great loss.
Knowing that darkness, Lucky transforms the lacerated heart
and reveals a pathway through to the light.

SIZE	20cm	25cm
SERVES	10-15	12-15

GRAPEFRUIT CONFIT (OPTIONAL)	
pink grapefruit	1
caster sugar	200g

TUTTI FRUTTI CURD		
eggs	2	3
yolks	2	3
caster sugar	100g	150g
freshly squeezed citrus juice and their zest (I use a combination of ruby grapefruit, limes, oranges and lemons)	100ml	150ml
unsalted butter	100g	150g

MACADAMIA ROCHER		
macadamias, toasted	100g	130g
almond meal	50g	65g
icing sugar	150g	200g
cream of tartar	¼ tsp	¼ tsp
cornflour (SEE NOTE)	1 tbsp	1½ tbsp
egg whites	3	4

LEMON DELICIOUS PUDDING	
eggs	3
caster sugar	150g
lemons, juiced and zested	1 tbsp
mascarpone	1
milk	50ml
self-raising flour, sifted (SEE NOTE)	50g

KUMQUAT AND TANGERINE COMPOTE		
kumquats	250g	350g
water	500ml	700ml
tangerines or mandarins, peeled and segmented	2	3
caster sugar	150g	200g

TO DECORATE	
icing sugar, for dusting	
pure cream	200g
calendula petals, for healing	

ORCHARD

(The day before)

GRAPEFRUIT CONFIT (OPTIONAL)

1. Slice the grapefruit in half vertically and squeeze out the juice (reserve for the curd below). Cut each half into quarters, then place in a medium saucepan and cover well with cold water. Bring to the boil, then drain the water off into the sink. This is called blanching and it releases the bitterness from the peel and needs to be repeated a minimum of three times. If you were to continue boiling the water without draining it off, the bitterness would just cook back into the peel. Once you have blanched the grapefruit segments three (or four times, for good measure), drain off the water and return the grapefruit to the saucepan with the caster sugar over low heat. The sugar will start to dissolve and there will be quite a lot of liquid in the pan. Continue to boil, stirring only occasionally with a heatproof spatula as too much agitation may cause the sugar to crystallise. Giving the pan a little shake is actually preferred to stirring, although, eventually as the sugar starts to really coat the fruit, it will be necessary to put your spatula in there and turn the fruit to prevent it from catching on the base of the pan. Heat can vary, as can the grapefruit segment sizes, so it is difficult to pinpoint how long the confit will take, but a rough guide of 40 minutes would be fair. The fruit will become a beautiful, transparent ruby colour and once this stage is reached, regardless of how much sugar is remaining, I usually turn off the heat to reserve the flavour of the fruit. It's possible to keep cooking to evaporate all the sugar, but this may caramelise the fruit and detract from its flavour. Use a pair of tongs or a fork to remove the grapefruit quarters from the pan and arrange them on a cooling rack to cool.

TUTTI FRUTTI CURD

1. Begin by cracking the eggs and yolks (set aside the egg whites for making the rocher) into a medium heatproof bowl. Add the sugar and use a hand whisk to beat for 1 minute or so until the eggs are slightly pale and the sugar is dissolved. Add the citrus juice and zest to the eggs and whisk again until well incorporated, then place the bowl over a saucepan of barely simmering water and heat, whisking every 3 minutes, for approximately 20 minutes. The curd will begin to cook around the edges first, so whisking the curd occasionally ensures an even temperature is maintained throughout the cooking process. The whisk is a great tool to use for scraping the cooked curd away from the sides of the bowl and into the middle. Don't worry about any little lumps at this stage, they will be smoothed out later. The curd will be cooked when it reaches 85°C on a digital thermometer or becomes the consistency of thick cream. Turn the heat off and allow the curd to sit for a further 10 minutes in the bowl over the saucepan. This step is an insurance policy to guarantee the thickness of the curd and its ultimate setting.

2. After 10 minutes, remove the bowl of curd from the saucepan and set it on the bench to cool down, whisking the curd occasionally so the heat can be released and the temperature reaches 45°C on a thermometer or is warm to touch. Once it has cooled to this temperature, start whisking in the butter, 1 tablespoon at a time, waiting until each addition is incorporated before adding the next. This step can also be done in a food processor or with a stick blender.

3. Cover the curd and refrigerate overnight or for a minimum of 6 hours until chilled and set.

MACADAMIA ROCHER

1. Preheat the oven to 160°C. Grease and line a 20 cm | 25 cm cake tin with baking paper and set it aside.

2. Place the macadamias in a food processor and blitz using the pulse function until they are as finely chopped as possible. Be aware the high oil content of the macadamias makes them prone to turning into a paste, so keep an eye on them, then add the almond meal and blitz again so the almonds soak up some of the oil and assist in making the macadamias finer.

3. Sift the icing sugar, cream of tartar and cornflour into a bowl together to remove any lumps and set the bowl beside your electric mixer. Place the egg whites (some of which have been reserved from making the curd) in the electric mixer fitted with the whisk attachment and begin whisking on high speed. Once you see soft ribbons forming in the egg white, reduce the speed to medium and very gradually add the icing sugar mixture, 1 tablespoon at a time, until all incorporated. This meringue has a high sugar content to make the rocher crunchy, so take your time adding it to the whites so as not to 'saturate' them, this will result in a heavy meringue. Aim to take 10 minutes to add all the sugar and, once the meringue is thick and glossy, remove the bowl from the mixer and fold through the macadamia crumb using a spatula.

4. Pour the meringue into the prepared cake tin and smooth the top using an offset palette knife or a tablespoon. Bake for 35 minutes or until crunchy on the outside and soft in the middle. You will be able to assess this by pressing your finger into the middle of the rocher, where it will feel slightly springy to touch, then remove the rocher from the oven and cool in the tin for at least 1 hour or overnight.

LEMON DELICIOUS PUDDING

1. Preheat the oven to 150°C. Grease and line a 20 cm | 25 cm cake tin with baking paper and set it aside.

2. Separate the eggs and place the yolks in the bowl of an electric mixer fitted with the whisk attachment. Start whisking on slow speed, then add only 100 g of the caster sugar. Increase the speed to medium and whisk the yolks for 5 minutes or until they are thick and fluffy. While the yolks are whisking, take this time to whisk the lemon juice and zest, mascarpone and milk together, then set the bowl aside. We do this now because the citrus will thicken the mascarpone, which will make the pudding fluffier later on.

3. Once the egg yolks are glossy, remove the bowl from the mixer and decant the mixture into a large bowl. This is called our 'sabayon'. Clean and dry the electric mixer bowl, add the egg whites and whisk on medium speed until soft ribbons start to form, then gradually add the remaining caster sugar, 1 tablespoon at a time, until it is all incorporated. Stop whisking the egg whites before they reach firm peaks so the meringue remains softly whipped. Fold the mascarpone mixture gently through the sabayon using a whisk.

4. Sift the flour for a second time directly over the surface of the mascarpone mixture and fold it through using the whisk. Once the flour is all incorporated, fold through the egg white, using a spatula to smooth out any lumps that have formed in the meringue. Once the last streak of egg white has disappeared give two final big folds to the bottom of the bowl using the spatula, then pour the mixture into the prepared cake tin. Place immediately in the middle of the oven for 30 minutes or until the centre of the cake is firm and springy to the touch. Remove from the oven and cool in the tin for 2 hours or overnight.

(*cont.*)

KUMQUAT AND TANGERINE COMPOTE

1. To prepare the kumquats, ensure that the stem has been removed completely with a sharp paring knife, then cut them in half lengthways. Place the kumquats and the water in a medium saucepan and bring to the boil, then reduce the heat so that they are just simmering. Continue to cook the kumquats for 30 minutes or until the fruit is tender, then remove from the heat and strain away any surplus water. Return the kumquats to the pan with the tangerine or mandarin segments and the sugar and place over medium heat, stirring to dissolve the sugar completely. Once the liquid starts to boil, reduce the heat to low and simmer for 20 minutes or until the sugar has turned syrupy and glossy and the tangerines look softened. Remove the compote from the heat and cool completely for 4 hours or overnight.

(On the day)

TO ASSEMBLE

1. This cake is best assembled directly on the platter you intend to present it on, as it is a very voluptuous cake and won't like being transferred. Begin by peeling the paper from the rocher layer and placing it onto the platter, then spread the tutti frutti curd evenly over the rocher using an offset palette knife. Roughly chop three or four wedges of the grapefruit confit (if using), then scatter these pretty jewels evenly over the curd. Remove the lemon delicious from the tin by inverting it onto a small plate and flipping it back the right way up, then place it on top of the grapefruit layer. It will likely be quite soft and mousse-y and will appreciate a gentle hand when manoeuvring it from the tin. Once the pudding layer is in place, I like to dust it with icing sugar to soften the edges and give it an ethereal appearance.

2. Whip the cream softly and smooth it over the top of the pudding layer, then spoon the kumquat and tangerine compote evenly over the cream. Thinly slice more slivers of the grapefruit confit (if using) and arrange them delicately over the top of the compote (I like to make sure everyone in the party will receive one), then finish the cake with a liberal amount of calendula petals.

3. The layers of Lucky can be made the day before and assembled on the day. I have also assembled this cake and kept it in the fridge overnight, finding that the layers meld into one another to form a different cake personality. No less delicious, albeit a little less light. Always leave the cake out of the fridge for 1 hour before serving to allow the flavours and textures to become their best selves. (*end.*)

NOTES.

It's important to me when writing recipes that I try to make them as accessible as possible and not overcomplicate them. There are many components to this cake and while the grapefruit is a lovely touch it isn't essential to the deliciousness of this cake.

To make this gluten-free, you can substitute the cornflour with gluten-free maize for the rocher and the self-raising flour with 50 g gluten-free flour plus ¼ tsp baking powder for the lemon delicious pudding.

MARIÚ
Grapes. Rosemary. Lemon.

A cake inspired by a night of theatre amongst vineyards,
olive groves and citrus trees anticipating a magician's twilight
spell to coax a sparkle of fireflies, a menagerie
of luminescent children looming.

It was there we met Mariú who painted her song onto us with her
starry eyes. She reminded me of the dreaming fire of youth.
That which is beautiful and terrifying at the same time.

1. Preheat the oven to 170°C. Line a 20 cm | 25 cm tin with baking paper.
2. Place the butter, sugar and vanilla in the bowl of an electric mixer fitted with the paddle attachment and whip together on medium speed until pale and fluffy, using a spatula to regularly scrape down the sides of the bowl including under the paddle where lumps of butter like to hide.
3. Crack the eggs into a small bowl and give them a light whisk with a fork, then gradually add them, a little at a time, to the creamed butter, ensuring that each addition has been incorporated before adding the next. Continue to scrape down the sides of the bowl using a spatula, then once all the egg has been added beat for a further 2 minutes to aerate the batter. Sift the flours together twice then place two-thirds of the grapes in a bowl with 2 teaspoons of the flour and toss to coat the fruit.
4. Decrease the speed of the mixer to low and gradually add the remaining flour in three batches, alternating with the buttermilk, also in three batches. Once the last trickle of buttermilk has been added, remove the bowl from the mixer and use a spatula to fold the batter a few times to incorporate any flour stuck to the sides of the bowl. Fold through the flour-dusted grapes and half the rosemary, then pour the batter into the cake tin and smooth the top using an offset palette knife.
5. Using your fingertips, rub the lemon zest through the extra 50 g of sugar and sprinkle the lemon sugar evenly over the cake. Bake the cake for 20 minutes then remove it from the oven momentarily and scatter over the remaining grapes and rosemary, then return it to the oven for a further 30 minutes. To test for readiness, insert the point of a sharp knife into the centre of the cake, if it comes out clean, it's ready. Remove the cake from the oven and cool in the tin.
6. This cake will keep for about 5 days at room temperature. (*end.*)

SIZE	20cm	25cm
SERVES	10-15	12-15
unsalted butter, softened	250g	275g
caster sugar, plus 50g for sprinkling	200g	220g
vanilla paste	1 tsp	1 tsp
eggs	3	4
self-raising flour	180g	200g
cornflour	20g	25g
plain flour	70g	75g
small black seedless grapes, stalks removed	300g	330g
buttermilk	90ml	100ml
rosemary sprigs, picked	3	4
lemons, zest finely grated	2	2

SAVARIN
Clementines. Toffee. Crème Anglaise.

Quanto basta (as much as is enough) is a term once used frequently in Italian recipes to indicate that our intuition will be our best guide in this scenario and that any further written instruction would be superfluous. It was so commonly used that the initials QB inserted into the text would be sufficient to inform the cook to move off-piste and engage the wealth of gut instincts they had acquired from simply exercising their intuition, over and over.

For fun, I've slipped QB into this recipe, because I like a bit of ambiguity to awaken my senses and yours.

SAVARIN

1. Place the yeast in a small bowl with half the warm milk and 1 teaspoon of sugar and give it a mix with a spoon to combine. Place the flour, salt and remaining sugar in the bowl of an electric mixer fitted with the hook attachment and mix on low speed. Whisk the eggs in a separate little bowl using a fork, then turn off the mixer and add the eggs, yeast mixture and remaining milk to the well that has formed in the middle. Start mixing on low speed again. It is very difficult to make savarin dough by hand because it's extremely sticky and developing the structure is dependent on working the dough to incorporate elasticity. This is best done with a dough hook. Beat on low speed for a few minutes until everything forms a sticky dough and all the flour has disappeared from the edges and bottom of the bowl.

2. Before increasing the speed, I usually tip the head of the machine back and remove the bowl from the mixer entirely, then use a spatula to scrape the bottom of the bowl completely to ensure all the flour has been incorporated. Now increase the speed to medium and beat the dough for approximately 5 minutes or until it is smooth and shiny. It will remain quite wet and, because of this, won't form a ball around the dough hook like other doughs. This is normal.

3. Continue to beat on medium speed then gradually add the softened butter, 1 tablespoon at a time. Watch as it is drawn into the centre of the dough and slowly disappears, then add the next tablespoon, and so on, until all the butter has been added. Beat the dough for a further 1 minute to ensure the butter is truly incorporated. If the butter doesn't seem to be incorporating, it usually means it's not soft enough, so take measures to make it so, then continue adding the butter.

4. Finally, reduce the speed to low again and add the sliced clementines, then mix the dough only until you see the fruit been distributed evenly, no longer. Remove the bowl from the mixer and scrape the dough into a lightly oiled bowl that is at least twice the size of the dough. Cover the bowl with a tea towel and prove the dough at room temperature until it has doubled in size.

5. Meanwhile, butter a 22 cm x 7 cm bundt tin and sugar it by rolling the sugar around the inside of the mould, being sure to coat the inner tube as well, then set it aside.

(cont.)

BUNDT TIN SIZE	22cm x 7cm-deep
SERVES	10-12
SAVARIN	
fresh yeast / dried yeast	15g / 7g
milk, warmed	75ml
caster sugar, plus extra 50g for sugaring	30g
plain flour, sifted	335g
fine salt	1½ tsp
eggs	4
unsalted butter, softened, plus extra 40g for greasing	200g
candied clementines, halved and finely sliced, plus 1 whole candied clementine to decorate	100g
SOAKING SYRUP	
water	300ml
caster sugar	150g
orange, zested and juiced	1
Cointreau	40ml
Grand Marnier	40ml
CRÈME ANGLAISE	
pure cream	360g
vanilla bean, split and seeds scraped	1
egg yolks	6
caster sugar	90g
TOFFEE	
caster sugar	200g

6   Knock back the dough by folding the edges into the middle and deflating the gases that have accumulated in the ball then cover the dough with plastic film and place in the fridge for 1 hour. This process slows the activity of the yeast and will in turn create a more open crumb. Dust the surface of your workbench lightly with flour then turn out the dough and fold the edges of the dough evenly into the centre to form a ball. Dust with more flour if necessary to stop the dough from sticking to your hands. At this stage, the bottom of the ball will be smooth and the top will be rougher where all the joins meet. Make a hole in the centre of the ball using your fingers then place the dough into the prepared bundt tin, smooth-side down, and use your hands to press it into the mould so that it sits level and evenly in the tin.

7   Dust the surface of your workbench lightly with flour, then turn out the dough and fold the edges of the dough evenly into the centre to form a ball. Dust with more flour, if necessary, to stop the dough from sticking to your hands. At this stage, the bottom of the ball will be smooth and the top will be rougher where all the joins meet. Make a hole in the centre of the ball using your fingers then place the dough into the prepared bundt tin, smooth-side down, and use your hands to press it into the mould so that it sits level and evenly in the tin. At this stage, you can preheat the oven to 175°C.

8   Once the savarin has doubled in volume it will probably reach three-quarters of the way up the sides of the bundt tin. This will take approximately 35 minutes. Bake for 30 minutes, then test it's ready by inserting a skewer into the savarin. If it comes out clean, it's ready. Alternatively, it will be 87°C when probed with a thermometer. Remove the bundt from the oven and immediately upturn onto a cooling rack, removing the tin, and allow it to cool completely. Keep the tin nearby as you will need it again later to soak the cake.

SOAKING SYRUP

1   Place the water, sugar, orange zest and juice in a small saucepan over low heat and stir until the sugar dissolves, then increase the heat to medium and simmer for 2 minutes. Turn off the heat then add the Cointreau and Grand Marnier and cool the syrup until it is just warm.

2   Once the savarin has cooled, use a skewer to poke holes all over the top and sides, then place the cooling rack with the savarin still on top over a deep tray and slowly pour one-quarter of the syrup over the top of the savarin. A lot of the syrup will run off the sides and won't appear to be soaking in, but be patient as this is a slow process to soak the savarin properly. Return the savarin to the tin you baked it in and poke more holes in the bottom of the cake, then pour another one-quarter of the syrup into the cake, including any syrup that has run off the sides in the first soak. Leave the cake to soak up the syrup for 30 minutes, then repeat this process every 30 minutes, soaking the savarin with one-quarter of the syrup at a time.

3   It's important to take the time to let the syrup soak in, as this makes the cake so wonderful. While you're soaking the cake, you can get on with making the crème Anglaise. Then once the final syrup has been added, turn the savarin back up the right way onto the cooling rack and position it over the deep tray so you can pour the toffee over the top.

CRÈME ANGLAISE

1. Have a bowl ready with a fine sieve sitting over the top. Bring the cream and vanilla bean and seeds to the boil over medium heat, then reduce the heat to low so that the cream is just simmering.

2. Meanwhile, beat the egg yolks with the sugar using a hand whisk until they are pale and fluffy, then pour one-quarter of the hot cream onto the eggs and give them a little whisk to temper the yolks before they are plunged into the hot cream. Use a spatula to scrape all the yolks into the pan of simmering cream and stir over gentle heat until the crème Anglaise thickens – this will take just a little over 1 minute. Use your spatula to test if it is thick enough by running your finger through the crème Anglaise on the paddle. If the path stays apart, it is ready. If it runs back together, return it to the heat for a little longer.

3. Remove the saucepan from the heat and pour the crème Anglaise into the sieve to remove any debris. Whisk for a few minutes to release the heat from the centre and cool it down quickly, as this is the stage when crème Anglaise can curdle. Cover the surface with plastic film to prevent a skin from forming.

4. The crème Anglaise can be made up to 3 days in advance and kept refrigerated. It's best served warm, so reheating should be done gently to avoid any overheating and scrambling.

TOFFEE

1. Place a small, non-stick frying pan over medium heat and sprinkle one-third of the sugar over the surface of the pan so that it covers the base evenly. The sugar will start to melt around the edges first and will gradually turn a glassy caramel all the way to the centre. The aim is not to stir the sugar, as this may make it crystallise, instead, just shake and roll the sugar in the pan to distribute it evenly so the caramel doesn't burn. Once the first amount of sugar has melted and is transparent, add another one-third and repeat the process, swivelling and turning the pan to distribute the sugar crystals into the molten caramel. Only add the final third when you can see the sugar in the centre is melted. Keep an eye on the heat and turn it down to low if you feel you are not managing the speed and evenness at which the caramel is colouring, there's no rush.

2. Once the toffee is clear and golden, QB, remove from the heat and pour over the top and sides of the savarin, as much as is enough to reach all the way to the base of the cake, then allow it to set for a couple of minutes. The savarin can be served immediately, decorated with more clementine, and is best cut with a sharp, serrated bread knife. A big jug of crème Anglaise in the middle of the table is all you need. (*end.*)

TAKUMI

Hōjicha. Dulce de leche. Cinnamon. Plums.

Takumi: (from Japanese) an artist of great skill. Often, having honed their craft over a lifetime.

I imagine the quietness and solitude of the artist's pursuit and the wisdom that emerges in tandem. A deeper understanding of self that at times wanders into darkness to find the truth and gives me a thrill that is unutterable. I soar.

SIZE	20cm	25cm
SERVES	10-12	12-15

DULCE DE LECHE OR CAJETA		
cow's or goat's milk (SEE NOTE)	750ml	1 litre
bicarbonate of soda	½ tsp	¾ tsp
granulated sugar	170g	225g
cinnamon quill (not cassia)	1	1
vanilla bean, split and seeds scraped	½	½

BAKED PLUMS		
fresh plums, halved and stones removed	8	12
vanilla bean	½	½
caster sugar	50g	50g
brown sugar	30g	30g
orange, zested and juiced	1	1

SPONGE		
unsalted butter	90g	120g
eggs	6	8
caster sugar	180g	240g
brown sugar	30g	40g
Japanese cake flour (SEE GLOSSARY)	180g	240g
hōjicha tea powder (SEE GLOSSARY)	15g	20g
ground cinnamon	1 tsp	1½ tsp
sea salt		big pinch

TO ASSEMBLE	
icing sugar	1 tbsp
ground cinnamon	1 tsp
hōjicha tea powder	½ tsp
pinch Davidson plum powder (optional)	

DULCE DE LECHE OR CAJETA

1. Place 2 tablespoons of the milk and the bicarbonate of soda in a small bowl and mix to combine. Combine the remaining milk, sugar, cinnamon quill and vanilla in a large saucepan over medium heat and stir gently until it starts to simmer. Remove the cinnamon and vanilla bean, then turn off the heat and immediately add the bicarb mixture to the hot milk and mix it through. This will cause the milk to bubble up slightly, which is completely normal. Return to the heat and simmer for approximately 45 minutes–1 hour or until caramel-coloured. Initially, stir only occasionally to check the caramel isn't catching on the base of the pan, then more regularly once you see the caramel colour starting to intensify. If the caramel does catch and burn on the bottom of the pan, pour it into a clean saucepan without scraping the bottom of the pan and continue to simmer. When the caramel is ready it will be the consistency of thick custard and you will need to stir it almost constantly to prevent it catching on the bottom of the pan. There will be no plumes of smoke that indicate readiness like normal caramel, however, the darker you make it the thicker the caramel will be. Cool the caramel at room temperature if you are assembling the cake the day it is made. If you have made it in advance, keep it stored in the fridge until you need it, then soften it with a good mix with a wooden spoon.

BAKED PLUMS

1. Preheat the oven to 160°C. Arrange the plums cut-side up on a flat baking dish. Scrape the half vanilla bean lengthways using a paring knife and while the seeds are still on the blade, spread them onto each plum half. Sprinkle the fruit with the sugars and orange zest, then squeeze the orange juice over the top.

2. Bake the plums for 15 minutes, then remove from the oven and turn the plums cut-side down in the juices. Bake for a further 10–15 minutes or until tender and almost falling apart. If you prefer to keep the plums firmer that's fine, but just consider the cake will be a little harder to cut through. Cool the plums on the tray. The plums can be baked up to 3 days in advance and kept refrigerated, sitting in as much of the cooking juice as possible.

SPONGE

1. Preheat the oven to 175°C. Lightly grease the sides of 2 x 20 cm | 2 x 25 cm cake tins with butter then pop in a base liner to help remove the cakes later.

2. Melt the butter in a small saucepan over low heat without boiling, then (*cont.*)

turn off the heat. Place the eggs in a heatproof bowl, preferably the bowl of the electric mixer as this is where you will transfer them to later, and give them a light whisk. Add the sugars and whisk together thoroughly using a hand whisk, then place the bowl over a saucepan of barely simmering water, ensuring the bowl isn't touching the water. Stir the eggs using a whisk until they are almost hot to the touch (50°C). This is an old school Genoese recipe that usually requires the baker to stand there whisking until the volume is created, but this method takes out the hard work with the aid of an electric mixer.

3 Remove the bowl from the heat and place it on the mixer fitted with the whisk attachment and whisk the eggs on high speed for 7 minutes or until they are cold. You will notice the volume triples during this time.

4 Meanwhile, sift the flour, hōjicha, cinnamon and salt twice, settling the ingredients back in the sieve in preparation for it to be sifted again when folding through the sponge.

5 Once the eggs are cold, remove them from the mixer and use a spatula to fold through the flour in two batches, sifting it over the surface of the sponge each time. It is not essential for every last speck of flour to be folded through before adding the next, since there is a lot more folding to do and this will just deflate the air you have whipped into the sponge. Scoop 1 cup of the sponge mixture into the saucepan with the butter and fold it through the butter to lighten it. This will prime the butter so that when it is folded into the sponge it won't deflate the total mass as much. Fold the lightened butter back into the sponge and once the eggs, flour and butter are nicely incorporated, pour the sponge into the prepared tins and gently smooth the tops using an offset palette knife.

6 Bake for 15 minutes | 17 minutes, pressing the centre of the cakes to test they're ready. You will hear a soft whisper and the sponge will bounce back ever so slightly. Remove the sponges from the oven and let them sit in the tins for only 2 minutes, then tilt the tins 45 degrees and use your fingertips to slip the sponges out onto a cooling rack to cool completely.

TO ASSEMBLE

1 Use a serrated knife to skim the top off one of the sponges and the base off the other. Just a couple of millimetres will do. This creates a line to help the sponges sit together more seamlessly, however, if you are happy to stack them on top of one another, that's fine, too.

2 Trimming the cakes is best done by using a serrated knife to score a mark around the circumference of the sponge first, then slicing little by little into the cake as you rotate it. The sponge without the top becomes your base cake and the sponge without the base will become your top cake.

3 Arrange the base sponge on a serving platter and spread over the dulce de leche, smoothing it to the edges using an offset palette knife, then spoon the plums on top of the caramel. Place the other sponge on top. Mix the icing sugar, cinnamon and hōjicha powder together with a spoon so they are well combined, then use a sieve to dust them evenly over the top of the sponge. Add a pinch of plum powder to the centre, if you wish. This cake really must be eaten on the day, although the dulce de leche and the plums can be prepared in advance. (*end.*)

> **NOTE.**
> Dulce de leche is a caramel made with cow's milk, while cajeta is the equivalent made with goat's milk. I prefer the tangy nature of goat's milk, however, feel free to use whatever dairy you wish.

THE WALTZING ORANGE TREE
Blood orange. Cardamom. Orange blossom.

The village orange orchard grew on the fringes of the dance hall. All year round, we would either be dancing to the scent of orange blossom or swapping orange cake recipes with the Aunties.

My favourite time of the year was when the fairy lights in the hall shone through the window onto the orange tree silhouettes outside. At Christmas.

It felt as if they were being celebrated even in their starkest hour.

(Two days before)

BLOOD ORANGE JELLY SLICES

1 Slice the oranges into 2 mm-thick rounds using a very sharp knife. Take your time as you want every slice to be completely round without tears. Place the orange slices in a large bowl and pour over boiling water from the kettle to cover the slices well, then wrap the bowl in plastic film for 6 hours until cold. Repeat the process twice more to make a total of three blanches over an 18-hour period. Don't worry, they can sit for longer if you need to leave them overnight. This is a technique used to soften citrus and remove the bitterness, while maintaining the vibrant colours. It's normally done by bringing the fruit to the boil in a saucepan, however, in the case of delicate orange slices they would be broken up in the process.

2 Place the sugar, water, cardamom and vanilla bean and seeds in a large, wide-based saucepan, bring to the boil and simmer for 5 minutes. Discard the blanching water from the oranges and gently add the orange slices to the cardamom syrup, laying them carefully over the base of the saucepan, then cover them with a round piece of baking paper (called a cartouche, SEE Techniques, page 259) to ensure the top of the slices don't dry out.

3 Continue to simmer the orange slices on the lowest heat possible for about 1 hour–1 hour 30 minutes or until the syrup reduces to a jelly and coats the slices in a glossy, translucent glaze. Turn off the heat and let them cool at room temperature. I have left these oranges at room temperature for three days without refrigerating them because the sugar will preserve them. After this time, they can be stored in the fridge stacked up in a jar with any remaining syrup poured over them for approximately 3 months.

ORANGE-SCENTED GANACHE

1 Place the cream, vanilla, cardamom pods, orange zest and orange blossom water in a small saucepan over medium heat and bring to the boil. Turn off the heat and allow the flavours to mingle for 30 minutes. Meanwhile, place the finely chopped chocolate into a medium bowl and set it beside the stove. Strain the aromatics out of the cream and return the cream to the boil, then pour it over the chocolate and stir the ganache until it is smooth and all the chocolate has dissolved. Pour the ganache into a container with a lid and cool in the fridge for 4 hours or overnight.

(cont.)

You'll need to begin this recipe 2 days in advance by making the orange jelly slices.

SIZE	20cm	25cm
SERVES	10-12	12-15

BLOOD ORANGE JELLY SLICES		
blood oranges	3	
caster sugar	250g	
water	250ml	
cardamom pods, crushed	1 tsp	
vanilla bean, split and seeds scraped	½	

ORANGE-SCENTED GANACHE		
pure cream	200g	240g
vanilla bean, split and seeds scraped	½	½
cardamom pods, crushed	1 tsp	1 tsp
blood orange, zested	1	2
tsp orange blossom water (optional)	¼ tsp	½ tsp
blond or white chocolate feves (buttons), finely chopped	55g	70g

CAKE		
natural almonds	90g	120g
blood oranges, zested and juiced to yield	2 (200ml)	3 (250ml)
cardamom pods, crushed	¾ tsp	1 tsp
blond or white chocolate feves (buttons)	100g	125g
ground almond meal	140g	175g
fine polenta	100g	125g
baking powder	½ tsp	1 tsp
eggs	4	6
caster sugar	150g	180g

(On the day)

CAKE

1. Preheat the oven to 150°C. Line a 20 cm | 25 cm cake tin with baking paper and set it aside.

2. Toast the almonds on a flat tray in the oven for 15 minutes or until light golden, this will extract the best flavour from the almonds.

3. Place the orange juice and crushed cardamom pods in a small saucepan and bring to the boil, then reduce the heat to low and simmer until the juice has reduced by half. Remove from the heat and allow the spice to infuse in the warm juice while you get on with making the cake. Once cooled, strain the juice to remove the pods.

4. Place the chocolate in the bowl of a food processor and blitz until it is finely chopped, then decant into a small bowl. Once the whole almonds are cool, add to the food processor and grind them as finely as possible using the pulse function. Once they are fine, add the almond meal and chocolate and blitz for a further 1 minute. The almond meal will absorb the oils from the natural almonds and the chocolate to assist in making them even finer. Decant the mixture into a medium bowl and add the polenta, orange zest and baking powder, then use a whisk or a fork to mix them through evenly.

5. Increase the oven temperature to 165°C. Place the eggs in the bowl of an electric mixer fitted with the whisk attachment and whisk on low speed for 10 seconds, then add the sugar, increase the speed to high and continue to whisk for 3 minutes or until the eggs have tripled in volume. This is called a 'sabayon'. Remove the bowl from the mixer and use a spatula to gently fold one-third of the almond and chocolate mixture through the sabayon, then fold through the strained orange juice. Fold through the remaining almond and chocolate mixture, taking care not to lose too much of the lovely air you have whipped into the sabayon. When you are confident the batter is evenly mixed, pour it into the prepared cake tin. Pop it straight in the oven for 30 minutes, then reduce the oven temperature to 150°C and bake for a further 25 minutes. Test the cake for readiness by inserting a skewer into the middle of the cake – if it comes out clean, it's cooked. Remove the cake from the oven and cool in the tin.

TO ASSEMBLE

1. Remove the cake from the tin by either inverting it onto a plate and then flipping it back the right way up onto a platter or, in the case of having used a springform tin, release it from the band.

2. Remove the orange-scented ganache from the fridge and give it a good whisk to incorporate any white chocolate that may have settled to the bottom or fat from the cream that may have floated to the top. Whip the ganache in the bowl of an electric mixer using the whisk attachment or use a hand whisk to whisk until firmly whipped, then spread or dollop evenly over the top of the cake. Arrange the blood orange jelly slices on top, noting that they're difficult to slice through when cutting the cake, so a bit of strategic placement based on the number of guests will make portioning much easier. Alternatively, you can place an orange on each plate then cut the cake afterwards. (*end.*)

SAKURA
Cherry. Almonds. Japanese whisky.

Watch the cherry blossoms fall to remind ourselves that this day is not promised to us. And every time you bake this cake write a letter to someone you love while it's in the oven. Because life is fleeting.

TART TIN SIZE	26cm
SERVES	12-15

BLOSSOM PASTRY	
plain flour, plus extra for dusting	300g
ground almonds	100g
baking powder	1 scant tsp
butter, slightly softened, plus extra for greasing	240g
caster sugar	220g
egg	1
yolk	1
orange, zested	1
lemon, zested	1
cherry blossom syrup or orange blossom water	1 tsp
vanilla paste	½ tsp

WHISKY CUSTARD FILLING	
milk	250ml
vanilla paste	1 tsp
egg yolks	3
caster sugar	50g
plain flour	30g
Japanese whisky (SEE GLOSSARY)	30ml

CHERRY COMPOTE	
frozen or fresh cherries, pitted	500g
orange, zested and juiced	1
lemon, zested and juiced	1
caster sugar	50g

BLOSSOM PASTRY

1. Sift the flour, almonds and baking powder together twice, adding any coarse almonds that remain in the sieve back into the dry ingredients. The purpose of this process is to remove any lumps from the ingredients and distribute the baking powder.

2. Place the butter and sugar together in the bowl of an electric mixer fitted with the paddle attachment and cream on low speed, being careful not to over aerate the butter. Crack the egg and extra yolk into a small bowl and give them a light whisk with a fork, then gradually add them to the creamed butter and sugar. Scrape down the sides of the bowl occasionally to incorporate any butter that has wandered up the sides of the bowl, then add the dry ingredients followed by the zests, cherry blossom syrup (or orange blossom water) and vanilla and mix until incorporated. Remove the bowl from the mixer and use a spatula to fold the pastry a few times to ensure any remaining butter on the bottom of the bowl is well combined with no streaks remaining.

3. Basque pastry has a very high butter content, making it extremely sticky to roll. So, unlike most other pastries, it is best rolled between two sheets of baking paper to stop it from sticking to the rolling pin. To do this, place two large sheets of baking paper on your bench and divide the pastry between the sheets. Place two-thirds of the pastry on one sheet (for the base) and one-third onto the other (for the top). Top each with another sheet of baking paper, then flatten the dough down slightly with your hands. Using a rolling pin, roll the base pastry out to a 7 mm-thick round that is 30 cm in diameter, and the top pastry out to a 7 mm-thick round that is 26 cm in diameter. Refrigerate the pastry while you get on with making the filling.

WHISKY CUSTARD FILLING

1. Prepare a shallow tray for pouring the custard into by setting it beside the stove. Pour the milk and vanilla into a saucepan and bring to the boil over medium heat. Meanwhile, whisk the egg yolks with the sugar until pale, then add the flour to the yolks and whisk until well combined.

(*cont.*)

2   When the milk comes to the boil, reduce the heat to low and pour half the milk over the egg yolks, giving it a little whisk to combine. This warms the yolks a little in preparation for being added to the scalding milk.

3   Pour the yolk mixture back into the boiled milk over low heat, ensuring you scrape all the yolk from the bowl with a spatula. Stir gently with a wooden spoon or heatproof spatula for 2 minutes or until the cream starts to thicken. If you can see lumps forming, swap your spoon for a whisk momentarily to obliterate any pesky lumps that have appeared and continue to whisk for 1 minute to cook the flour completely. Remove from the heat and add the whisky, then whisk thoroughly to combine and spread the custard out on a shallow tray. Cover the custard with plastic film, pressing it directly onto the surface to prevent a skin from forming, then refrigerate until cold.

CHERRY COMPOTE

1   Place half the cherries and the remaining ingredients in a saucepan over medium heat and stir until the sugar has dissolved and the syrup starts to boil. Allow the cherries to simmer for 10 minutes before adding the remaining cherries, then bring the compote back to a simmer for a further 10 minutes, stirring occasionally to ensure the fruit is not sticking to the base of the saucepan. Remove the compote from the heat, pour into a container and cool in the fridge. By cooking the cherries in two stages, there will be a contrast of cherry texture in your finished cake with pops of juice from the whole fruit and a jammier texture that maintains the moisture throughout the cake.

LINING THE SAKURA CAKE

1   Remove the pastry top from the fridge. Peel off the top sheet of baking paper, then flip over the pastry disc and peel away the base paper. Place the disc on a fresh sheet of baking paper on your bench, so it doesn't stick. This pastry is very difficult to mould because, as it becomes warmer, it either melts or splinters, making the lining of a tart tin quite awkward. Follow me here for the best results.

2   Cut the pastry for the top of the cake by using the actual tart tin as a cutter. Invert the tart tin over the pastry disc on the bench and press down to use the sharp rim of the tin to cut the top to exactly the right size, then return the disc to the fridge while you cut and line the base.

3   Grease the base and sides of the tart tin with butter and sprinkle with flour to stop the pastry from sticking. Remove the base pastry from the fridge and remove the top sheet of paper. Place the tart tin on top of the pastry disc and use a small paring knife to cut round the circumference just 2 cm bigger than the tin to eliminate any surplus pastry, then flip the pastry into the tart tin. Peel away the other sheet of paper and press the pastry into the sides of the tin. The pastry may splinter and crack, but that's OK, just press it back into the sides of the tart ring and mould it evenly all the way around the edges of the tin. This pastry will become sticky quite quickly, so if you feel you need to return the pastry to the fridge to firm up, don't be afraid to do so – take your time. Once the pastry is in the tart tin you can mould it into shape quite easily and fill in any gaps with the softer pieces, then place the tart case into the fridge to chill for 15 minutes.

TO ASSEMBLE

1   Preheat the oven to 160°C. Bring the pastry base out of the fridge and use a sharp paring knife to trim any surplus pastry sitting above the rim. Spread the whisky custard into the base of the pastry case using an offset palette knife and scatter the cherry compote evenly over the top. Remove the pastry top from the fridge, release it from the paper and place it on top of the cake, then

seal the base to the top by pressing the seam together. Remove any surplus trim to form a neat edge.

2 Place in the oven for 35 minutes, then reduce the temperature to 150°C and bake for a further 15 minutes or until the top is golden round the rim and a paler, buttery shortbread colour in the middle. Remove the cake from the oven and allow it to rest for 1 hour before dusting with the cherry blossom stencil *(SEE NOTE)* and cutting. As this pastry is very buttery and crumbly, I would recommend cutting it with a sharp, fine-pointed knife. (*end*.)

> NOTE.
> I have used a cherry blossom stencil here that I purchased online. There are lots of options available. You can also easily cut your own stencil using a scalpel and a piece of acetate.

WHERE THE ORCHARD MEETS THE MEADOW
Nectarine. Chamomile. Honey.
166

LOVE CAKE
Tonka bean. Bay. Citrus. Rose. Summer berries. Herbs from the meadow.
171

ATHENA
Raspberry. Grappa. Lime. Mascarpone cream heart.
177

CAKE FOR THE ANGELS
Pear. Bay. Sage.
181

FLORA
Fennel pollen. White chocolate. Gooseberries. Fennel seeds.
185

DOW

LAYERS OF MEMORIES
Caramel. Passionfruit. Macadamia.
189

**BETWEEN A THOUSAND
LEAVES OF DELIGHT**
Vanilla. Wild strawberries.
193

ODE TO JOHN OLSEN
Pistachios. Rhubarb. Ginger.
197

OUR FRIENDSHIP CAKE
Quince. Rose.
201

TROPÉZIENNE
Mulberries. Orange blossom. Vanilla.
205

MEADOW

These meadows of cake celebrate the ethereal nature of floral scent and its kinship with what attracts us to one another.

Like the romance between the quince and the rose whose heady perfumes have drifted into many a love story over time.
My love cake ensues, with layers of sponge tinted in rose vermouth and berries for feminine allure.

A cake for the angels with bay, sage and pears, earthy and herbaceous, because I'm certain angels are tired of cloud cake.

These cakes express the charming unions that exist within nature. The places where the orchard meets the meadow or the way that the relationship of nectarines, honey and chamomile is not unlike the enamoured encounter between pavlova and sponge.

There's the meadow where I imagine meeting artist John Olsen, as though I was transported into the brushstrokes of one of his paintings. A quivering rhubarb custard falls from the tip of his brush over the landscape. I believe he loved to bake and I am attracted to the freedom and courage of his creativity.

Possibly the most significant muse for this book is the goddess Athena who appears in this chapter. My adoration for Athena is founded in her dedication to strategies for civilised war over bloodshed. That is the epitome of 'fierce' in my mind. I met her in the kind of meadow that has barely a kiss of clover on the ground, nowhere to hide, and just a bejewelled shield of raspberries and a mascarpone cream heart to carry her.

This chapter ultimately inspires an element of hope in divine meadows like the Elysian Fields with my Tarte Tropézienne. A lusciously feminine cake that I bring with me into this paradise to share with all the women who have loved and supported me. Sage mulberries for wisdom and orange blossom to impart a sense of new beginnings and possibilities for the future.

MEADOW

These meadows of cake celebrate the ethereal nature of floral scent and its kinship with what attracts us to one another.

Like the romance between the quince and the rose whose heady perfumes have drifted into many a love story over time.
My love cake ensues, with layers of sponge tinted in rose vermouth and berries for feminine allure.

A cake for the angels with bay, sage and pears, earthy and herbaceous, because I'm certain angels are tired of cloud cake.

These cakes express the charming unions that exist within nature. The places where the orchard meets the meadow or the way that the relationship of nectarines, honey and chamomile is not unlike the enamoured encounter between pavlova and sponge.

There's the meadow where I imagine meeting artist John Olsen, as though I was transported into the brushstrokes of one of his paintings. A quivering rhubarb custard falls from the tip of his brush over the landscape. I believe he loved to bake and I am attracted to the freedom and courage of his creativity.

Possibly the most significant muse for this book is the goddess Athena who appears in this chapter. My adoration for Athena is founded in her dedication to strategies for civilised war over bloodshed. That is the epitome of 'fierce' in my mind. I met her in the kind of meadow that has barely a kiss of clover on the ground, nowhere to hide, and just a bejewelled shield of raspberries and a mascarpone cream heart to carry her.

This chapter ultimately inspires an element of hope in divine meadows like the Elysian Fields with my Tarte Tropézienne. A lusciously feminine cake that I bring with me into this paradise to share with all the women who have loved and supported me. Sage mulberries for wisdom and orange blossom to impart a sense of new beginnings and possibilities for the future.

WHERE THE ORCHARD MEETS THE MEADOW
Nectarine. Chamomile. Honey.

Chamomile grows in furrow, dancing with blades of ochre weed.
Wish after wish, we bury ourselves in dandelion rain,
puffing at downy clocks,
and watching as our dreams drift in barbed seeds beyond us.

RECTANGLE SIZE	25cm x 30cm
SERVES	15-20

VANILLA SUGAR	
caster sugar	500g
vanilla bean	1

HONEY CUSTARD	
vanilla bean (from above)	1
pure cream	400g
honey	40g
dried chamomile flowers	1 tbsp
egg yolks	5
caster sugar	60g

ROASTED NECTARINES	
ripe nectarines, halved and stones removed	5
light soft brown sugar	50g
orange, juiced	1

CHAMOMILE CAKE	
unsalted butter, softened	200g
vanilla sugar (from left)	200g
eggs	3
self-raising flour	160g
cornflour	40g
baking powder	1 tsp
dried chamomile petals, crushed or ground	1 tbsp
buttermilk	100ml

PAVLOVA	
pink peppercorns	2 tsp
egg whites (from the 5 eggs used for honey custard)	180g
sea salt	½ tsp
vanilla sugar (from above left)	300g
cornflour	1 tbsp
white vinegar	2 tsp

TO SERVE	
dried chamomile petals	
icing sugar	

> **NOTE.**
> As a little prelude to this recipe, you will be making some vanilla sugar to use for both the sponge and the pavlova, and you will use the bean in the infusion for the honey custard.

VANILLA SUGAR

1. Using the tip of a sharp paring knife, slice lengthways down the centre of the vanilla bean and open the bean so it sits flat on your chopping board. Now using the middle part of the blade, scrape along the length of the bean to extract the seeds onto your board. Every seed is precious, so carefully push any seeds on the blade onto the board, along with any on your fingertips. Separate the bean from the seeds, reserving the bean to use for the honey custard. Sprinkle 1 tablespoon of caster sugar directly on top of the seeds on the chopping board and use a little offset palette knife or a butter knife to rub the blade through the sugar and seeds. The abrasion of the sugar will separate the seeds and the little clumps will disappear. Continue to work the sugar through the seeds and, once you're happy you have dispersed the seeds fully through the sugar, use a larger knife or palette knife to transfer the seeds and sugar to a bowl.

2. Add the remaining caster sugar to make the weight up to 500 g, which is what you need for this recipe, then mix the sugar together so the vanilla distributes through the whole amount. This is also a perfect amount of sugar to put in a jar to use for later. Generally, 1 vanilla bean to 500 g sugar is a good ratio. If you're not using the bean to infuse as you are today for the honey custard, you can store the bean in the sugar jar for extra flavour. Remember, you can always use that bean at a later date to infuse into a custard or such, it's there waiting for you. Once a vanilla bean is 'spent' by infusing it in heat, it can be boiled up in water for 5 minutes then dried in the open air and returned to the vanilla sugar jar.

HONEY CUSTARD

1. Place the reserved vanilla bean, cream, honey and chamomile in a medium saucepan over low heat and bring the cream almost to the boil, then remove from the heat and allow the flavours to infuse for 1 hour.

2. When you are separating the eggs for the yolks here, set the whites aside to use for the pavlova later, as the egg white whips much better at room temperature. Place the egg yolks in a medium bowl with the caster sugar and whisk together immediately using a hand whisk. It's important to never allow sugar to rest on egg yolks for longer than it takes to pick up a whisk, because it will burn the yolks (essentially cooking them). The protein (setting) qualities of the yolks will be lost, thus rendering a component of the yolks worthless in their capacity to thicken custard. Continue to whisk the yolks and sugar together for 1 minute or until pale and a little fluffy.

3. After 1 hour infusing, set a medium bowl beside the stove and place a sieve on top in preparation for making the custard. Return the cream to the boil over medium heat then remove from the heat momentarily and pour approximately 125 ml of the boiling cream directly onto the whipped yolks, whisking to incorporate. Pour this yolk mixture back into the saucepan with the remaining cream and stir to combine all the ingredients thoroughly. Return the saucepan to low heat, stirring calmly and constantly with a heatproof spatula or wooden spoon as the custard thickens. If the custard looks like it's starting to bubble around the outside, take it off the heat and stir it to cool down, then return it to the heat when you feel confident. The custard should take approximately 2 minutes to thicken and can be tested as follows.

4. Remove the saucepan from the heat and lift the spatula out of the custard, holding it up over the saucepan with the paddle facing you. Draw a line through the custard with your finger (like parting the sea). If the line doesn't run back together the custard is ready. If the custard is still running on the spatula, return (*cont.*)

it to the heat to continue to thicken. When you're satisfied it's ready, remove it from the heat and pour the custard immediately through the sieve and into the prepared bowl to remove all the aromatics and any pesky lumps. Give the custard another good whisk to release more heat and prevent it from curdling, then cover the surface of the custard directly with plastic film to prevent a skin from forming. Cool the custard in the fridge for a couple of hours.

ROASTED NECTARINES

1. Preheat the oven to 160°C. Prepare a medium ceramic baking dish by greasing the inside with butter. Set aside.

2. Slice each nectarine half into 4 mm-thick slices and place in a bowl. Sprinkle over the sugar and orange juice and toss everything together to coat the fruit. Scatter the nectarines evenly over the base of the ceramic dish. Bake the nectarines in the oven until they are tender, shaking the dish every now and then to distribute the juices. The length of time will depend on the ripeness of the fruit, somewhere between 10–20 minutes should be a fair guide. Remove the roasted nectarines from the oven and allow them to cool completely.

CHAMOMILE CAKE

1. Preheat the oven to 160°C. Grease and line a deep 25 cm x 30 cm baking tray with baking paper and set it aside.

2. Place the softened butter and vanilla sugar in the bowl of an electric mixer fitted with the paddle attachment and cream together on medium speed until pale and fluffy. Use a spatula to scrape down the sides of the bowl regularly to ensure all the butter is being whipped.

3. Crack the eggs into a small bowl and give them a light whisk with a fork to make them more fluid and easier to incorporate into the batter. Gradually add the eggs to the butter, a little trickle at a time, ensuring each addition is incorporated before adding the next. Again, continue to scrape down the sides of the bowl to ensure the eggs combine with all the butter. Once all the egg is combined continue to whip for a further 1 minute while you prepare the dry ingredients.

4. Sift the self-raising flour, cornflour, baking powder and chamomile flowers twice, pressing through as many of the flowers as possible and discarding any stems that remain in the sieve.

5. Reduce the mixer speed to low and use a tablespoon to gradually add the dry ingredients to the batter in three batches, alternating with the buttermilk, also in three batches. I usually start with the dry ingredients and end with the buttermilk, which helps to dissolve any last traces of flour. Once everything has been added, scrape down the sides of the bowl and increase the speed to medium-high for just 3 seconds to aerate the batter and activate the baking powder. Remove the bowl from the mixer, then pour the batter into the prepared baking tray and use an offset palette knife or a spoon to spread evenly to the edges of the tray.

6. Pop the cake straight in the oven for 20 minutes, then reduce the temperature to 150°C and bake for a further 5–10 minutes. The cake is cooked if the centre bounces back when pressed with your finger. It will be extremely light and may even whisper to you. Remove the cake from the oven and slide out of the tray to cool completely on a cooling rack.

7. Re-line and grease the same baking tray you have just removed the cake from and set it aside in preparation for the pavlova top. Reduce the oven temperature to 140°C.

PAVLOVA

1. Toast the peppercorns to enhance their flavour by placing them in a frying pan over medium heat for 1–2 minutes, shaking to distribute the heat, until you start to notice their colour changing to a deeper red. Shake them out of the pan into a pestle and mortar or straight onto your chopping board and allow them to cool. Crush roughly to maintain some texture for the top of the pavlova. If you don't have a pestle and mortar, place them in a pile on your chopping board and use the base of a small saucepan to crush them, pressing and rolling the pan over the top of the peppercorns using your weight. You will be able to hear the pepper cracking. Set aside for now.

2. Prepare all the ingredients for the pavlova before you start whisking the egg whites, so they are ready to fold through the meringue the moment it is ready. Place the reserved egg whites (from the honey custard) and a pinch of salt into a scrupulously clean bowl of an electric mixer fitted with the whisk attachment and begin whipping on high speed. This will aerate the egg whites and lift them up around the balloon of the whisk, this part of the process is for volume in your pavlova. As soon as you start to see soft ribbons forming in the meringue, reduce the speed to medium and start adding the vanilla sugar, 1 tablespoon at a time, leaving 5 seconds between each addition and sprinkling it over the surface of the beating meringue. The reason for turning down the speed here is to allow for a slow addition of the sugar without the egg whites over-whipping. As you add more sugar, you should increase the gap between each addition so the egg whites aren't saturated in sugar, unable to absorb it. Once all the sugar has been added, beat the meringue for a further 2 minutes to ensure the sugar has dissolved completely, then remove the bowl from the mixer. Sprinkle the cornflour, half the cracked peppercorns and the vinegar evenly over the surface of the meringue and gently fold through until you are confident everything is well incorporated. Pour the meringue into the prepared baking tray and use an offset palette knife to spread almost to the edge of the tray, leaving a 5 mm gap for air to circulate and create a crunchy outside.

3. Place the pavlova in the oven and once the door is closed immediately reduce the temperature to 110°C. Bake for 1 hour, then turn the oven off and allow the pavlova to remain in the oven with the door closed for a further 1 hour to set and stabilise. Afterwards, remove the pavlova from the oven and slide it out of the tray onto a cooling rack. Allow it to cool completely before assembling the cake.

TO ASSEMBLE

1. Place the chamomile cake onto your serving platter, ensuring that you peel the baking paper away first. Using an offset palette knife, spread half the honey custard over the top of the cake all the way to the edges, then spoon half the roasted nectarine evenly over the custard. Slide the pavlova layer onto the nectarines and spoon the remaining custard and roasted nectarines on top. Sprinkle the cake with extra chamomile flowers and remaining crushed peppercorns and dust with icing sugar, if you wish.

2. Serve the cake immediately. This cake is best eaten on the day it is assembled, although all the components of this cake can be prepared the evening before it is presented. (*end*.)

LOVE CAKE
Tonka bean. Bay. Citrus. Rose. Summer berries. Herbs from the meadow.

Floral scent speaks to us of higher elements of nature.
That heady euphoria encourages a romantic notion, more and more,
and we ourselves are transported within every note
of fragrance that floats through the air.

SIZE	20cm	25cm
SERVES	10-12	12-15

TONKA BEAN CUSTARD

double cream	200g	250g
pure cream	200g	250g
tonka bean, finely grated	1	1
vanilla bean	1	1
egg yolks	4	5
caster sugar	60g	75g
mascarpone	200g	250g

BERRY COMPOTE

strawberries, hulls removed	250g
raspberries	250g
blackberries	125g
blueberries	125g
caster sugar	80g
lemon, zested	1

SPONGE

plain flour	75g	90g
cornflour	25g	30g
eggs, separated	5	6
vanilla paste	1 tsp	1 tsp
egg whites, extra	2	2
icing sugar, sifted	225g	270g
rosé vermouth	80ml	95ml

WOODLAND CRUMBLE

unsalted butter, well-softened	50g
caster sugar	50g
flour	50g
almond meal	50g
ground cinnamon	½ tsp
ground cloves	¼ tsp
dried chamomile flowers	1 tsp
dried rose petals	2 tsp
orange, zested	1

DRIED FOREST TWIGS AND BERRIES

vanilla bean (reserved from the tonka bean custard)	1
strawberries, hulled	5
icing sugar, for dusting	

FLORAL MOSS

freeze-dried fruit (such as raspberries, strawberries, mandarin segments)	50g
Davidson plum powder	2 tsp
freeze-dried citrus powder (such as lemon, lime or orange)	2 tsp
dried rose petals	2 tbs
quantity dried forest twigs and berries (from above)	1
quantity woodland crumble (from above)	1

(The day before)

TONKA BEAN CUSTARD

1. Place the creams, tonka bean and vanilla bean in a medium saucepan over low heat to infuse the aromatics into the cream. Once the cream comes to the boil, turn off the heat and allow the cream to sit and infuse for 30 minutes. Meanwhile, whisk the egg yolks and sugar together using a hand whisk until light and fluffy.

2. Return the cream to medium heat until it comes to the boil again, then pour over the egg yolks and whisk well to combine. Pour the custard mixture back into the saucepan and return to the stove over low heat, stirring calmly and slowly with a heatproof spatula or a wooden spoon until the custard thickens. Use the spatula to scrape the bottom of the pan as you go to avoid the custard sticking. The custard should take approximately 5 minutes to thicken, keep the heat on low and don't be tempted to turn it up. To test if the custard is ready, dip the spatula into the custard then remove it and run your finger through the custard on the back of the spatula. If the path made by your finger doesn't close again the custard is thick enough. When the custard is ready, remove it from the heat and strain through a fine sieve, then place in the fridge to cool. Retain the vanilla bean and rinse it well under a running tap. Set it aside for the vanilla twigs.

3. Cover the surface of the custard directly with plastic film to prevent a skin from forming, then refrigerate for 4 hours to cool. Once the custard has cooled, whip with mascarpone, being careful not to overwhip it, and fold the custard through the mascarpone. Set this aside in the fridge until ready to assemble the love cake.

BERRY COMPOTE

1. Slice the strawberries into quarters and place in a heatproof bowl with the remaining ingredients. Cover the bowl tightly with plastic film and place over a saucepan of gently simmering water with the heat on the lowest setting. The steam from the saucepan will heat the berries and the sugar will melt, forming a syrup they'll poach in. This is the most beautiful way of gently cooking berries that will also retain their shape and flavour. Leave the berries to cook for 20 minutes, then turn the heat off and allow them to sit over the saucepan for a further 15 minutes. Leave the bowl covered as you remove it from the saucepan and place in the fridge to cool completely.

SPONGE

1. This cake has five layers of sponge, which are shaped freeform onto baking paper. Follow the 'how to shimmy with sponge' method on page 256 and begin by preparing the baking paper circles needed for the layers of love cake.

2. Preheat the oven to 160°C. Sift the flours together twice into a bowl and set them aside with the sieve, as they will be sifted once more later on.

3. Place the egg yolks, vanilla paste and half the icing sugar in the bowl of an electric mixer fitted with the whisk attachment and whip for 5 minutes or until pale and fluffy. Remove the yolks from the mixer and decant them into a separate large bowl. Thoroughly clean and dry the mixer bowl, add the egg whites and whisk on high speed until soft peaks form, then reduce the speed to medium and gradually add the remaining icing sugar, 1 tablespoon at time, allowing 5 seconds between each addition, until a thick and glossy meringue appears. Waiting between each addition of sugar will enable the egg whites to absorb the sugar and for the meringue to stabilise.

4   Using a spatula, fold one-third of the egg whites into the egg yolk mixture, then sift one-third of the flour over the surface and fold through. Repeat this process, alternating the egg whites and flour, until everything is combined. It's not necessary to fold each ingredient through completely after each addition. For instance, a few streaks of egg white and a dusting of flour is fine for the first two-thirds. It's only until you fold through the final third of each that you need to ensure everything is incorporated properly. Remember, every fold you make is depleting air from the sponge.

5   Divide the sponge equally between the five baking paper circles you have prepared as part of the shimmy method. You could use a scale for this to get them exactly even, if you like. Use an offset palette knife to gently spread the batter evenly to the edges of the circles. Bake each sponge layer for 12–15 minutes or until the centre springs back when pressed with your finger, then remove from the oven and slide onto a wire cooling rack until cool.

WOODLAND CRUMBLE

1   Preheat the oven to 140°C. Cream the butter and sugar together in a bowl using a wooden spoon. If your butter is truly soft, this shouldn't be too much of a challenge. There is no need to aerate the butter excessively here, you just need the sugar to dissolve and marry with the butter. Add the remaining ingredients and stir well to form a paste, then wrap the dough in baking paper and place in the freezer to set.

2   Once the crumble dough is completely hard, remove from the freezer and grate it directly and evenly onto a tray lined with baking paper. Ideally, you should use the largest side of a box grater to do this, although, at a pinch, you could use a coarse microplane grater, but it won't produce the best textural crumb.

3   Bake the crumble for 20 minutes or until dry, but without attracting too much colour. Remove crumble from the oven and cool on the tray. This will later be mixed with the other ingredients for the floral moss.

DRIED FOREST TWIGS AND BERRIES

1   Preheat the oven to 50°C. Line an oven tray with baking paper. Dry the reserved vanilla bean by patting it with some kitchen paper, then slice it finely lengthways using a sharp paring knife. Spread the vanilla strips onto one half of the baking tray, so the heat can circulate around them. Cut the strawberries lengthways into 2 mm slices and place alongside the vanilla, then dust them with a conservative layer of icing sugar. Pop in the oven for 40 minutes to dry out, then turn off the oven and leave the fruit and vanilla to cool in the oven for a further 1 hour. I favour using a dehydrator for dried fruit since it preserves the flavour much better than in the oven, but either method is suitable here.

TO ASSEMBLE

1   Line a 22 cm | 25 cm round cake tin with baking paper. To make getting the cake out of the tin easier the next day, I recommend using two 5 cm x 40 cm-long strips of baking paper to line the base of the tin. Cross them over one another in the base of the tin, then run the strips up the sides and let them fall over the rim. Then line the tin as you usually do. This tin will be what you set the layers of sponge and custard in overnight. Alternatively, you could line the tin with plastic film, making sure the plastic is snugly pressed into the tin groove for a sharp-looking cake.

(*cont.*)

2. Peel away the base papers from your sponges and place one, golden-side up, into the bottom of the prepared cake tin, trimming with a pair of scissors to fit, if necessary. Using a pastry brush, brush this layer with one-fifth of the rosé vermouth, then pipe or spread one-fifth of the custard evenly over the sponge. Drain the liquid from the compote and evenly spoon over one-quarter of the berries.

3. Repeat this layering until you reach the top layer of sponge, which should be placed golden-side down in order to form a flat top for your finished cake. Brush with the final amount of vermouth. You should have one-fifth of the custard remaining to coat the cake with on the following day, which can be stored in the fridge until you need it. Cover the moulded cake with baking paper and refrigerate overnight or for a minimum of 4 hours.

(On the day)

1. Just before you unmould the cake, prepare the floral moss by tossing all the ingredients in a bowl and using your hands to crush everything together to create a union of fragrance and texture.

2. Unmould the cake from the tin by levering it out using the paper strips and place it onto your cake platter. Using a palette knife, skim the final amount of custard over the top and sides of the cake, then completely cover it in the floral moss. I always try to make the cake look as natural as possible by imagining what it would look like if you found it in the meadow. Arranging the dried strawberry slices and vanilla twigs can be a lot of fun. (*end.*)

NOTES.

This recipe is best started the day before you intend to serve the cake. Then, on the day, all you need to do is ice the cake and scatter over the crumble. If you'd like, you can also make the tonka bean custard, the crumble and the berry compote 2 days in advance.

A couple of different size tins feature here. As part of my signature recipe writing style, I've done the maths for you. You will only notice variation in the sponge and the custard, though, because the other components of this cake yield an amount that will cover both sizes with some to spare.

ATHENA
Raspberry. Grappa. Lime. Mascarpone cream heart.

Goddess of war, handicraft and practical reason. Athena is in the breath between what provokes us and how we choose to react to it. She is the easy restraint of our untarnished self. The one we started out in this world with.

These layers of cake are woven from the day I met Athena and realised she had been by my side all these years, I just needed to call her.

SIZE	20cm	25cm	35cm
SERVES	10-12	12-15	20-30

RASPBERRY, GRAPPA AND LIME JAM			
fresh raspberries	250g	350g	750g
caster sugar	125g	175g	375g
limes, zested and juiced	1	1½	3
grappa	20ml	30ml	40ml

AMARETTI			
blanched almonds	200g	240g	570g
egg white	90g/ 3 eggs	110g /4 eggs	240g /6 eggs
caster sugar	200g	240g	570g
vanilla paste	1 tsp	1½ tsp	2 tsp
amaretto (or ½ amount in almond extract)	½ tbsp	¾ tbsp	1 tbsp

MASCARPONE CREAM HEART			
vanilla bean(s), split and seeds scraped	1	1½	2
caster sugar	60g	120g	200g
mascarpone	175g	250g	500g
cream cheese, softened	120g	170g	335g
crème fraîche or natural yoghurt	140g	200g	400g
pure cream	285g	405g	820g
grappa	30ml	45ml	80ml

TO ASSEMBLE			
mascarpone	100g	150g	300g
pure cream	100g	150g	300g
limes, zested and juiced	1	1½	2
fresh raspberries	450g	650g	1kg
freeze-dried raspberries (optional)	50g	50g	50g

RASPBERRY, GRAPPA AND LIME JAM

1 Place the raspberries and caster sugar in a medium saucepan over low heat, stirring the fruit with a wooden spoon to coat in the sugar. After a few minutes all the sugar will be melted and the fruit will start to boil. Add the lime juice and stir to combine, then increase the heat to medium and boil, stirring occasionally, to ensure the jam isn't catching on the bottom of the pan. The purpose of the rapid boiling is to maintain the colour of the raspberries, however, if the jam starts to splutter everywhere, turn the heat down a little. It's not essential for the jam to reach setting point as this will be spread inside a cake – it's far more important to preserve the flavour of the fruit. Boiling the jam for 10 minutes will be sufficient and, along the way, you will notice the bubbles become a more consistent size – this is also an indicator that the jam is thick enough. Remove the jam from the heat, cover the saucepan with a lid and allow to cool while you get on with making the amaretti layers.

AMARETTI

1 Preheat the oven to 160°C. Line the base only of 3 x 20 cm | 3 x 25 cm | 3 x 35 cm cake tins with baking paper. Alternatively, because not everyone has three tins the same size, the layers can be shaped free-form on sheets of baking paper and then baked. Later, they will be moulded into one single cake tin along with the filling and set in the fridge for 4 hours. To create the shape, you need to draw three circles the size of the cake you are making on three pieces of baking paper and either pipe or spread the amaretti mixture onto the paper. I have explained how to do this below, but you can also refer to the 'how to shimmy with sponge' method on page 256.

2 Prepare three squares of baking paper by drawing a 20 cm | 25 cm | 35 cm circle on each of them using your cake tin as a template. Assess the space in your oven and how many amaretti layers you will be able to bake at once and scout around for the equivalent number of trays to place the baking circles onto. Don't worry if you don't have enough trays – these layers can be baked in batches.

3 To make the amaretti, scatter the almonds onto a baking tray and pop them in the oven for 10–15 minutes or until they are lightly toasted and golden. Remove from the oven and allow to cool completely on the tray, then place the cooled almonds in a food processor and blitz until fine crumbs form. *(cont.)*

4   Increase the oven temperature to 170°C. Ensure the egg whites are weighed to the specifics in the ingredients list, as not all egg whites weigh the same and this will affect the recipe, then weigh the sugar in preparation for making the meringue.

5   Place the egg whites in an electric mixer fitted with the whisk attachment and whip on high speed until soft ribbons start to form. Reduce the speed to medium and gradually add the sugar, 1 tablespoon at a time, leaving 5 seconds between each addition, until all the sugar is added and the meringue is firm and glossy. Continue to beat the meringue for a further 2 minutes to make sure it is really firm, then remove the bowl from the mixer and fold through the vanilla, followed by the ground almonds and finally the amaretto, ensuring everything is well combined.

6   Divide the mixture between your three baking circles or tins by either weighing each one on a scale (for perfection) or using your eye to estimate the same size (you only live once). Spread the amaretti out using a small offset palette knife until it reaches 2 mm inside each circle – this is just to give you a buffer for expansion. Bake the amaretti layers for 20 minutes | 25 minutes | 30 minutes or until they are crisp. Remove from the oven and cool on a wire rack.

MASCARPONE CREAM HEART

1   Prepare the vanilla sugar by using the back of a palette knife to rub the seeds of the vanilla through 1 tablespoon of caster sugar on a chopping board. This will disperse the seeds in order to distribute the precious vanilla through the cream. Add the vanilla sugar to the remaining sugar and stir to disperse. See the note about making vanilla sugar on page 262.

2   Using a food processor, blend half the mascarpone together with the cream cheese and vanilla sugar until smooth and creamy. Pay extra attention to scraping down the sides of the bowl to ensure any lumps of cream cheese are caught by the blade and eliminated. They can ruin a beautiful cake. Finally, add the crème fraîche (or yoghurt) and blend for a further 1 minute to combine, then decant the cream cheese mixture into a large bowl.

3   Whip the pure cream with the remaining mascarpone in a separate bowl using a hand whisk until firmly whipped, then fold the cream through the cream cheese mixture. This will lighten the cream for the filling, making it like clouds, then fold through the grappa.

TO ASSEMBLE

1   Prepare a 20 cm | 25 cm | 35 cm cake tin by lining it with plastic film, making sure you press snugly into the groove where the base of the tin meets the sides and allow the plastic film to hang over the rim of the cake tin and down the sides. You can also use baking paper, although the plastic film makes it easier to remove from the tin. A springform tin is also handy in this situation. I find wetting or oiling the cake tin ever so slightly will make the plastic cling to the inside of the tin, so you can achieve a neat lining and subsequently a sharper shape to the cake.

2   Begin by placing one of the cooled amaretti layers in the base of the tin, even with your best efforts previously shaping the amaretti, you may still need to trim it to fit the tin (I find scissors the easiest). Spoon half the jam over the top of the amaretti and gently spread it all the way to the edges of the tin. Pour half the mascarpone cream heart over the top of the jam and smooth it evenly all the way to the edges of the tin using an offset palette knife, then add another layer of amaretti and repeat the jam and cream layer once more, finishing with the

final sheet of amaretti. Cover the cake with the excess plastic film hanging over the sides of the tin and refrigerate for 4 hours or overnight.

3   Whip the mascarpone and cream together using a hand whisk until softly whipped, then fold through the lime zest and juice. The juice will naturally thicken the cream once added, so don't go overboard with the initial whipping, it only needs to be loosely whipped.

4   Remove the cake from the fridge and invert it onto your cake stand or serving platter. Use the plastic film to lever it out of the tin, then remove the film. Dollop the lime cream into the centre of the cake and, working in a circular motion, use an offset palette knife to smooth the cream to the edges. Decorate the top of the cake with fresh upturned raspberries. If you have freeze-dried raspberries at hand, they can be useful to fill any gaps on the top and they add a little texture for interest, too.

5   This cake needs to be kept refrigerated until serving, but can generally sit out for 1 hour (weather dependent) before cutting. (*end*.)

NOTE.

Grappa is a fragrant grape-based pomace brandy of Italian origin. It is not essential to put it in the jam, however, it is crucial for the flavour of the mascarpone cream heart in the cake. To make this cake alcohol-free, omit the amaretto (or extract) and the grappa. Substitute the grappa with an extra two vanilla beans in the mascarpone filling. The toasted almonds in the amaretti will give you enough of the almond flavour without using amaretto or extract, but perhaps you could whisper to the almonds when you put them in the oven that they might sing with more flavour.

CAKE FOR THE ANGELS
Pear. Bay. Sage.

Our capacity to feel everything enables us to live what can be a blissful life. Vedic philosophy tells us that the Angels and Devas are envious of us because they can only feel love and live purely in a state of joy. It's breathtaking to me that our senses are really a gift in disguise and make our experiences more nuanced and meaningful. I made this cake for the angels so grounded and earthy. Bay for protection, as often angels do. Sage for purity.

SIZE	20cm	25cm
SERVES	10-12	12-15
BEURRE NOISETTE		
unsalted butter	280g	300g
bay leaves	3	4
sage leaves	6	8
vanilla bean, split and seeds scraped	1	1
POACHED PEARS		
water	500ml	500ml
caster sugar	250g	300g
bay leaves	2	2
lemon, zested	1	1
orange, zested	1	1
Packham or Beurre Bosc pears, peeled, halved and cored	3	4
CAKE		
beurre noisette (from above)	160g	180g
olive oil	1 tbsp	1½ tbsp
caster sugar, plus 50g | 60g for the topping	145 g	160g
eggs	2	3
plain flour	110g	130g
baking powder	¾ tsp	1 tsp
polenta	50g	60g
milk	75ml	90ml
lemon, zested	1	1
poached pear halves (from above)	6	8
sage leaves	6	8
TO SERVE		
cultured cream		

BEURRE NOISETTE

1. Set a small heatproof bowl beside the stove. Combine all the ingredients in a small saucepan over medium heat and bring to the boil. Keep an eye on the butter as it starts to transition through all its colours until it reaches a nut-brown colour called 'noisette'. The colour past this point is called 'noir', otherwise known as black, and if it reaches this point it should be discarded. Apart from being carcinogenic, it will be bitter and inedible. Actually, I like to catch the butter just before it reaches nut-brown since it continues to colour a little after it has been removed from the heat. In savoury cooking the colour is usually arrested with a squeeze of lemon juice, but we don't have that advantage in baking. Remove the saucepan from the heat and pour the infusion immediately into the small bowl in order to prevent the colour from turning darker. Allow the butter to cool for 30 minutes. After this time, pour the butter through a fine sieve to remove the herbs and discard them. Allow the butter to set opaque. This can be hastened in the fridge.

POACHED PEARS

1. Combine the water, sugar, bay leaves, lemon and orange zests in a large saucepan over medium heat and bring to the boil. Simmer for 3 minutes, then drop the pears into the syrup and cover with a cartouche (SEE Techniques, page 259) in order to keep them submerged. Simmer the pears until they are tender, using a sharp paring knife to test their tenderness; depending on the ripeness of the pears, they may take anywhere between 10–20 minutes on low heat to cook. You're looking for a little resistance so they retain some of their 'bite', then turn off the heat and cool the pears in the syrup. You can reserve a bay leaf for decorating.

(*cont.*)

CAKE

1. Preheat the oven to 170°C. Line a 20 cm | 25 cm cake tin with baking paper.

2. Once the beurre noisette is cool, place it in the bowl of an electric mixer fitted with the paddle attachment along with the olive oil and sugar and beat on medium speed until pale and fluffy. The aroma coming from the bowl at this stage is incredible. Scrape down the sides of the bowl every now and then with a spatula. Whip the eggs lightly with a fork and gradually add to the whipped butter, one-third at a time, waiting for each addition to be incorporated before adding the next.

3. Sift the flour, baking powder and polenta together twice. Remove the bowl from the electric mixer and use a spatula to fold the flour mixture through the whipped butter, one-third at a time, alternating with the milk, also one-third at a time. Ensure that all the butter at the bottom of the bowl has been folded through properly before pouring the batter into the prepared cake tin, then smooth the top using an offset palette knife.

4. Rub the extra caster sugar and the lemon zest together between your fingertips and sprinkle half over the surface of the cake. Bake for 30 minutes, then remove the cake from the oven and arrange the pear halves gently and evenly over the top. Top with the sage leaves, reserved bay leaf from the poaching syrup, and remaining lemon sugar, reduce the oven temperature to 165°C and pop the cake back in the oven for a further 20 minutes | 25 minutes. During the baking process some of the pears will fall to the bottom and some will remain on top. Test the cake for readiness by gently pressing the centre – if it bounces back, it's cooked. Remove the cake from the oven and cool completely in the tin.

5. Serve with cultured cream. *(end.)*

TO ASSEMBLE

1 Remove the sponges from the tins and set them aside. Re-use one of the tins to assemble the cake layers into (kind of like a mould) by lining the tin with plastic film. You may need to wet the inside of the tin a little to make the plastic stick, then run the plastic film over the sides of the tin so you have something to pull the cake out with once set.

2 Begin by slicing the sponges evenly in half horizontally through the middle using a serrated knife. Now you have four sponge rounds. Place the first sponge into the base of the tin and dollop one-third of the caramel mousse on top, smoothing it over evenly. Sprinkle over a generous amount of praline, then cover this layer with one-third of the passionfruit curd and smooth it over evenly. Repeat this process with the remaining sponges, mousse, praline and curd, finishing with a layer of sponge. Place the cake in the fridge for 4 hours to set.

CRÈME FRAÎCHE FROSTING

1 Place the softened cream cheese in the bowl of an electric mixer fitted with the paddle attachment and whip until smooth, being sure to scrape down the sides of the bowl frequently using a palette knife. Add the sifted icing sugar and beat until fluffy, then remove the bowl from the mixer and fold through the crème fraîche by hand using a flexible spatula until evenly combined. Gently fold through half the fresh passionfruit.

2 Once the cake is set, remove from the tin by inverting it directly onto your serving platter, then remove the tin and plastic film. Use an offset palette knife to ice the cake with the crème fraîche frosting, beginning with the sides and then smoothing over the top. Finish the frosting by using the palette knife to ripple the remaining fresh passionfruit into the sides and top of the icing, so it sits just below the surface.

3 This cake is best iced on the day it will be eaten, but can be stored un-iced in the fridge for 2 days beforehand. The frosting can be made ahead of time, but will need to be re-whipped to aerate the cream. (*end.*)

(On the day)

SPONGE

1. Preheat the oven to 150°C. Grease 2 x 22 cm cake tins and set aside. Sift the flours together into a bowl and set them aside. Place the egg yolks and half the sugar in the bowl of an electric mixer fitted with the whisk attachment and whisk for 5 minutes or until fluffy. Decant the yolks into a large bowl so you can fold all the ingredients of the sponge together, then clean and dry the mixer bowl.

2. Place the egg whites in the clean mixer bowl fitted with the whisk attachment and whip on high speed until soft peaks form, then add the remaining sugar and whip until a thick meringue forms. Fold one-third of the egg whites through the egg yolk mixture, alternating with one-third of the flour. Continue this process until all the ingredients have been combined. Divide the batter between the prepared tins and bake for 15 minutes or until the centre springs back when pressed with your finger. Remove from the oven and allow to cool in the tins. Keep the oven on for the macadamias.

MACADAMIA PRALINE

1. Toast the macadamias in the oven for 10 minutes, then remove and set aside. Line a baking tray with oiled baking paper and set it aside also. Place the sugar and water in a saucepan over low heat and stir the sugar continuously until all the crystals have dissolved, brushing down the sides of the saucepan with a wet pastry brush to remove any sugar crystals that may be forming. Once the syrup starts to boil, stop stirring and increase the heat to medium, then cook the caramel until golden. Add the macadamias to the saucepan and stir with a wooden spoon to combine evenly, then pour the praline out onto the prepared baking tray and allow to cool completely for at least 1 hour. Crush the cooled praline by placing it in a plastic bag and bashing it with a rolling pin to create pebble-sized pieces.

CARAMEL MOUSSE

1. Begin by soaking the gelatine in cold water to rehydrate it. Meanwhile, make a dry caramel by placing the sugar in a small saucepan over medium heat to melt. The edges of the sugar will melt first, then the centre. As this is happening, swirl the pan to evenly distribute the sugar as it caramelises. Continue to cook the caramel until it is dark-golden and clear, then remove from the heat and pour 160 g of the pure cream into the caramel to stop it from colouring. Be careful as the caramel may spit and splutter at this stage. Mix the caramel well with a spatula and allow to cool for 10 minutes before mixing through the chocolate. Squeeze the water from the gelatine leaves and add them to the caramel, mixing well to combine, then add the egg yolks and use a spatula to mix through. Cool the caramel mixture in the fridge for approximately 30 minutes, stirring occasionally, until it thickens, then whip the remaining 100 g pure cream together with the double cream or mascarpone to firm-whip stage. Fold the cream through the caramel one-third at a time, then set the mousse aside.

LAYERS OF MEMORIES
Caramel. Passionfruit. Macadamia.

What remains of the layers of our memories?
All the souvenirs, narratives and dreams we collect.
Blurred photographs and counting candles on the cakes to remember where we were.
I believe all the layers of cake must be my memoire.
My life expressed through whipping butter and sugar together.

CAKE TIN SIZE	2 x 22cm
SERVES	12-15

PASSIONFRUIT CURD	
egg	3
eggs yolks	3
caster sugar	160g
passionfruit pulp	150g
lemons, juiced	2
unsalted butter	160g

SPONGE	
plain flour	75g
cornflour	25g
egg yolks	5
icing sugar	225g
egg whites	7

MACADAMIA PRALINE	
macadamias, toasted	100g
caster sugar	200g
water	30ml

CARAMEL MOUSSE	
titanium-strength gelatine leaves	2
caster sugar	150g
pure cream	260g
white chocolate	200g
egg yolks	2
double cream or mascarpone	110g

CRÈME FRAÎCHE FROSTING	
cream cheese, softened	200g
icing sugar, sifted	50g
crème fraîche	300g
fresh passsionfruit pulp	80g

(The days before)

PASSIONFRUIT CURD

1 Begin by cracking the eggs and yolks into a medium heatproof bowl. Add the sugar and use a hand whisk to beat for 1 minute or so until the eggs are slightly pale and the sugar is dissolved. Add the passionfruit pulp and lemon juice to the eggs and whisk again until well incorporated, then place the bowl over a saucepan of barely simmering water and heat, whisking every 3 minutes, for approximately 20 minutes. The curd will begin to cook around the edges first, so whisking it occasionally ensures an even temperature is maintained throughout the cooking process. The whisk is a great tool to use for scraping the cooked curd away from the sides of the bowl and into the middle. Don't worry about any little lumps at this stage, they will be smoothed out later. The curd will be cooked when it reaches 85°C on a digital thermometer or becomes the consistency of thick cream. Turn the heat off and allow the curd to sit for a further 10 minutes in the bowl over the saucepan. This step is an insurance policy to guarantee the thickness of the curd and its ultimate setting.

2 After 10 minutes, remove the bowl of curd from the saucepan and set it on the bench to cool down, whisking the curd occasionally so the heat can be released and the temperature reaches 45°C on a thermometer or is warm to touch. Once it has cooled to this temperature, start whisking in the butter, 1 tablespoon at a time, waiting until each addition is incorporated before adding the next. This step can also be done in a food processor or with a stick blender.

3 Now, it's up to you if you want to leave the passionfruit pips in the curd, I usually remove 80 per cent of them by straining the curd, then return a few back to the curd as a gesture. Cover the curd and refrigerate overnight or for a minimum of 6 hours until chilled and set.

(cont.)

(On the day)

GOOSEBERRY COMPOTE

1. Place all the ingredients for the compote in a large saucepan over medium heat and stir the fruit to coat in the sugar. Once the fruit comes to the boil, reduce the heat to low and simmer for approximately 10 minutes or until the fruit is tender, then remove the saucepan from the heat and allow to cool in the pan.

FENNEL AND PINE NUT PRALINE

1. Line a baking tray with a sheet of lightly oiled baking paper and set it beside the stove. Toast the pine nuts in a small frying pan over medium heat, tossing until they're evenly coloured, then tip them into a small bowl. Return the pan to the heat to repeat this process with the fennel seeds until they are toasty and aromatic, then tip them onto the pine nuts. Once again, return the pan to the heat and sprinkle half the caster sugar evenly over the base of the frying pan. The sugar will begin to melt and become glassy, but instead of stirring the sugar, just swivel and shake the pan until it dissolves. Add the remaining sugar and heat and swivel until it has dissolved. The sugar will become dark quite quickly, so don't be afraid to remove the frying pan from the heat as you're swivelling to let the sugar melt in the residual heat. Once the sugar is completely transparent with no sugar crystals remaining, remove the caramel from the heat. Add the pine nuts and fennel to the pan and stir with a wooden spoon to coat them in the caramel, then pour the praline out onto the prepared tray and allow it to cool and set completely. Once cooled, blitz the praline in a food processor to form a fine crumb.

TO SERVE

1. Remove the parfait from the freezer and invert it onto a chopping board or flat tray. Remove the tin and the paper, then coat the sides and top of the parfait in fennel praline, pressing it into the surface with the palm of your hand. At this stage, the parfait can be returned to the freezer until you are ready to serve it.

2. Lift the parfait onto a serving platter and sprinkle the top with more fennel pollen and fennel blossoms before you take it to the table. Have your dessert plates chilling in the freezer and either slice the parfait at the table with a bowl of gooseberry compote in the middle or slice the parfait in the kitchen and present on your chilled plates alongside the compote. (*end.*)

NOTES.

A parfait is the same as a semifreddo. It is made using the same method as a mousse and doesn't require churning because the air incorporated into the mousse is then trapped during the freezing process, resulting in a very creamy dessert. Because it begins as a stable mousse when it comes out of the freezer, it doesn't melt like ice-cream. So it maintains its shape for longer when serving.

I have chosen gooseberries here because of their tartness and their colour, which is pale and lovely against the fennel cream. However, you could use brambles or just about any berry you fancy. If berries are in season, you could serve them fresh or follow the recipe for the gooseberry compote, but omit the water and just use 10 per cent sugar to the weight of fruit.

FLORA
Fennel pollen. White chocolate. Gooseberries. Fennel seeds.

Flora is the goddess of flowers who brings new hope to our hearts carried by the first scent of spring. When the shadows of winter start to lift and the afternoons draw longer, Flora arrives, giving new life and promise to our dreams.

(The days before)

PARFAIT

1. Place 425 g cream, the fennel pollen and vanilla bean and seeds in a small saucepan over medium heat and bring almost to the boil. Pour the cream into a plastic container and refrigerate for 3 hours or until completely cold.

2. Prepare a 25 cm x 10 cm x 10 cm loaf tin to mould the parfait by lining it with either baking paper or plastic film. It helps to lightly oil the tin first so the lining sticks and doesn't move around while you're trying to create neat edges and corners. Place the tin in your freezer to chill while you get on with making the parfait.

3. Melt the chocolate in a heatproof bowl over a saucepan of barely simmering water, ensuring the bowl doesn't touch the water, then turn off the heat. Bring the remaining 200 g cream to the boil in a small saucepan, then pour this over the top of the melted chocolate. Using a spatula, stir until the ganache is smooth. Leave the bowl over the saucepan for now.

4. Place the egg yolks in the bowl of an electric mixer fitted with the whisk attachment and wait for me to give you the go ahead to start whisking. Have your sugar thermometer ready and make sure it's working by checking the battery isn't flat. Combine the sugar and water in a small saucepan over medium heat and stir the syrup until it starts to boil. If there are sugar crystals up the sides of the saucepan, use a wet pastry brush to sweep them back down into the syrup. At this stage, you can begin whisking the egg yolks on high speed so they become pale and fluffy, then go back to watching the syrup.

5. When the sugar syrup reaches 120°C, remove it from the heat and reduce the speed of the electric mixer to medium. Slowly trickle the syrup down the inside of the bowl onto the egg yolks. Once all the syrup has been added, increase the speed to high and beat the eggs until they are completely cold, then remove the bowl from the mixer. What you have just made here is called pâté à bombe. Remove the fennel cream from the fridge once it is completely cold and remove the vanilla bean, then whisk the cream until it is softly whipped.

6. Take the chocolate off the saucepan and, using a spatula, gently fold the pâté à bombe into the chocolate ganache in two batches, trying to preserve as much air as possible. Fold through the whipped fennel cream, also in two batches, then pour the parfait into the prepared tin and freeze for at least 12 hours. *(cont.)*

You will need a sugar thermometer to make this recipe.

LOAF TIN SIZE	25cm x 10cm x 10cm
PARFAIT	
pure cream	625g
fennel pollen	1 tsp
vanilla bean, split and seeds scraped	1
white or blonde chocolate	625g
egg yolks	5
caster sugar	150g
water	150ml
GOOSEBERRY COMPOTE	
gooseberries	600g
caster sugar	100g
water	50ml
FENNEL AND PINE NUT PRALINE	
pine nuts	100g
fennel seeds	10g
caster sugar	100g
TO SERVE	
fennel pollen	
fennel blossoms	

BETWEEN A THOUSAND LEAVES OF DELIGHT
Vanilla. Wild strawberries.

A watchful heart is vigilant in tending to delight
like sowing wild strawberry seeds between the cracks of sorrow.

PASTRY CREAM

1. Place the milk, cream and vanilla beans in a medium saucepan and bring to the boil. Turn off the heat and allow the vanilla to infuse for a couple of hours, or better still, overnight.

2. Place the egg yolks and sugar in a bowl and use a hand whisk to whisk until pale, then add the cornflour and plain flour and whisk through. Remove the vanilla beans from the milk, then return the milk to the boil and reduce the heat to low. Pour one-third of the milk onto the egg yolk mixture and whisk together to temper the yolks before they are beaten into the scalding milk. Pour the yolk mixture back into the saucepan and whisk through the milk. This will take 30 seconds or so for the pastry cream to come back to the boil. Whisk gently and calmly for a further 2 minutes to cook the flour, then remove from the stove and cool to approximately 40°C. Once cooled, whisk through the softened butter, a little at a time, until it is all incorporated and the cream is glossy. Pour the pastry cream onto a shallow tray and cover with plastic film, pressing it directly onto the surface of the custard to prevent a skin from forming. Cool it completely in the fridge for a minimum of 4 hours.

MILLE-FEUILLE LAYERS

1. Lightly flour your bench, then place the block of puff pastry in the centre and lightly dust the top also. Before you begin to roll the puff, use your rolling pin to firmly tap down the pastry in both directions, as if you're tapping a grid pattern onto the top. This will balance the pastry and prevent it from going skew-whiff when you begin to roll.

2. Roll the puff out to a 40 cm x 45cm x 3 mm-thick rectangle using as little flour as possible, then transfer the pastry to a flat tray lined with baking paper and rest the sheet in the fridge or freezer for a minimum of 1 hour. Meanwhile, preheat the oven to 160°C. Prepare a large baking tray the same size as the pastry you have rolled by lining it with baking paper or a silicone baking mat.

3. After the puff has rested, cut the sheet into three equal rectangles that are approximately 15 cm x 13 cm each using a sharp paring knife then transfer them to the baking tray leaving a 2 cm gap between each strip. Use a fork or a pastry docker to pierce holes all over the surface of the rectangles to prevent the pastry from puffing up and shrinking too much. Beat the egg together with the milk using a fork then brush the egg wash over the top of the pastry. Sift the icing sugar evenly over the top. Bake the pastry for 30 minutes, then reduce the temperature to 150°C and bake for a further 35 minutes or until the pastry is golden and very crisp. Remove it from the oven and slide onto a wire rack to cool completely.

(cont.)

MILLE-FEUILLE SIZE	30cm x 10cm
SERVES	10-12
PASTRY CREAM	
milk	400ml
pure cream	180g
vanilla beans, split and seeds scraped	3
egg yolks	6
caster sugar	115g
cornflour	20g
plain flour	40g
unsalted butter, softened	70g
MILLE-FEUILLE LAYERS	
strong bakers or plain flour (for rolling)	100g
quantity full butter sourdough puff (page 248; SEE note)	½
egg	1
milk	1 tsp
icing sugar	3 tbsp
VANILLA CREAM	
quantity pastry cream (from above)	1
mascarpone	200g
crème fraîche	250g
wild strawberries or small strawberries	400g

4 To trim the pastry layers, use a large, sharp serrated knife and a ruler to mark out the pastry where you will cut. Sometimes the pastry will shrink in the corners and it seems like a waste when you look at how much you cut off. It's up to you how fussy you want to be.

5 The size I have given you at the top of this recipe is just a guide, so don't be disheartened if the pastry has shrunk a little and you're unable to achieve three rectangles this size, just trim the cut the pastry into three equal rectangles making the best use of the pastry. Set them aside.

VANILLA CREAM

1 Remove the pastry cream from the fridge and scrape into a medium bowl. You'll notice that it has taken on the shape of the tray and will need smoothing out before you can fold through the whipped creams.

2 Use a spatula to gently press the pastry cream to smooth it out. I can't stress enough how important it is that you don't start beating or stirring the cream, as this will just cause it to lose its thickness and capacity to hold up the mille-feuille. Just a gentle smoothing with the spatula and a few turns is all that's needed.

3 Whip the mascarpone and crème fraîche together until very firmly whipped. Some might say, on the verge of being overwhipped, but not quite. Again, this is to give the filling strength and definition in the piping.

4 Fold one-third of the mascarpone mixture through the pastry cream by initially adopting the same pressing technique you used before, then following on by folding the two creams together to form a consistency closer to the whipped mascarpone. Gently fold through another one-third of mascarpone mixture, scraping to the bottom of the bowl to ensure all the pastry cream is incorporating properly, then fold through the final third.

5 You should have a very firm vanilla cream in front of you now.

TO ASSEMBLE

1 Place one of the pastry layers on a serving platter. Fit a piping bag with a #7 star nozzle and fill the bag with one-quarter of the vanilla cream. Pipe the cream onto the pastry using whatever pattern you wish and cover with wild strawberries all the way to the edges. Top the strawberries with another quarter of the cream, so they sit in the middle of the cream layers. Alternatively, just pipe the cream once and have the strawberries on top or don't pipe at all and go for a more rustic aesthetic by just piling the cream on and spreading it gently to the edges with a palette knife – it's up to you.

2 Place the second pastry layer on top and press it down ever so lightly to create stability. Repeat the piping and filling as before. Top with your final pastry layer and press it down a little, then stand back and check that all the layers are aligned and give yourself a round of applause.

3 To slice the mille-feuille, use the same serrated knife you used to cut the rectangles earlier and have the plates ready, as the slices will be topsy-turvy in transit. (*end*.)

NOTE.
My full butter sourdough puff recipe in this book is double what you need for this mille-feuille, however, making puff pastry takes a lot of time, so it's best to make a bigger batch and freeze half for another day.

ODE TO JOHN OLSEN
Pistachios. Rhubarb. Ginger.

John Olsen was inspired by many of the great poets and their philosophies on the human condition, especially its metaphoric link to the wilderness. Through the medium of paint, he portrayed both the textures of the Australian landscape and his own nature in every brush stroke. His call to explore under every rock and in every crevice to uncover what makes us unique as artists is an eternal driving force for me. Meeting in a meadow with cake is what I imagined when I looked into Olsen's *Coopers Creek in Flood* (1975-76), dated 1981, with its palette of pistachio and rhubarb. It gave me the feeling of cake painted onto a canvas.

SIZE	20cm	25cm
SERVES	10-12	12-15

BAKED RHUBARB

1. Preheat the oven to 160°C. Wash the rhubarb to remove any soil and trim off the ends and leaves using a sharp cook's knife. Slice the stalks lengthways down the centre, so that they are no thicker than 1 cm. If the stalks are really thick you may need to slice them into three pieces lengthways to achieve the correct thickness. Cut each length into 7 cm batons then toss with the sugar, ginger, and orange juice and zest. Arrange the rhubarb in a deep baking dish, all in a row and in the same direction like matchsticks, and place in the oven for 20 minutes. Check the fruit and you will see the sugar has melted and the rhubarb is half-immersed in the liquid. Give the dish a shake so the fruit rolls over and the other side can be cooked, then return to the oven for a further 15–20 minutes or until soft and tender. You need the fruit to be soft enough so that when it goes into the layers of the cake you can cut through it with a knife. Remove the rhubarb from the oven and cool completely in the baking dish.

BAKED RHUBARB		
bunch rhubarb (minimum 6 | 9 stalks)	1	1½
caster sugar	150g	250g
small piece fresh ginger, peeled and thinly sliced	1	1
oranges, juiced and zested	1	2

GINGER CUSTARD

1. Combine the creams, ginger, cardamom and vanilla in a small saucepan over medium heat and bring everything almost to the boil, then turn off the heat and allow the flavours to infuse for 30 minutes.

2. Whisk the egg yolks and sugar together using a hand whisk until pale and fluffy. Set them beside the stove with a sieve sitting over the top of the bowl. Place a shallow tray beside the stove ready to pour the custard into.

3. Return the cream almost to the boil and pour the hot liquid through the sieve directly onto the yolks. Use a spatula to press the ingredients through the sieve to extract every last possible drop of cream into the eggs and discard the ginger. Whisk the cream and yolks together and return to the saucepan over low heat, stirring constantly and gently using a heatproof spatula, for 1–2 minutes or until the custard thickens. Test it's ready by running your finger through the custard on the spatula. If the custard doesn't run back together, it's done. Remove it from the heat and pour into the shallow tray, then cover the surface directly with plastic film to prevent a skin from forming and pop in the fridge to cool and set for 3 hours.

(cont.)

GINGER CUSTARD		
double cream	200g	250g
pure cream	250g	300g
large piece fresh ginger, peeled and thinly sliced	1	1
ground cardamom	¼ tsp	¼ tsp
vanilla paste	1 tsp	1 tsp
egg yolks	5	6
caster sugar	60g	70g

PISTACHIO SPONGE		
unsalted butter, plus 50g | 70g for greasing	50g	70g
pistachio paste	40g	55g
eggs	6	8
caster sugar	200g	260g
cake flour or combine 100g | 140g plain flour with 50g | 60g cornflour	150g	200g
pistachios, shelled and finely ground	100g	135g

TO ASSEMBLE		
pure cream	150g	200g
double cream	150g	200g
pistachios, shelled and roughly chopped	80g	100g

PISTACHIO SPONGE

1. Preheat the oven to 175°C. Lightly grease 3 x 20 cm | 3 x 25 cm cake tins with butter and pop in a base liner of baking paper to make removing the cakes easier. No need to flour the tins.

2. Melt the butter in a small saucepan on the stove, turning off the heat before it starts to boil. Add the pistachio paste and whisk through the butter thoroughly then set aside.

3. Choose a heatproof bowl (preferably the bowl from an electric mixer) and crack the eggs into the bowl. Add the sugar and roughly whisk together using a hand whisk. Place the eggs and sugar over a saucepan of barely simmering water, ensuring the bowl isn't touching the water, and whisk every now and then so they don't sit idle and scramble. It's not necessary to engage any fierce whisking action here as the electric mixer or electric beaters will do that later, you just need to keep the eggs and sugar moving as they are warming. Once the mixture is slightly hot to the touch (50°C on a thermometer), remove it from the heat and place the bowl onto an electric mixer fitted with the whisk attachment. Beat on high speed for 5–7 minutes or until completely cool.

4. Meanwhile, sift the flour twice to aerate and wake up the flour and have the finely ground pistachios at hand.

5. By now the eggs will be cool and have tripled in volume, so remove the bowl from the mixer. Sift half the flour onto the surface of the eggs and gently fold it through using a spatula or metal spoon. Repeat with the remaining flour. Once all the flour is combined, gently fold through the pistachios. Remove 3 tablespoons of the sponge mixture and fold it through the melted butter to lighten the liquid. Now fold this back through the sponge – this process will cause less deflation in the finished sponge.

6. Divide the sponge batter equally between the prepared cake tins and gently smooth the tops using an offset palette knife or a spoon. Bake the cakes for 20 minutes | 25 minutes. The sponges are ready when the middle bounces back slightly when pressed with your finger. Remove the sponges from the oven and allow to set in their tins for 2 minutes only. Remove them by tilting the tins at a 45-degree angle and slipping them out onto a cooling rack using your deft fingertips. Cool the sponges completely before assembling the cake.

TO ASSEMBLE

1. Remove the ginger custard from the fridge and place in the bowl of an electric mixer fitted with the whisk attachment along with the creams. Whip together until thick and fluffy. Don't walk away from the mixer at this stage as double cream can whip very quickly and curdle.

2. Place one of the sponges onto a cake platter and spoon one-third of the ginger cream on top, spreading it evenly to the edge of the cake using an offset palette knife. Cover the custard with half the baked rhubarb, being mindful not to add too much of the syrup at this stage, then top with the second sponge and repeat the layering of ginger cream and rhubarb. Place the third sponge on top and take a moment to jig all the layers together so the cake looks straight. Ripple a little of the rhubarb poaching syrup through the final third of the ginger cream then spoon it all over the top of the cake. Push the cream gently over the edges of the cake using a large palette knife and rotate the cake as you go to cover the sides. Try to move the cream only in one direction, so you don't sweep crumbs back into the icing. Smooth over the top, drizzle with a little more rhubarb syrup, if you like, and sprinkle with the chopped pistachios. (*end.*)

OUR FRIENDSHIP CAKE
Quince. Rose.

We have an abiding desire, you and me, to see the best in one another, regardless of what may separate us. To recognise the gifts the other brings to the world and to encourage their abundance is testament to our devotion.

This is a story of a quince and a rose who may never have met through the seasons, though they were always meant to be the most intimate of friends. They see themselves in each other and so when they are together the quince becomes more quincy and the rose becomes more rosy.

CHIFFON TIN SIZE	25cm
SERVES	10-12

(The night before)

SUGARED ROSE PETALS

1. Pluck the petals from the roses and wash them carefully. Place on a cooling rack to dry. Sprinkle the sugar onto a flat tray and brush the rose petals lightly with egg white on both sides. Place the petals on the bed of sugar and turn to coat. Once they are all coated, dry your hands and sprinkle the tops of the petals with sugar. Allow to dry and become crisp overnight.

SUGARED ROSE PETALS	
organic roses	2
caster sugar	150g
fresh egg white or 50ml pasteurised egg white	1

(On the day)

QUINCE PREPARATION

1. You will be happy to know that no arduous quince cooking is required here. The cake is made with raw, grated quince and the frosting is whipped with the cooked purée from around the core, which will be ready in the same time as it takes to make the chiffon.

2. Grate the peeled quince using the second-largest side of a box grater, turning the quince as you grate all the way down to the core until you have 180 g grated quince flesh to use for the chiffon sponge. Use a large cook's knife to roughly chop the remaining quince, core and all, and place in a small saucepan. Add the caster sugar, water and lemon juice and place over medium heat until it comes to the boil. Reduce the heat to low and cover the fruit either with a lid or a piece of baking paper to prevent the water from evaporating. Simmer the quince for 1 hour, while you get on with making the chiffon.

QUINCE PREPARATION	
large quinces, peeled	3
caster sugar	150g
water	200ml
lemon, juiced	1

CHIFFON

1. Preheat the oven to 170°C. Set aside a 25 cm chiffon tin with the tube inserted and check that your oven racks are set to fit the tin with the addition of a 5 cm rise.

2. Place the egg whites and salt in the bowl of an electric mixer fitted with the whisk attachment and leave on standby until you have weighed up all the ingredients.

(cont.)

CHIFFON	
large eggs, separated	9
salt	pinch
brown sugar	40g
water	70ml
rose liqueur	30ml
grated quince (from above)	180g
coconut oil, melted	70ml
Japanese cake flour or 140g plain flour plus 20g cornflour	160g
caster sugar	160g
cream of tartar	½ tsp
cornflour	20g

QUINCE FROSTING	
pure cream	200g
mascarpone	200g
cooked quince purée (from above)	200g

3. Place the egg yolks in a large bowl big enough to be able to fold all the ingredients together. Whisk in the brown sugar, followed by the water, rose liqueur and grated quince. The next addition will be the coconut oil, however, if you add it now, it can set in the time it takes for you to whip the egg whites, making it difficult to combine them and resulting in loss of air. Instead, leave the coconut oil somewhere warm until the meringue is almost ready.

4. Sift the flour twice to aerate it, but leave the sieve nearby. Weigh the caster sugar, cream of tartar and cornflour into a small bowl and roughly mix together with a spoon. Set the bowl beside the whites in the electric mixer. Now begin whipping the egg whites on medium-high speed until soft ribbons form. Reduce the speed to medium and begin adding the sugar and cornflour mixture, 1 tablespoon at a time, leaving 5 seconds between each addition. This will give the egg whites enough time to absorb the sugar. Add the coconut oil to the yolk mixture now and sift the flour over the top of the yolks, whisking it through also. Once all the sugar has been added to the whites and they are thick and glossy, remove from the mixer. Using a spatula, fold the whites through the egg yolk mixture, one-third at a time, ensuring there are no large lumps of egg white being folded through. If you do see egg white lumps on top, use the back of your spatula to flatten them gently before folding them through, as it will be almost impossible to eliminate them later without a heavier hand, which again results in loss of air.

5. Once the sponge is free from egg white streaks, pour it into the chiffon tin and use a small offset palette knife or a dessert spoon to smooth over the top gently so the batter meets the edge of the tin. This will create a flat foot to the chiffon, preventing it from doming too much. If you have a skewer handy, insert it all the way into the sponge and draw a spiral through the batter from the outer edge of the tin to the centre tube. This will pull through any air pockets in the sponge. If you don't have a skewer, just tap the chiffon ever so slightly on the bench before placing it in the oven. Bake for 50 minutes.

6. Meanwhile, be prepared for when the chiffon comes out of the oven, as it will need to be inverted immediately and hung until it cools. If the batter rises above the little feet on the rim of the tin, it will be necessary for you to quickly trim this off before inverting the chiffon so it doesn't touch the bench and squash back up into the tin. So have a large, serrated knife ready in preparation for this.

7. The chiffon can be tested for readiness by inserting a skewer into the sponge, if it comes out clean, its cooked. Remove the chiffon from the oven, trim only the necessary amount from the top (if any) and invert onto the bench, so that the sponge is just kissing the bench. Cool for 2 hours or overnight.

8. Once the chiffon is out of the oven, check the quince to see if it's cooked. The fruit should be very soft and mushy when pressed with the back of a fork. Remove it from the heat if you feel it's ready and drain off any surplus water before cooling at room temperature. Once the quince is cooled, purée the fruit using a hand-held blender or a high-performance blender. This will create a very fine purée, whereas a food processor will leave it more coarse. Whatever machine you use, be sure to press the purée through a fine sieve to remove the seeds and any unwanted texture. Place in the fridge to chill completely.

QUINCE FROSTING

1. Whip the cream and mascarpone in the bowl of an electric mixer fitted with the whisk attachment until firmly whipped, being careful not to overwhip. Using a spatula, fold the quince purée gently through the cream by hand, then set aside while you remove the chiffon from the tin.

2. To remove the chiffon from the tin, tilt the tin and slide a large offset palette knife or a long knife with a thin blade between the sponge and the tin. Angle the knife blade toward the tin and cut all the way around the outside of the sponge. Press the tube insert out of the tin to release the chiffon, then use a large, serrated knife to cut the top off the chiffon to make it flat. I know you want the chiffon to be really tall and cutting away sponge seems a waste, but it will be reflected in the profile of the cake, so cut down to the line marking around the outside of the chiffon.

3. Next, use a small paring knife to cut round the inside hole of the chiffon, between the tube and the sponge. Finally, put the chiffon tube flat on the bench and use the thin knife to cut between the tin and what will be the top of the chiffon. Invert the chiffon onto a plate and use your hands to brush away as many crumbs as possible. Clean down the bench and any crumbs that may find their way into the frosting, then place the chiffon onto a serving platter or cake stand for frosting.

TO DECORATE

1. Dollop one-quarter of the quince frosting on top of the chiffon and use an offset palette knife to coat the entire chiffon with a skim of cream. This is called a crumb coating and will trap any crumbs into the first layer. When working with a frosting that sets this would be put into the fridge to really set the crumbs in there before the next layer is applied. That is not the case with this frosting because it's just cream. So go ahead and dollop another one-quarter of the frosting evenly over the top of the chiffon.

2. Using the palette knife in a circular motion, sweep the frosting over the top in one direction only, before moving onto the sides. Continue loading your palette knife with a generous amount of frosting and working on small spaces at a time until the entire cake is covered. Neaten up the line between the top and the sides and decorate the edges with the sugared rose petals. Naturally, the rose petals will absorb the moisture from the frosting and, in time, will revert to their soft state, so if you are decorating the cake in advance, place the rose petals flat on the surface otherwise they will droop.

3. Refrigerate this cake if the weather is warm and bring it to room temperature 30 minutes before serving. (*end.*)

TROPÉZIENNE
Mulberries. Orange blossom. Vanilla.

An ethereal cake for a garden party in the fields of Elysium
among all the women who have imbued my life with beauty and meaning.
With mulberries for abundance and orange blossom for loveliness.

SERVES	15-20
PASTRY CREAM	
egg yolks	3
caster sugar	50g
plain flour	20g
milk	20ml
vanilla bean, split and seeds scraped	1
BRIOCHE	
fresh yeast or dried yeast	12g / 6g
milk, warmed	100ml
caster sugar	1 tbsp
strong bakers flour, plus extra for dusting	300g
salt, plus extra for egg wash	1 tsp
eggs, lightly beaten with a fork, plus 1 extra for egg wash	3
unsalted butter, well-softened and roughly chopped	150g
pearl sugar	100g
MULBERRY COMPOTE	
mulberries, stems removed	500g
caster sugar	50g
orange, zested and juiced	1
CRÈME MADAME	
quantity pastry cream (from above)	1
double cream or mascarpone	125g
pure cream	125g
orange blossom water	20ml
TO ASSEMBLE	
icing sugar (optional)	2 tbsp

PASTRY CREAM

1. Before you begin, place a flat container or tray beside the stove ready to pour the pastry cream into the minute it is cooked. Place the egg yolks and sugar in a bowl and beat together using a hand whisk until pale and fluffy, then add the flour and whisk again briefly to form a smooth paste.

2. Combine the milk and vanilla bean and seeds in a medium saucepan over medium heat and bring to the boil. Reduce the heat to low so the milk doesn't boil over, then with your whisk at the ready, tip one-third of the boiling milk over the egg yolk mixture and whisk gently to combine. This will 'temper' the egg yolks and prevent the custard from curdling. Reduce the heat to low so the milk is just simmering and pour the tempered yolks back into the saucepan. While it remains on the heat, whisk the milk and yolks until they from a thick custard. Swap your whisk for a wooden spoon and continue to stir for a further 2 minutes or until the custard has thickened. During this time you may need to swap back to the whisk to smooth out any lumps that appear. The most important thing to remember is that the pastry cream needs to cook on the stove for 2 minutes to cook out the raw flour. It might bubble and splutter, so if this happens, remove it from the heat momentarily to diffuse the heat before returning to the stove, stirring and whisking calmly to make a smooth and delicious cream. Pour the cooked custard into the waiting container or tray. Remove the vanilla bean and cover the surface directly with plastic film to prevent a skin from forming. Pop into the fridge until cold.

BRIOCHE

1. Combine the yeast, half the milk and 1 teaspoon sugar in a bowl and mix to dissolve the yeast. Place the flour, salt and remaining sugar in the bowl of an electric mixer fitted with the dough hook and beat on low speed to incorporate everything together. Turn off the mixer and pour the yeast mixture, remaining milk and lightly beaten eggs into the well formed by the dough hook and mix again on low speed, regularly scraping down the sides and bottom of the bowl to incorporate all the flour. When you can't see any loose flour remaining, increase the speed to medium and beat for a further 10 minutes (*cont.*)

or until the dough is glossy and elastic. Don't worry if it looks sticky – this is good and will create a fluffier cake. Start to add the butter, little by little, allowing each addition to be almost fully incorporated before adding the next. Continue until all the butter has been added, then beat for a further 5 minutes to develop the dough's structure. If the butter isn't incorporating, it usually means it isn't soft enough. If this happens, take measures to soften it more, then continue beating.

2 Scrape the dough from the mixer bowl using a pastry scraper and place in a large, lightly oiled bowl. Cover with a cloth and place the bowl somewhere warm to prove for 1 hour or until doubled in volume. After this time, fold the dough over itself twice, like a piece of paper, to knock it back. Cover the bowl with plastic film and place in the fridge for 3–4 hours for the butter to set and stabilise the dough so you can shape it.

3 Line a baking tray with baking paper then remove the dough from the fridge, by which time it will have hopefully doubled in volume again. This time the butter will have set and the dough will be more manageable. Lightly dust your bench with flour and use your hands to shape the dough into a ball by tucking the circumference under itself all the way around. Place the dough on a lightly floured surface and flatten slightly using your hands. Let the dough rest on the bench for 10 minutes covered with a cloth, this will allow the protein to relax so you can roll it to the required diameter.

4 Keep the dough lightly dusted with flour and use a rolling pin to roll out to 3 cm-high and 22 cm-wide. Refine the round shape as you roll and use your sense of touch to locate uneven pockets in the dough, using the rolling pin to redistribute. Place the dough onto the prepared baking tray and cover with an upturned bowl (that won't inhibit the dough if it doubles in volume) or a light tea towel and set aside in a warm place to prove for 2–4 hours or until the dough has doubled in volume. To test the dough is ready, gently press the side and you will feel pockets of fermentation under the surface. If it still feels resistant to the touch, leave it for a bit longer.

5 Preheat the oven to 180°C. Beat the extra egg with a pinch of salt using a fork. The salt breaks down the albumen and makes the wash more fluid, so you will have less streaks in the glaze. Brush the dough with the egg wash using a pastry brush and cover the top generously with pearl sugar. Don't put pearl sugar on the sides because it just falls off and burns at the base creating black spots on the bottom layer of the brioche.

6 Bake the brioche for 30 minutes, then reduce the temperature to 170°C and bake for a further 20 minutes. The brioche can be tested for readiness by inserting a skewer into the centre and checking for a little moisture, but no stickiness. Remove the brioche from the oven and slide it (paper and all) onto a cooling rack to cool completely.

MULBERRY COMPOTE

1 Place the mulberries and sugar in a heatproof bowl and toss to combine, then add the orange zest and juice and cover tightly with plastic film. Place the bowl over a saucepan of simmering water for 15 minutes to steam the mulberries. Turn off the heat and leave the mulberries to cool in the syrup over the pan of hot water. This mulberry compote can be made up to 5 days ahead and stored in the fridge.

CRÈME MADAME

1. Once the pastry cream has cooled, gently decant it into a medium bowl. It will have taken on the shape of the flat tray but don't be tempted to whisk or beat it. Instead, take a spatula and gently press the cream with a flattening motion into the surface of the bowl to smooth it out. Turn the cream over itself a few times and search for any large lumps that can also be pressed out.

2. Whip the double cream or mascarpone and pure cream together until very firm. Look for the point where it's just about to overwhip then use a spatula to gently fold through one-third of the pastry cream. Engage the same pressing action you used to smooth out the pastry cream to create a union between the creams so they bond. Don't whip or beat them. Fold through the remaining cream, one-third at a time, before folding through the orange blossom water to your taste.

TO ASSEMBLE

1. Using a large, serrated knife slice the brioche in half horizontally. Before you make the cut all the way across the middle, use the knife to 'score' around the brioche first to make sure your slicing will be even all the way through. Once you are happy with this mark, cut a little deeper, rotating the brioche all the way around, but only going about 5 cm-deep at first. Don't be tempted to cut straight from one side to the other, as you may not come out on the line you marked. Go around a second time, rotating the cake again, until you reach the centre with the knife. Lift the top off the brioche and fill the centre with the crème madame, spreading it to the edge of the brioche using an offset palette knife. Top the cream with the drained mulberry compote and pop the lid on. Dust the top lightly with icing sugar. (*end.*)

SIREN
Bitter chocolate. Sour cherries. Sea salt.
213

CAKE FOR JOY
Coconut. Passionfruit. Finger lime.
217

YOUR SONG FOR THE SEA
Verbena. Lavender. Hemp seeds. Pink grapefruit. Rose. Chervil.
221

HONEYMOON CAKE
Speculaas. Pineapple. Lime. Coconut.
225

LUNA
Lemons. Limoncello. Mascarpone.
231

ROCKPOOLS OF FIGS & PLUMS
Plums. Figs. Cultured cream.
241

MANGO EXTRAVAGANZA
*Mango for happiness and the magical power to grant wishes.
Coconut. Lime.*
237

SEA

At the edge of the sea the feathered fringes of the waves roll to shore carrying with them a sorrow.

Ernest Hemingway said 'write hard and clear about what hurts' and I think there is an importance in acknowledging pain but then sending it back out to the horizon along with all your moods and secrets. By nurturing our spirit with this tenderness and vigilance we can, in turn, make way for joy.

The sea carries so much just beneath its surface. All the unrequited love of the Sirens but also the delight, healing and wonderment of us all. My cake for the Siren Parthenope has a wreath of sour cherries for immortality. She can still be seen running along the sand and watching over Naples from the stars.

In my sea of cakes, botanicals of citrus, finger lime, coconut and passionfruit remind us of holidays, weekends at the beach and reconnecting with our carefree self. I can't pretend to know the sea. I find it quite daunting actually. Although its power to dissolve our worries is undeniably magical. As with mangoes and their ability to grant wishes.

My cake for Luna is inspired by the Amalfi cake Delizie al Limone and the way both sunshine and moonlight reflect from the sea to change our moods.

The herbs in my gateau Breton are elixirs for the soul – lavender for devotion, hemp for happiness and joy giving, with chervil for sincerity. These botanicals speak to my purpose, but you can create your own story, your own song to sing to the sea.

SIREN

Bitter chocolate. Sour cherries. Sea salt.

A cake baked by the gods of the sea in celebration of an immortal Siren's odyssey.
Of bewitching songs to tempt a king's heart that are still being sung.
Feathered and finned all gather in a festival of flowers and fruit to set her free.
A wreath of cherries floating on twilight waters met on the horizon
by a sky of Napoli stars.

1. Preheat the oven to 140°C. Line a 20 cm | 25 cm round cake tin with baking paper using the following instruction. This cake will be baked in a water bath, so you need to use a conventional tin, not a springform tin, to ensure it doesn't leak. On this occasion, you won't be tipping the cake upside down to get it out, instead, you will be levering it out with the aid of two paper strips lining the base of the tin. So before you line the tin, lay a couple of long baking paper strips approximately 5 cm-wide and 40 cm-long crossing over one another so they meet in the centre of the tin, then run the strips up the sides and let them fall over the rim. Now line the tin as you usually do and set it aside.

2. Half-fill a deep tray large enough to fit your cake tin with water and place it in the preheating oven.

3. Combine the 180 g | 220 g Manjari chocolate, all the Jivara chocolate, and the butter in a large (sounds excessive but bear with me) heatproof bowl and place over a saucepan of barely simmering water, making sure the bowl isn't touching the water, to half-melt. Once half-melted, turn the heat off and leave the bowl on top of the saucepan.

4. Meanwhile, place the extra 80 g | 100 g Manjari chocolate in a food processor and blitz to a fine crumb using the pulse function or pausing intermittently between 4 second spurts. This method allows the chocolate to fall from the sides of the processor back into the bowl and will ultimately form a fine, even crumb without the chocolate overheating or melting. Decant the chocolate into a bowl, then add the toasted almonds to the food processor and blitz using the same method until they are just roughly chopped. Remove 50 g of the coarsest almonds to use for the top of the cake and continue to blitz the remaining almonds until they form fine crumbs, then add these to the bowl with the Manjari crumb.

5. Place the egg yolks in the bowl of an electric mixer fitted with the whisk attachment and whisk on medium speed, then add half the caster sugar, increase the speed to high and beat until very pale and tripled in volume. Remove the bowl of chocolate from the saucepan and stir it to thoroughly combine the chocolate and butter, then, half at a time, gently fold through the whipped yolks using a spatula. Sift the cocoa directly over the chocolate mixture and fold it through until well combined. Add the ground almonds and chocolate crumbs and fold to combine. You'll find that large bowl coming into play now. *(cont.)*

SIZE	20cm	25cm
SERVES	10-12	12-15
FIG LEAF SYRUP		
Valrhona Manjari chocolate (minimum 64% cocoa solids), plus extra 80g / 100g	180g	220g
Valrhona Jivara chocolate (minimum 40% cocoa solids)	65g	80g
unsalted butter	80g	100g
whole almonds, skin on and toasted	120g	150g
eggs, separated	6	7
caster sugar	130g	160g
good-quality cocoa powder	40g	40g
salt	pinch	pinch
sea salt flakes, plus extra to serve	½ tsp	¾ tsp
frozen sour cherries	200g	250g
clotted or thick cream, to serve (optional)		

6 Whip the egg whites with a pinch of salt in a clean and dry electric mixer bowl fitted with the whisk attachment on high speed. When soft ribbons start to form, reduce the speed to medium and gradually add the remaining caster sugar, then beat until glossy and firm peaks form. Be careful not to overwhip.

7 Gently fold half the whipped meringue into the chocolate, pressing out any lumps of meringue that may have formed. Fold in remaining meringue, then pour the cake batter into the prepared tin and smooth the top with an offset palette knife. Scatter the coarsely chopped almonds evenly over the top of the cake and sprinkle with sea salt.

8 Place the cake tin into the water bath in the oven, ensuring the water comes halfway up the sides of the tin. If the tin starts to float, remove some of the water until it makes contact with the base of the tray again. Bake the cake for 25 minutes, then open the oven door and scatter the sour cherries over the top of the cake like a wreath. Reduce the oven temperature to 130°C and bake the cake for a further 50 minutes.

9 Once this time is up, the cake will spring back when pressed in the middle, although, it will still seem a little wobbly. Turn the oven off, leaving the cake in the oven with the oven door slightly ajar to cool for 1 hour. If your oven door doesn't stay ajar by itself, use a wooden spoon wedged into the door to allow the heat to escape. Cooling the cake this way will help it to set and reduces the dramatic sinking that flourless chocolate cakes usually encounter.

10 After 1 hour the cake can be removed from the oven and from the water bath to cool completely in the tin. Ideally, this cake should be set overnight or 'express set' in the fridge for 4 hours because it is very mousse-y and this will make it easier to remove from the tin. To unmould the cake, gently tug at the four strips of baking paper hanging over the rim to release the cake from the base. Then pull upwards, angling the cake at 45 degrees to slide it out onto a serving platter. Even better if you have a friend who can pull up on two of the strips as you pull up on the other two. I recommend using a hot knife to cut this cake. Sprinkle with extra sea salt to serve. I like to serve it with clotted or thick cream.

11 There is no need to refrigerate this cake after it has been removed from the tin. If you have leftovers, just leave it out at room temperature. (*end.*)

CAKE FOR JOY
Coconut. Passionfruit. Finger lime.

Unmoored, and swept by the ocean tides
she lay with her arms splayed wide like a starfish
luminescent and waiting for joy.
All the flying fish leapt from the depths around her
and she glowed like lime caviar ready to burst.

SIZE	20cm	25cm
SERVES	10-12	12-15

PASSIONFRUIT CURD		
eggs	3	4
egg yolks	3	4
caster sugar	100g	150g
passionfruit pulp	100g	150g
lemons or limes, juiced	2	3
unsalted butter, well-softened	80g	120g

COCONUT SPONGE		
eggs	2	3
egg yolks	2	3
caster sugar	280g	320g
plain flour	100g	120g
cornflour	50g	60g
baking powder	1 tsp	1¼ tsp
bicarbonate of soda	¾ tsp	1 tsp
almond meal	50g	60g
coconut oil, melted	200ml	240ml
coconut cream	250g	300g
lemon, zested and juiced	1	1
desiccated coconut	¼ cup	½ cup
flaked coconut	½ cup	¾ cup
egg whites (2 / 3 reserved from egg yolks above in passionfruit curd)	4	6
sea salt	pinch	¼ tsp

FROSTING		
crème fraîche	100g	150g
pure cream (preferably double cream)	100g	150g
quantity passionfruit curd (from above)	1	1

TO DECORATE		
passionfruits, pulped	2	3
finger limes	6	8
flaked coconut	½ cup	¾ cup

PASSIONFRUIT CURD

1. Begin by cracking the eggs and yolks into a medium heatproof bowl (reserve the whites to make up the quantity of egg whites needed for the sponge below). Add the sugar and use a hand whisk to beat for 1 minute or so until the eggs are slightly pale and the sugar is dissolved, then add the passionfruit pulp and lemon or lime juice (seeds and all) to the eggs and whisk again until well incorporated.

2. Place the bowl over a saucepan of barely simmering water, whisking every 3 minutes, for approximately 20 minutes. The curd will begin to cook around the edges first, so whisking the curd occasionally ensures an even temperature is maintained throughout the cooking process. The whisk is a great tool to use for scraping the cooked curd away from the sides of the bowl and into the middle. Don't worry about any little lumps at this stage, they will be smoothed out later. The curd will be cooked when it reaches 85°C on a digital thermometer or becomes the consistency of thick cream. Turn the heat off and allow the curd to sit for a further 10 minutes in the bowl over the saucepan. This step is an insurance policy to guarantee the thickness of the curd and its ultimate setting.

3. After 10 minutes, remove the bowl of curd from the saucepan and set it on the bench to cool down, whisking the curd occasionally so the heat can be released and the temperature reaches 45°C on a thermometer or is warm to touch. Once it has cooled to this temperature, start whisking in the butter, 1 tablespoon at a time, waiting until each addition is incorporated before adding the next. This step can also be done in a food processor or with a stick blender. Press the curd through a fine sieve using a spatula to remove the seeds and any lumps, then cover the curd with plastic film and press onto the surface to prevent a skin forming. Cool completely in the fridge.

COCONUT SPONGE

1. Preheat the oven to 165°C. Line 2 x 20 cm | 2 x 25 cm cake tins with baking paper and set them aside. Place the eggs, egg yolks and only 200 g | 220 g of the sugar in the bowl of an electric mixer fitted with the whisk attachment and whip on medium-high speed until pale and fluffy.

(cont.)

2   Meanwhile, sift the plain flour, cornflour, baking powder, bicarbonate of soda and almond meal together to aerate and distribute the raising agents evenly. You may find some coarser parts of the almonds won't go through the sieve, but just return these bits to the flour mixture, making sure there are no lumps of bicarbonate of soda accompanying them.

3   Once the eggs are pale and fluffy, reduce the mixer speed to medium and add the coconut oil, a little at a time, trickling it down the inside of the bowl until all combined. Remove the bowl from the mixer and decant the mixture into a larger bowl, then thoroughly clean and dry the electric mixer bowl in preparation for the egg whites. Using a spatula and working in four batches, gently fold the dry ingredients through the eggs, alternating with the coconut cream, also in four batches. Add the lemon juice and zest and the desiccated and flaked coconut to the batter and fold the mixture gently again to combine.

4   Place the egg whites and salt in the clean bowl of an electric mixer fitted with the whisk attachment and whip on high speed until soft ribbons start to form. Reduce the speed to medium and gradually add the remaining sugar, 1 tablespoon at a time, until firm peaks form and the meringue is thick and glossy. Allow the egg whites to beat for a further 1 minute after the final addition of the sugar to ensure the meringue is stable and all the sugar has dissolved. Working with one-third at a time, fold the meringue gently through the cake batter until no streaks of egg remain, then divide the mixture evenly between the prepared cake tins and smooth the tops using an offset palette knife. Bake the cakes for 40 minutes | 55 minutes. Test for readiness by pressing the centre of the cake with your finger, if it bounces back the cake is cooked. Remove the cakes from the oven and allow to cool in the tins.

FROSTING

1   Place the crème fraîche and cream in the bowl of an electric mixer fitted with the whisk attachment or use a hand whisk to whisk to firm-whip stage, being careful not to overwhip. Remove the passionfruit curd from the fridge, then use a spatula to fold the curd through the cream, one-third at a time, being mindful that the consistency of the curd and cream are very different and need to be introduced to one another gradually and gently. This is for two reasons; firstly, so that the thickness of curd isn't compromised by too much mixing and, secondly, so that the cream isn't introduced too quickly, resulting in lumps throughout the frosting. Fold one-third of the curd through the cream in order to create a smooth union between both. No lumps of cream should be visible before adding the next third of the cream. This time, fold it through more gently to preserve the thickness of the frosting, which needs to be firm enough to coat the sides of the cake without running off. Finally, add the last of the curd, folding it through until there are no streaks remaining.

TO DECORATE

1   Remove the cakes from their tins and place one cake onto your serving platter. Dollop one-third of the frosting onto the cake and use an offset palette knife to spread it evenly to the edges. Spoon the passionfruit pulp over the frosting, then top with the second cake. Cut the finger limes in half and scoop half the pearls into the remaining frosting. Smooth the frosting over the top and sides of the cake to completely cover it, then spread the remaining finger lime pearls over the top of the cake. Decorate with flaked coconut. (*end.*)

YOUR SONG FOR THE SEA
Verbena. Lavender. Hemp seeds. Pink grapefruit. Rose. Chervil.

Brittany herbs have long had a place in folklore and witches' spellbooks for their healing properties and the elemental virtues they instil. There's some kind of magic in choosing favourite botanicals and seeking out their spirit, only to find you embody them in life or purpose. Gateau for devotion, happiness, creativity, sincerity, joy and love.

1. Preheat the oven to 160°C. Line a 20 cm | 25 cm round cake tin with baking paper.

2. Blitz the sugar in a food processor with the lavender, half the ruby grapefruit zest, salt flakes and the vanilla seeds only (not the bean) to release the aroma. If you don't have a food processor, just rub everything together with your fingertips or use a pestle and mortar, adding only 1 tablespoon of sugar to the bowl for friction to create the infusion and release the flavours.

3. Combine all the sugar and flour in the bowl of either a food processor or an electric mixer fitted with the paddle attachment and blend briefly to combine, then add the butter and blitz or beat until fine breadcrumbs form. Add the egg yolks to the mixture and beat to combine everything until a thick paste forms. Remove the bowl and use a spatula to fold the mixture a few times, scraping all the way to the bottom of the bowl to incorporate the mixture evenly, then fold through half the chervil leaves and half the lemon verbena leaves (no stems).

4. Spoon the batter into the prepared cake tin and smooth the top using an offset palette knife, then brush the top of the cake with the extra beaten egg yolk, adding a splash of water for fluidity. Score the top of the cake with a knife in a diamond pattern and sprinkle with hemp seeds, more salt flakes, the remaining grapefruit zest and extra lavender. Finish the top with the nasturtium leaves and flowers, the rose geranium leaves, spent vanilla bean, and remaining chervil and lemon verbena (stems on this time). Bake for 30 minutes | 40 minutes or until the top is golden brown and an even colour all over. This is generally an indicator the cake is cooked, as the colour and heat will reach the centre last.

5. Remove the cake from the oven and allow it to cool in the tin. Once cooled, tilt the cake at a 45-degree angle to remove it from the tin. This cake is very durable and is known as a travelling cake, having traditionally been sent all over France by post. With a texture described as 'sandy' like shortbread, it is even great eaten stale but keeps on the kitchen bench for days and days.

6. The botanicals I've used in this recipe are my favourite, but you can use any you like, depending on your nature. (*end.*)

SIZE	20cm	25cm
SERVES	10-15	15-20
PASSIONFRUIT CURD		
caster sugar	180g	270g
organic dried lavender, plus extra for sprinkling	2 tsp	3 tsp
ruby grapefruit, zested	1	1
sea salt flakes, plus extra for sprinkling	½ tsp	¾ tsp
vanilla bean, split and seeds scraped	1	1
spelt or rosella wheat flour (or 200g / 300g plain flour)	180g	270g
unsalted butter, cold	250g	375g
egg yolks, plus extra 1 yolk for the glaze	6	9
bunch of chervil	¼	½
bunch of lemon verbena	¼ (6 dried leaves)	½ (8 dried leaves)
hemp seeds	2 tsp	3 tsp
nasturtium leaves and flowers	3	3
rose geranium leaves	2	3

HONEYMOON CAKE
Speculaas. Pineapple. Lime. Coconut.

Spice awakens the most primitive of our senses and whispers
into the batter all the magic spells of sunshine, lust and promise.
I imagined love would stay in the same form, but it changes
to something richer that can't always be seen on the surface.

LOAF SIZE/ROUND TIN SIZE	30cm x 7cm	25cm
SERVES	10-12	12-15

LIME CURD		
eggs	3	3
egg yolk	1	1
caster sugar	160g	160g
lime juice	150ml	150ml
limes, zested	2	2
unsalted butter	160g	160g

TOASTED COCONUT CUSTARD		
flaked coconut	75g	90g
double cream	220g	260g
pure cream	200g	220g
star anise	1	1
egg yolks	4	5
caster sugar	60g	75g

SPECULAAS SPONGE		
cornflour	125g	150g
self-raising flour	55g	70g
cocoa powder	3 tsp	3½ tsp
ground cinnamon	1 tsp	1½ tsp
ground nutmeg	1 tsp	1½ tsp
ground cloves	½ tsp	¾ tsp
ground aniseed or fennel	½ tsp	¾ tsp
white pepper	¼ tsp	½ tsp
ground ginger	1½ tsp	2 tsp
ground cardamom	1 tsp	1½ tsp
ground mace	¼ tsp	½ tsp
unsalted butter	20g	25g
golden syrup	60g	75g
eggs, separated	5	6
caster sugar	225g	275g

TOASTED COCONUT CREAM		
double cream	100g	120g
pure cream	100g	120g
toasted coconut custard (from left)	230g	280g

TO ASSEMBLE		
freeze-dried pineapple	50g	80g
fresh pineapple, halved, cored and cut into 2mm-thick slices	½	½
flaked coconut	100g	150g

> NOTE.
> There are two sizes and shapes for this cake. The first column is for a long loaf 30 cm x 7 cm x 7cm and the second column is for a 25 cm round celebratory cake. The sponge for the loaf shape is first baked in a baking tray then cut into rectangles and layered into the loaf tin. The 25 cm round cake's layers are baked using the shimmy method, because hardly anyone in the world has five round cake tins the same size. It is then layered into a single round tin, which becomes the mould to set the cake in overnight.

(The day before)

LIME CURD

1. This recipe for curd will be plenty for both sizes. Begin by cracking the eggs and yolks into a medium heatproof bowl. Add the sugar and use a hand whisk to beat for 1 minute or so until the eggs are slightly pale and the sugar is dissolved. Add the lime juice and zest to the eggs and whisk again until well incorporated.

2. Place the bowl over a saucepan of barely simmering water and heat, whisking every 3 minutes, for approximately 20 minutes. The curd will begin to cook around the edges first, so whisking the curd occasionally ensures an even temperature is maintained throughout the cooking process. The whisk is a great tool to use for scraping the cooked curd away from the sides of the bowl and into the middle. Don't worry about any little lumps at this stage, they will be smoothed out later. The curd will be cooked when it reaches 85°C on a digital thermometer or becomes the consistency of thick cream. Turn the heat off and allow the curd to sit for a further 10 minutes in the bowl over the saucepan. This step is an insurance policy to guarantee the thickness of the curd and its ultimate setting.

3. After 10 minutes, remove the bowl of curd from the saucepan and set it on the bench to cool down, whisking the curd occasionally so the heat can be released and the temperature reaches 45°C on a thermometer or is warm to touch. Once it has cooled to this temperature, start whisking in the butter, 1 tablespoon at a time, waiting until each addition is incorporated before adding the next. This step can also be done in a food processor or with a stick blender. Press the curd through a fine sieve using a spatula to remove any lumps, then cover the curd with plastic film and press onto the surface to prevent a skin forming. Cool completely in the fridge.

TOASTED COCONUT CUSTARD

1. Preheat the oven to 150°C. Scatter the coconut onto a baking tray lined with baking paper and toast for 10–15 minutes or until golden. It may be necessary to give the coconut a bit of a shake so that it toasts evenly.

2. Place the coconut, double cream, pure cream and star anise in a saucepan over medium heat and bring to the boil, then reduce the heat to low and simmer for 1 minute to infuse the coconut. Turn off the heat and allow the cream to sit for 1 hour, then strain the cream to remove the coconut.

3. Whisk the egg yolks and sugar together using a hand whisk until pale and fluffy and set them beside the stove. Prepare a flat tray for pouring the custard onto when it is cooked and place it beside the stove also.

4. Return the cream almost to the boil then pour half the cream directly onto the yolks. Whisk the cream and yolks together then return them to the saucepan over low heat, stirring constantly and gently using a heatproof spatula for 1–2 minutes or until the custard thickens. The custard can be tested by running your finger along the paddle of the spatula. If the custard doesn't run back together, its ready. Remove it from the heat and pour onto the prepared flat tray, then cover the surface directly with plastic film to avoid a skin from forming and pop the custard in the fridge to cool and set.

SPECULAAS SPONGE

1. Preheat the oven to 170°C. Line a 30 cm x 40 cm x 3 cm baking tray with baking paper or, if you are making the round cake, refer to the 'how to shimmy with sponge' method on page 256 and prepare five pieces of baking paper with a 25 cm circle drawn on each of them.

2. Sift the flours, spices and cocoa three times to aerate the flour and evenly distribute the spices. Melt the butter and golden syrup together in a small saucepan over medium heat. Place the egg yolks in a small bowl and give them a light whisk with a fork. Place the egg whites in the bowl of an electric mixer fitted with the whisk attachment and whisk until soft peaks form, then gradually add the sugar, a little at a time, continuing to whip until the egg whites have formed stiff peaks. Reduce the speed to low and trickle in the egg yolks, then increase the speed to medium for 10 seconds to incorporate the yolks into the meringue. Remove the bowl from the machine and use a spatula to fold through the flour and spices, sifting them into the bowl in two batches. When I fold dry ingredients into eggs, I sift them directly into the eggs rather than sifting them into a bowl and tipping them in, as this stops any lumps from forming and you can shower a thin film of flour over the top of the meringue; it's lighter and won't sink to the bottom until you fold it through, giving you more control.

3. Once you see that almost all the flour has been incorporated, trickle in the butter and syrup, then fold through until well incorporated. It is better to start folding the butter through when there are still streaks of uneven colour in the sponge, as those final few turns will fold in any residual flour and the butter at the same time. Fewer turns mean a fluffier sponge. Stop folding the second you see the colour of the sponge is even with no streaks. Pour the sponge into the baking tray and smooth the top using an offset palette knife or, if you are making the round cake, use the 'shimmy' method to create round layers. Bake the sponge for 10–12 minutes or until the top of the cake bounces back when pressed with your finger. Listen to the sponge, too. A perfect sponge will whisper with a little moisture when you press it, telling you it's time to take it out of the oven. Remove the sponge from the oven and slip the sponge (or layers) from the baking tray and onto a wire rack to cool.

TOASTED COCONUT CREAM

1. Place the double and pure creams into the bowl of an electric mixer fitted with the whisk attachment and whip until very firmly whipped, to the point where you think it's about to overwhip, then remove the bowl from the mixer. Using a spatula and working in two batches, fold the toasted coconut custard gently through the cream, trying to maintain the thickness of the cream as you do so. Place the toasted coconut cream in the fridge while you prepare the sponge layers for assembly.

TO ASSEMBLE

1. Line a 30 cm x 7 cm x 7 cm loaf tin | 25 cm round tin with plastic film to make it easier to remove the cake from the tin the next day. You can also use baking paper, but I would recommend cutting two 5 cm x 40 cm strips of baking paper to line the base of the tin with. Overlap them to make a cross in the centre of the tin, then run the strips up the sides and let them fall over the rim. Then line the tin as you usually do. This tin will be what you use to set the layers of sponge and custard in overnight.

(*cont.*)

2   If making the loaf, cut the rectangle sponge into 5 x 30 cm x 7 cm pieces. These will form the layers of your cake. If you're making the 25 cm round cake, peel the paper away from your cake layers and trim the layers, if necessary, so that they fit into the tin.

3   For both shapes, place the first layer of sponge in the base of the tin then spread evenly with one-third of the toasted coconut cream. Crush some of the freeze-dried pineapple over the cream and place another layer of sponge into the tin. Next, spread half the lime curd over this layer and cover with half the sliced pineapple. Add another layer of sponge followed by another one-third of the coconut cream and crush more freeze-dried pineapple on top (reserving some for the final decoration). The fourth layer of sponge can be added now and spread with the remaining lime curd. Top with the remaining sliced pineapple and, finally, the last sponge layer. Cover the cake and set it in the fridge overnight. Place the remaining coconut cream into a covered container and refrigerate.

(On the day)

1   The following day, unmould the cake from the tin by pulling it out using the plastic film (or baking paper) and place it on a serving platter. Using a palette knife, skim the final amount of coconut cream over the top and sides of the cake then completely cover it in the flaked coconut and remaining freeze-dried pineapple.

2   This cake should be refrigerated until you're ready to serve. It's best to slice it using a large serrated knife. *(end.)*

LUNA

Lemons. Limoncello. Mascarpone.

Every evening Luna shoots an arrow of stars and constellations into the night sky. Her light leaps and dances amongst clouds of springtime lemons as she settles on a tree of dreaming blossoms. Luna tickles the petals of happiness, pleasure and enjoyment from the branches and tosses them like confetti in her wake, as she drives her golden chariot back across the Amalfi sky.

PUDDING BOWL SIZE	900ml, 22cm diameter
SERVES	10-12

LUNA'S CITRUS ROSETTE	
lemons	4
caster sugar	200g
lemon juice	200ml
water	100ml

LEMON-SCENTED GANACHE	
good-quality white chocolate, finely chopped	85g
pure cream	320g
lemons, zested	2

LEMON CURD	
eggs	4
egg yolks	2
caster sugar	200g
lemons, zested and juiced	4 (180ml)
unsalted butter, softened	160g

LIMONCELLO BATH	
caster sugar	150g
water	150ml
lemons, zested and juiced	2
limoncello	50ml

LEMON SPONGE	
plain flour	60g
cornflour	40g
large eggs, separated	5
icing sugar, sifted	150g
salt	pinch
lemon, zested and juiced	1

TO ASSEMBLE	
pure cream	100g
mascarpone	100g

(The day before)

LUNA'S CITRUS ROSETTE

1. For Luna's rosette, you first need to make the lemon confit peel. This is the process of cooking lemon peel very slowly until it becomes transparent and glossy, while being sweet and tender to eat.

2. Begin by peeling the lemon skin into strips using a vegetable peeler. First you need to blanch the peel to remove the bitter flavour of the pith and soften it before it is cooked slowly in the sugar syrup. The blanching is important, because if the peel isn't cooked properly before it goes into the confit syrup, it will not become transparent and it will be tough. So, place the peel into a medium saucepan, cover well with cold water and bring to the boil over medium heat. Be generous with the amount of water as the bitterness of the peel will escape into the water. If you are scant with the water, the bitterness will remain in the peel. Once the water comes to the boil, remove the saucepan from the stove and drain the water into the sink. Repeat this process three more times to make a total of four blanches. After the fourth time, drain the peel and set it aside.

3. Clean the saucepan and place the sugar, lemon juice and water in the saucepan over low heat. Cook, stirring, until the sugar is dissolved. Once the syrup comes to the boil, stop stirring and simmer for 2 minutes, then add the peel to the syrup. Return to the boil, then reduce the heat to the lowest setting, so that the syrup is just 'ticking over' with minimal bubbles. Cover the peel with a cartouche (*see* Techniques, page 259) that fits perfectly into the saucepan to keep the peel submerged and retain the heat in the pan. Continue to simmer for 1 hour or until the peel is translucent. The syrup will reduce a little along the way – that's OK, so long as you don't start to see the syrup turning a caramel colour, as that means the heat is too high and the confit will be caramelising. Once you're happy the peel is glossy and transparent, turn off the heat and cover the saucepan, leaving it at room temperature until cool.

LEMON-SCENTED GANACHE

1. Place the chocolate into a medium bowl and set it beside the stove, then place the cream and lemon zest into a small saucepan over medium heat and bring to the boil. Turn off the heat and allow the lemon to infuse for 20 minutes. Return the cream to the boil and pour it over the chocolate, then use a hand whisk to mix the ganache until there are no lumps of chocolate remaining. Refrigerate the ganache overnight.

LEMON CURD

1. Begin by cracking the eggs and yolks into a medium heatproof bowl. Add the sugar and use a hand whisk to beat for 1 minute or until the eggs are slightly pale and the sugar is dissolved. Add the lemon juice and zest to the eggs and whisk again until well incorporated.

2. Place the bowl over a saucepan of barely simmering water, whisking every 3 minutes, for approximately 20 minutes. The curd will begin to cook around the edges first, so whisking the curd occasionally ensures an even temperature is maintained throughout the cooking process. The whisk is a great tool to use for scraping the cooked curd away from the sides of the bowl and into the middle. Don't worry about any little lumps at this stage, they will be smoothed out later. The curd will be cooked when it reaches 85°C on a digital thermometer or becomes the consistency of thick cream. Turn the heat off and allow the curd

to sit for a further 10 minutes in the bowl over the saucepan. This step is an insurance policy to guarantee the thickness of the curd and its ultimate setting.

3   After 10 minutes, remove the bowl of curd from the saucepan and set it on the bench to cool down, whisking the curd occasionally so the heat can be released and the temperature reaches 45°C on a thermometer or is warm to touch. Once it has cooled to this temperature, start whisking in the butter, 1 tablespoon at a time, waiting until each addition is incorporated before adding the next. This step can also be done in a food processor or with a stick blender. Press the curd through a fine sieve using a spatula to remove any lumps, then cover the curd with plastic film and press onto the surface to prevent a skin forming. Cool completely in the fridge.

LIMONCELLO BATH

1   Combine the sugar, water, lemon juice and zest in a small saucepan over medium heat and bring to the boil, then reduce the heat to low and simmer for 2 minutes. Remove the saucepan from the heat and allow the syrup to cool for 30 minutes, then add the limoncello, cover and place in the fridge overnight to chill.

(On the day)

LEMON SPONGE

1   Preheat the oven to 170°C. Line a 30 cm x 40 cm x 2 cm baking tray with baking paper. If you don't own a tray this size, just use a couple of smaller ones.

2   Sift the plain flour and cornflour together twice and keep the sieve nearby. Separate the eggs then place the yolks and half the icing sugar in the bowl of an electric mixer fitted with the whisk attachment and whip on high speed until thick and very fluffy. Once the mixture has tripled in volume, remove the bowl from the mixer and decant the yolks into a larger bowl. Thoroughly clean and dry the mixer bowl.

3   Whisk the egg whites and salt in the clean mixer bowl on high speed until soft ribbons start to form, then reduce the speed to medium and add the remaining icing sugar, 1 tablespoon at a time, leaving 5 seconds between each addition. When the meringue is thick and glossy, remove the bowl from the mixer and fold the meringue through the yolks, one-third at a time, alternating with the flours, also one-third at a time. It's good practice to sift the flour over the surface of the sponge during this process to avoid lumps from forming. Finally, fold through the lemon zest and juice and pour the batter into the prepared baking tray, smoothing the top gently with an offset palette knife. If you are using two trays (it doesn't matter if they are different sizes) the most important thing is that the sponge is the same thickness in both tins to ensure the layers are even. Pop the cake in the oven and bake for 18 minutes. Test it's ready by pressing the centre of the sponge and looking for a slight bounce. Remove the sponge from the oven and slip out onto a wire cooling rack.

TO ASSEMBLE

1   Prepare the pudding bowl by lining it with plastic film, draping the excess over the rim of the bowl and down the sides. I usually wet the bowl a little to enable the plastic to cling more easily and make for a smoother finish and more snug fit. Set the bowl aside for now.

2   The layers for this cake are cut from a single sheet of sponge and the number of layers and sizes you can achieve in your cake depends on how many rounds of cake you can cut from that sheet. I have cut six layers all increasing in size (*cont.*)

gradually from the base of the cake to the top. I used all sorts of things as templates – cookie cutters, saucers and buckets lids. It really doesn't matter what you use, but spend some time figuring out how many circles you can get out of the trays you have used before you cut. The filling is designed to be spread between however many layers you have.

3 Once you have cut the sponge into round layers, use a pastry brush to brush each layer on both sides with the limoncello bath or, if you're brave, just dip the sponge layers into the bath. Whisk the pure cream and mascarpone together until firmly whipped, then fold through half the lemon curd using a spatula. Clouds of Amalfi lemons will ensue, forming a lemon cream.

4 Begin by placing the smallest sponge layer (the point) into the bottom of the pudding bowl and spread with one-third of the lemon cream, smoothing it over with the back of a spoon. Place the next layer of sponge on top of the cream and cover with one-third of the lemon curd, also smoothing it over with the back of a spoon. Continue layering the sponge, alternating with the lemon cream and lemon curd, and finishing with a layer of sponge. If you have any of the limoncello bath left, you can brush some on the layers as you go. Cover the cake with the excess plastic film and place in the fridge for 2 hours or overnight to set.

5 To remove the cake from the bowl, invert onto a serving platter or cake stand and pull down on the plastic film as you lift the bowl off, then remove the plastic film.

6 Remove the lemon ganache from the fridge and give it a good whisk to incorporate any chocolate that has floated to the top and set. Using a hand whisk, whip the lemon ganache to medium-firm whip. I say medium because, as you are piping the cream onto the cake, it will naturally continue to set in the piping bag and so a firm whip may cause it to split. It's important that it's not too soft, either, as you won't achieve the definition in the piping.

7 Fit a piping bag with a #11 plain nozzle and scoop one-third of the lemon ganache into the bag at a time. Working with this small amount at a time will give you more control and prevent your hands from warming the cream, potentially causing it to become runny. Begin piping with a little spiral of cream to cover the top of the cake to get a feel for the weight of the bag and your own dexterity. Then decorate the sides by piping the cream in an upwards direction, letting go of the pressure in the bag on the approach to the top so that you can form little peaks. Turn the cake as you go until the sides are all covered. You can practice on something that isn't the cake first, just to establish a rhythm before piping on the actual cake. I believe this decorative finish looks better when you go back over it, piping into the gaps between each pillar so that it isn't exactly perfect. But, of course, that's up to you.

8 To make the rosette, begin by curling a piece of peel into a cone shape for the centre of the rosette and place in the centre-top of the cake. Follow by wrapping the rest of the peel loosely around the outside to eventually form a rose.

9 This cake can keep decorated in the fridge overnight. (*end.*)

MANGO EXTRAVAGANZA

Mango for happiness and the magical power to grant wishes. Coconut. Lime.

To be a cake maker is to be woven into the sweetness of people's lives
through belonging and celebration of one another.
A threshold between us for all those coveted wishes
to be granted as they fall silently over the crumbs.

SIZE	25cm	35cm
SERVES	15-20	20-30

LIME CURD		
eggs	2	4
egg yolks	1	2
sugar	100g	200g
lime juice	65ml	120ml
lemon juice	30ml	60ml
limes, zested	1	2
unsalted butter, softened	100g	200g

LIME CREAM		
pure cream	110g	200g
double cream	110g	200g
1 quantity lime curd (from above)		

COCONUT CAKE		
unsalted butter, well-softened	120g	220g
caster sugar	145g	260g
eggs	2	4
self-raising flour	220g	400g
baking powder	1 tsp	2 tsp
coconut cream	220ml	400ml
desiccated coconut	2 tbsp	3 tbsp
flaked coconut	2 tbsp	4 tbsp

COCONUT MERINGUE		
egg whites	10 (300g)	15 (450g)
salt	pinch	¼ tsp
icing sugar, sifted	380g	580g
desiccated coconut	70g	100g
flaked coconut	35g	50g

TO DECORATE		
flaked coconut, toasted	2 tbsp	4 tbsp
icing sugar	1 tbsp	1½ tbsp
fresh mangoes, cut into small wedges	2	4
passionfruit, pulped	2	5
limes, zested	2	3

LIME CURD

1. Place the eggs, additional egg yolks and sugar in a heatproof bowl and mix to roughly combine, then add the lime and lemon juices and lime zest and whisk together well. Place the bowl over a saucepan of barely simmering water, whisking every 3 minutes, for approximately 20 minutes. The curd will begin to cook around the edges first, so whisking the curd occasionally ensures an even temperature is maintained throughout the cooking process. The whisk is a great tool to use for scraping the cooked curd away from the sides of the bowl and into the middle. Don't worry about any little lumps at this stage, they will be smoothed out later. The curd will be cooked when it reaches 85°C on a digital thermometer or becomes the consistency of thick cream. Turn the heat off and allow the curd to sit for a further 10 minutes in the bowl over the saucepan. This step is an insurance policy to guarantee the thickness of the curd and its ultimate setting.

2. After 10 minutes, remove the bowl of curd from the saucepan and set it on the bench to cool down, whisking the curd occasionally so the heat can be released and the temperature reaches 45°C on a thermometer or is warm to touch. Once it has cooled to this temperature, start whisking in the butter, 1 tablespoon at a time, waiting until each addition is incorporated before adding the next. This step can also be done in a food processor or with a stick blender. Press the curd through a fine sieve using a spatula to remove any lumps, then cover the curd with plastic film and press onto the surface to prevent a skin forming. Cool completely in the fridge for at least 4 hours or overnight.

LIME CREAM

1. Whip the pure and double creams together using a hand whisk until firmly whipped. Using a spatula, fold the lime curd through the cream half at a time, then refrigerate until needed.

COCONUT CAKE

1. Preheat the oven to 160°C. Prepare to make two cake layers by lining 2 x 25 cm | 2 x 35 cm cake tins with baking paper. I recommend that you run two long lengths of baking paper across the base and sides of each tin, so that you can just pull the cake out of the tin once it is cooked. It's very difficult to remove cakes this large from tins unless you have a springform tin, so putting some thought into how you will remove them once baked will save heartache later.

2. Place the butter and sugar in the bowl of an electric mixer fitted with the paddle attachment and whip on medium speed until pale and fluffy. Remember to have the butter very soft and scrape down the sides of the bowl regularly using a spatula, as half the butter will wander up the sides of the bowl. Taking the extra time to turn the machine off and tilt the paddle back in order to scrape the butter from the bottom of the bowl will also reward you for your efforts.

3. Crack the eggs into a small bowl and give them a light whisk with a fork. Gradually add them to the creamed butter, ensuring that each addition is completely incorporated before adding the next. Once all the egg is combined, turn the machine off and tilt the paddle back one last time to scrape any butter that has not mingled with the eggs from the base of the bowl, then return to whip again briefly.

4. Sift the flour and baking powder twice to aerate it and remove any small lumps that may hinder the fluffiness of your cake, then set it beside the electric mixer. Reduce the mixer speed to low and use a tablespoon to add the flour in four batches, alternating with the coconut cream, also in four batches. Remove the bowl from the mixer, add the desiccated and flaked coconut to the batter and

fold the mixture thoroughly using a spatula, scraping all the way to the bottom of the bowl until the coconut is evenly distributed. Pour the batter into one of the prepared cake tins and smooth the top using an offset palette knife or a tablespoon until it is level, then bake for 35–40 minutes. Test for readiness by pressing the middle of the cake with your finger, if it bounces back, it's cooked. Remove the cake from the oven and allow to cool in the tin.

COCONUT MERINGUE

1 Place the egg whites and salt in the clean bowl of an electric mixer fitted with the whisk attachment and whip on high speed until soft ribbons form. Reduce the speed to medium and gradually add the sugar, 1 tablespoon at a time, leaving 7 seconds between each addition. Once all the sugar has been added, whisk the meringue for a further 2 minutes on medium speed to ensure the sugar is completely absorbed, then remove the bowl from the mixer and fold through the desiccated coconut and flaked coconut using a spatula. Scoop the meringue into the remaining prepared cake tin and use an offset palette knife to smooth over the top and create some swirls in the meringue. Bake the meringue for 20 minutes, then reduce the oven temperature to 150°C and bake for a further 20 minutes. The meringue is ready when the top is golden and crisp, but the centre is still marshmallow-like. Remove the meringue from the oven and allow it to cool in the tin.

2 Once the meringue is out of the oven, this temperature (150°C) is perfect for toasting the coconut that you will need to decorate the top. Just scatter it onto a baking sheet and toast in the oven for 10–15 minutes or until the edges are tinged golden.

TO ASSEMBLE

1 Slip the two layers of cake from the tins by tilting them at a 45-degree angle and pulling on the baking paper to gently leverage them from the tins. Place the coconut cake onto a cake stand or platter and cover it with the lime cream, pushing it to the edges of the cake. Place the meringue layer on top of the lime cream, then dust with a little icing sugar. Arrange the mango wedges on top of the meringue and spoon over the passionfruit pulp, then use a microplane to zest the lime directly over the top of the cake and sprinkle with the toasted coconut.

2 I have always made this cake on the same day of the party, although the lime curd can be made up to 3 days in advance with the cream being folded through just before assembling the cake. (*end.*)

TECHNIQUES

FULL BUTTER SOURDOUGH PUFF

(to accompany the mille-feuille, page 193)

Puff pastry is the union of a dough called détrempe and a block of butter shaped into a sheet, which becomes known in this application as beurrage. The two are folded together in harmony with consideration to temperature and texture in order to create hundreds of layers.

The difference between full butter puff and rough puff is mainly the resulting texture of the layers with the rough puff being crumblier, rather than flaky, because the flour and butter are merely rubbed together. Full butter puff layers become more developed and stable through the laminating process, where distinct and even separation of the détrempe and the beurrage occurs. When they go in the oven, steam forces them apart causing the 'puff'.

If making a sourdough starter from scratch, you will need to start this recipe at least one week in advance.

MAKES	puff for 4 x 30 cm tarts
BEURRAGE	
unsalted butter, well-softened	500g
DÉTREMPE	
strong bakers flour	675g
fine salt	20g
unsalted butter, cut into dice-sized cubes	130g
ripe sourdough starter *(SEE RECIPE AND NOTE PAGE 254)*	150g
iced water	250ml
apple cider vinegar or white vinegar	20ml

(The day before)

BEURRAGE

1 The purpose of this step is to create a sheet of butter that is 20 cm x 20 cm x 1 cm-thick. The easiest way to do this is to soften a block of butter and place it between two sheets of baking paper. Use a rolling pin to tap and flatten it down to create a flat square. When purchasing the butter, aim to buy a single 500 g block, if that exists in your supermarket. If not, just buy 2 x 250 g blocks.

2 Cut 2 x 30 cm squares of baking paper. After ensuring the butter is very soft, place the block in the centre of one square and place the other square on top. Simply tap down the butter to shape into a 20 cm x 1 cm-thick square. Use the rolling pin to create an even thickness by rolling it across the finished block and make last-minute alterations to the corners to ensure they are sharp 90-degree angles (I find using a pastry scraper is the best tool for shaping the corners), then place the butter block (beurrage) in your fridge overnight.

DÉTREMPE

1 Sift the flour and salt onto your benchtop and scatter the butter over the surface of the flour. Start rubbing the butter and flour together between your fingertips until it resembles fine breadcrumbs. Alternatively, this step can be done in the bowl of an electric mixer fitted with the paddle attachment.

TECHNIQUES & GLOSSARY

2. Make a well in the centre of your flour and add the starter, water and vinegar, then using your fingertips, start drawing the flour into the well in a circular motion until it forms a thick paste. Gradually incorporate the rest of the flour into the centre to form a rough ball. The dough will be quite shaggy to begin with but continue to knead the dough only for 1 minute or so, as it doesn't need to be completely smooth. Don't overwork the dough, you just need it to come together, ensuring that everything is mixed cohesively.

3. If using an electric mixer, be aware the finished dough will be quite heavy on domestic machines and could become unmanageable, depending on the capacity of your motor. The machine could, for instance, be thrown off the bench, so you may need to hold onto it toward the end of the dough-making.

4. Shape the dough into a 20 cm square that will be approximately 5 cm-thick, taking care to create the sharp 90-degree corners here, too, then wrap it in baking paper and a tea towel to stop it from drying out and rest in the fridge overnight.

(On the day)

1. For the détrempe and the beurrage to be laminated together successfully they need to be the same consistency. Obviously, the butter is very cold having been in the fridge and the dough is much softer, so you will need to remove the butter from the fridge until it is a similar consistency to the dough. It needs to be pliable but not too soft. If you're using cultured butter, this process will take about 15–20 minutes, but other butter may take around 30 minutes. Once the beurrage has softened enough, remove the dough from the fridge and begin by 'locking in' the butter.

2. During the rolling process, you should try to use as little flour and possible, as this will hinder the layers developing. Of course, it is nearly impossible to use none, but just be mindful to use a minimal amount. Dust your bench with a small amount of flour and a little more on top of the dough, then roll the dough into a rectangle that is 20 cm-wide x 40 cm-long, paying attention to keeping the corners a sharp 90 degrees. The dough should now be about 1 cm-thick, the same as the butter.

3. Remove the butter from the paper and place it in the centre of the dough.

4. Fold the two ends of the pastry into the centre to meet in the middle so that the dough now envelopes the butter, then pinch the ends together ever so slightly.

5. You will notice the butter is exposed down the sides of the package, so just pinch the sides to join them. It's important that there isn't too much surplus dough pinched at the sides, as this will just end up as dough without butter in it.

6. The first turn happens now. Turn the dough so the middle seam is perpendicular to your body (like an arrow pointing toward you). Dust the bench again lightly and roll the dough in the opposite direction as you rolled it before until it is 20 cm x 40 cm.

7. If bench space is an issue, you can turn the dough to make it parallel to your body, then travel along the bench rolling the pin to create the length and even out the thickness, which should be 1 cm-thick. Again, pay attention to the right-angle of the corners and keep them sharp.

8. At this stage, the ends could be a bit curved and, at closer inspection, may look to have no butter in them. Trim the ends to make them straight.

9. Fold the ends of the rectangle into the centre of the dough so they meet in the middle.

(*cont.*)

10 Fold the dough in half again to create your first book fold.

11 Press your finger gently into one of the corners of the block to make a single indent to represent the first turn. Wrap the dough up in baking paper and a tea towel and pop back in the fridge to rest for 2 hours.

12 When you open the pastry again you'll see the little indent and remember you have made one turn. As you progress through the turns, add an indent to the corner to help you remember how many you have made. It's surprisingly easy to forget.

13 When you remove the pastry from the fridge to make the second turn and every turn thereafter, tap down on the top of the block with your rolling pin to help seal the open seam and make it more stable. That way, you're able to roll the pastry without the rectangle going skew-whiff.

14 In fact, a good tap down in both directions, as if drawing a noughts and crosses grid, will set you straight.

(On the day) 2

(On the day) 3

(On the day) 4

(On the day) 5

(On the day) 6

(On the day) 7

15 Repeat the book fold three more times, making a total of four book folds (four turns), leaving 2 hours between each turn. The most important thing to remember each time is that the 'spine' of the book will always run perpendicular to your body, so you're always rolling the dough in the opposite direction to the last turn. Even if you do need to eventually turn the dough so that it is parallel to your body to create the length (because of your bench width), it's good practice to always start rolling away from yourself.

16 This is quite a large dough for domestic application, but the process takes so long you may as well make a big batch and freeze half. Or better still, roll it into sheets and freeze it already rolled. You can keep the dough in the freezer for up to 3 months.

17 Once you have the finished puff, don't try and roll the whole block out at once. It's best to 'tap' it into a flattened rectangle then cut it in half, so you can tackle it in two portions. Personally, I don't believe the starter imparts much fermentation to the dough, but it does add a lot of flavour.

(On the day) 8

(On the day) 9

(On the day) 10

(On the day) 11

(On the day) 12

(On the day) 13

FULL BUTTER SOURDOUGH PUFF

SOURDOUGH STARTER

Once upon a time, you were labelled a hipster if you could keep a sourdough culture alive and thriving. Nowadays there is a movement that is empowering us all to try these old methods that don't subscribe to the novelty value of the concept. It is, after all, how it used to be before all the artificial stuff came in. Making your own starter is easy, and if you have always wanted to give it try, all you need is seven days and a jam jar.

You can use raisin water for this, if you like. The water absorbs the yeast from the fruit and improves the flavour of the ferment. Just place a couple of handfuls of raisins in a bowl, cover with filtered water and leave for a few days.

HOW THE STARTER WORKS

1 When the flour and water are mixed together they make enzymes that convert the starches to sugar, which in turn forms the food source for all the yeasts and bacteria in the atmosphere. Once this exchange occurs the microbes will multiply more quickly, resulting in the alcohol that flavours the dough and the carbon dioxide that makes it rise.

2 Using rye flour will create a foolproof starter because of all the nutrients in it, but feel free to supplement the weight with other flours such as wholewheat, which has more natural yeast than plain old white flour (though this is fine, too).

3 It's important to use filtered water to begin your starter because tap water has chlorine in it – which is added to kill bacteria and therefore has a counterproductive effect on creating a culture. Once you have the starter established (after 7 days) you can then start to add tap water and progress to using any form of flour you like.

DAY 1

filtered water or raisin water	500ml
rye flour	250g
wholewheat flour or plain white flour	250g

1 Place 50 ml filtered or raisin water, 25 g rye flour and 25 g wholewheat flour in a 500 ml jam jar and mix together well with a clean tablespoon. Place the lid loosely on top of the jar (or use a square of muslin fastened with an elastic band, like we do), then place the jar in a warm spot in the kitchen for 24 hours.

DAY 2

1. In order to increase the activity of the starter you need to feed it. To do that, pour 50 g of the starter into a bowl on the scale, then discard it. Place the jam jar with the remaining starter in it on the scale and return it to zero, then add 50 g filtered or raisin water, 25 g rye flour and 25 g wholewheat flour and mix it well with a tablespoon. Replace the lid or muslin and put it back in a warm place for just 12 hours this time. For the starter to be kicked into action you now need to increase the feeds, a bit like increasing metabolism in our bodies to increase its ability to burn fat.

2. Repeat the feeding process 12 hours later.

DAYS 3 TO 7

1. Continue to feed the starter every 12 hours for the next 5 days – perhaps at 7 am then at 7 pm. After day 3 and over the course of the starter's life, it will rise when the sugars accumulate and fall once the culture eats all the sugars, making it necessary to feed it again and increase the activity of the sourdough, and ultimately its quality when baking with it.

2. The smell of the starter will be pleasantly sour after day 2, progressing to a more tangy smell after day 7, which is normal. Its structure will become stronger as the gluten develops, and the consistency will be thicker, requiring you to scoop it from the jam jar instead of pouring it.

3. The starter is ready to use and you can now reduce the feeding schedule to every 24 hours to keep your starter active. Continue this schedule if you intend to make crumpets or bread regularly, increasing the feeds to every 12 hours a couple of days before you want to bake with it.

4. If you are not baking for a while, just pop the starter in the fridge, then take it out 3 days before you want to use it and resume feedings as normal. (*end.*)

NOTE.

Making sourdough puff pastry is not meant to be arduous. Feeding a starter for seven days before you can even begin to make the pastry may seem excessive in the pursuit of flavour, and you would be right! I'm not trying to put you off learning the skill of creating a starter, because its uses will bring you a lot of pleasure. If you don't feel the need to make a starter, just omit it altogether and add 100 ml more iced water instead. Alternatively, use an existing starter, if you have one, or visit your local baker, who is usually happy to share some with you.

HOW TO SHIMMY WITH SPONGE

Making a layer cake without lots of cake tins can be challenging, however, if you have just a couple of flat baking trays you can achieve the same result. The following is a method tried and tested by many pastry chefs and, in particular, the makers of Russian honey cake, which has more than eight layers.

TO BAKE MULTIPLE LAYERS OF SPONGE USING ONE CAKE TIN, FOLLOW THESE STEPS

1. Preheat the oven to the instructed temperature for the recipe.

2. Cut five squares of baking paper 2 cm bigger than the sponges you need to make. Using a lead pencil, draw a circle on each piece of paper using your cake tin as a template. Place the baking paper squares onto as many baking trays as you own and line the rest of the squares up along your bench or at least on a flat surface. The more baking trays you have, the more squares can be placed down ready to be prepared with sponge.

3. Make the sponge according to the recipe then divide the mixture between the five sheets of baking paper, placing it in the middle of each circle. Using a small offset palette knife, spread the sponge batter evenly to the edge of the first circle, then place it straight in the oven and cook for the required time.

4. Or, if you are deft with a piping bag, this method can also be achieved by piping a spiral of sponge batter into the middle of the circle. The advantage of this is that you will achieve a more even layering. Although, there is an argument that pouring the sponge batter into a piping bag and squeezing it will deflate it somewhat. All of these factors depend on your skills with a piping bag.

5. How many baking trays you own and how many racks you have in your oven will determine the amount of sponges you can bake at once. Continue to shimmy the sponges through the oven as the space becomes available until they are all baked, then cool them on a wire cooling rack.

6. Once the sponges have cooled, trim them by placing the cake tin over each sponge and cutting around the outside using a sharp paring knife. This will be necessary if you are making a moulded layer cake where all the layers are built into the cake tin with the filling in between. If this is the case, after you have cut the first circle of sponge, test to see that it fits into the tin before cutting the rest. There can be a variation in how pliable sponges are and you may need to cut a little bit more off than you had anticipated to fit them in the tin. (*end.*)

ROCKPOOLS OF FIGS & PLUMS

Plums. Figs. Cultured cream.

If you look inside to see what's been left by the last tide,
deep within the chasms and crevices and caves
you will see rockpools shimmering with tropical liveliness
urchins and jewels
even volcanic fire.

We are the ebb and flow of the ocean
the water against the rocks
and the ripple of every moment we touch.

PIE DISH SIZE	25cm	28cm
SERVES	10-12	12-15

FIG LEAF SYRUP		
fig leaves	20	20
water	250ml	250ml
granulated or caster sugar	250g	250g

FIG LEAF OLIVE OIL PARFAIT		
pure cream	500g	500g
vanilla bean, split and seeds scraped	½	½
fig leaves, dried (from above quantity)	6	6
white chocolate	100g	100g
egg yolks	3	3
fig leaf syrup, leaves removed (from above)	180ml	180ml
olive oil	80ml	80ml

ROUGH PUFF PASTRY		
strong bakers flour, plus extra for dusting and rolling	300g	400g
salt	1 tsp	1¼ tsp
unsalted butter, at room temperature (but not soft), plus extra for greasing	300g	400g
ice-cold water	100ml	130ml
apple cider vinegar	20ml	25ml

CULTURED CREAM CAKE		
unsalted butter, melted	40g	60g
vanilla bean, split and seeds scraped	½	½
eggs	2	3
caster sugar	300g	430g
crème fraîche (cultured cream)	75g	100g
egg whites	3	4
salt flakes	pinch	pinch
soft cake flour or 90g / 100g plain flour and 20g / 25g cornflour, sifted	110g	125g
plums, halved and stones removed	4	5
figs, halved	4	5
fig leaf syrup (from left), for brushing	20ml	40ml
icing sugar, for dusting (optional)		

(One week before)

FIG LEAF SYRUP

1. Preheat the oven to 50°C. Prepare the fig leaves by cutting the stem off as closely as possible to the leaf. Tear up the fig leaves and place on a baking tray. Place the tray into the oven for 20 minutes to dry out the sap that is found in fig leaves. Meanwhile, combine the water and the sugar in a medium saucepan over medium heat and bring to the boil. Once the fig leaves are dry, remove from the oven and add two-thirds of the leaves to the syrup (reserving the remainder for making the parfait). Simmer for 5 minutes. Turn off the heat and pour the leaves and syrup into a clean glass jar. Place in the fridge for a minimum of three days to infuse. A week is better.

(Two days before)

FIG LEAF OLIVE OIL PARFAIT

1. Combine 400 g cream, the vanilla bean and seeds and reserved dried fig leaves in a small saucepan over medium heat and bring almost to the boil. Turn off the heat and pour the cream into a plastic container to refrigerate overnight.

2. The next day, place a container for freezing the parfait into the freezer in preparation. Place the chocolate in a heatproof bowl over a saucepan of barely simmering water until melted, ensuring the bowl doesn't touch the water. Turn off the heat and pour in the remaining 100 g cream. Using a spatula, stir until the ganache is smooth. Leave the bowl over the saucepan for now.

3. Place the egg yolks in the bowl of an electric mixer fitted with the whisk attachment and wait for me to give you the go ahead to start whisking. Have your sugar thermometer ready and check that it is operational. Place the fig leaf syrup in a small saucepan over medium heat and bring to the boil. At this stage, you can begin whisking the egg yolks on high speed so they become pale and fluffy, then go back to watching the syrup.

4. When the sugar syrup reaches 120°C, remove it from the heat and reduce the speed of the electric mixer to medium. Slowly trickle the syrup down the side of the bowl onto the egg yolks. Once all the syrup has been added, increase the speed to high and beat the eggs until they are completely cold. What you have just made here is called pâté à bombe.

5. Now, reduce the speed to the lowest setting and gradually trickle the olive oil into the pâté à bombe until all combined. Remove the bowl from the machine. Remove the cream from the fridge and strain to remove the fig leaves and vanilla bean. Using a hand whisk, whip the cream until softly whipped.

6. Take the chocolate off the saucepan and use a spatula to fold approximately one-quarter of the pâté à bombe into the chocolate ganache to lighten it. Pour the chocolate mixture back into the pâté à bombe, trying to preserve as much air as possible, then fold through the whipped cream in two batches. Pour the parfait into the prepared tin and freeze for a minimum of 12 hours.

(The day before)

ROUGH PUFF PASTRY

1. Begin by sifting the flour and salt directly onto your clean work surface. Return any unground salt flakes that get trapped in the sieve back into the flour.

2. Cut the butter into 1 cm dice and scatter over the flour. Using your fingertips, rub the butter into the flour, ensuring there are still chunks of butter remaining throughout. These lumps of butter will be transformed into pockets of steam later on, contributing to the flakiness of the pastry. Combine the iced water and vinegar together in a small bowl and trickle the liquid evenly over the flour. I used to make a well in the centre of the flour to pour the liquid into, but I feel this method distributes it more evenly.

3. Use a dough scraper or cutter to turn the flour over itself, pulling it to the centre of the pile until the dough eventually forms a shaggy ball. It will require some coaxing from your hands, but try to handle it as little as possible. Flatten the dough out to make an approximately 22 cm x 12 cm x 3 cm-high rectangle and rest in the fridge for 30 minutes. I like to swaddle the pastry in a clean tea towel at this stage – it saves plastic film and makes it easier to move the pastry from bench to fridge during the upcoming turns. It's worth noting that you can leave your pastry to rest longer than 30 minutes, if necessary. But if it rests longer that 2 hours you will usually need to let it soften before you start rolling it again. This may take around 20 minutes.

4. Dust your clean work surface with flour. Remove the dough from the fridge and place in the centre of the flour with the short side parallel to the bench and the long side pointing away from you. Dust a little more flour over the top and roll the dough away from you until it is three times the length, adding a little flour along the way to prevent the dough from sticking to the rolling pin. You may even notice the dough sticking to the bench. If it does, just stop rolling and use your hands to release it from the bench. Hold it up as you sprinkle more flour on the work surface and continue to roll it out. Try to keep the dough looking like a rectangle with sharp corners and neat edges. The more care you take during this process the better the pastry will be.

5. Now fold the two ends of the pastry into the centre of the rectangle so they meet in the middle, then fold them over one another. You should now have what looks like a book sitting in front of you; this is your first 'book' turn. Use your finger to mark an indent in the corner of the pastry so you can remember this was the first turn, then wrap the pastry and rest in the fridge for 30 minutes. Remove the pastry from the fridge and roll it again, making sure the 'spine' of the book fold is perpendicular to the bench and that you roll the pastry in the opposite direction as before. Fold again using another book turn, mark with two indents this time, then cover and return to the fridge for 30 minutes before repeating the rolling process to make a third book turn to complete the pastry. Rest the pastry overnight.

(On the day)

LINING AND BAKING THE PASTRY

1. Preheat the oven to 160°C. Grease a deep 25 cm | 28 cm pie dish with butter and dust with flour.

2. Remove the pastry from the fridge and give it a light tap down in both directions using your rolling pin. Imagine you are using the rolling pin to tap a grid onto *(cont.)*

the pastry. This balances the pastry and prevents it from going skew-whiff during the rolling process.

3. Dust your bench again with flour and a little on the surface of the pastry. Roll the pastry out to a 30 cm | 35 cm round that is 5 mm-thick then transfer the pastry to a large sheet of baking paper and rest in the fridge for 20 minutes.

4. Remove the pastry from the fridge and peel the baking paper from the top. Place the pie dish in the centre of the pastry and use a paring knife to trim any pastry that seems like it will be surplus to lining the dish. By this I mean that you do not want the pastry to be hanging over the rim of the pie dish too much as it may tear. By now the pastry will be pliable, so set about tucking it into the dish to fit snugly into the seams and scallops (if there are any). Pop the pastry case back into the fridge for 15 minutes to set, then remove it and use a scalpel or paring knife to trim the pastry so it's level with the rim of the dish. The advantage of using such a sharp blade is that it exposes all the layers of puff. However, if you don't have a sharp blade, just use a paring knife.

5. Fill the case with baking beads and blind bake for 25 minutes, then remove the case from the oven and remove the baking beads. You'll notice that some of the pastry looks a bit opaque and raw. Return the case to the oven for a further 10 minutes. Remove and set aside while you make the cream cake.

CULTURED CREAM CAKE

1. Reduce the oven temperature to 150°C. Melt the butter and the vanilla bean and seeds gently together without boiling. Turn off the heat and allow to cool slightly.

2. Whisk the eggs and just 140 g | 180 g sugar together in a bowl using a hand whisk until pale and fluffy. Add the crème fraîche and whisk again until the mixture is smooth and there are no more lumps of cream. Pour the butter into the batter (removing the bean) and whisk to thoroughly combine.

3. Whip the egg whites and salt in the bowl of an electric mixer fitted with the whisk attachment on high speed until soft ribbons form, then reduce the speed to medium and gradually add the remaining sugar, 1 tablespoon at a time, until thick and glossy. Remove the bowl from the mixer and use a spatula to fold the meringue gently through the batter, one-third at a time, alternating with the flour, also one-third at a time. As you are adding the flour, sift it over the surface of the batter to add more air. Gently, gently.

4. Pour the batter into the baked pastry dish where it should only fill the pastry case by three-quarters. Any surplus is the result of your pie dish not being as high as specified in the recipe. Bake the pie for 20 minutes, then remove the pie from the oven momentarily and cover the surface evenly with the plums and figs. During the cooking process some fruit will fall to the bottom and some will remain on top, forming rockpools of fruit.

5. Reduce the temperature to 140°C and bake for a further 40 minutes. The cake filling will be ready when the centre slightly bounces back when pressed with your finger. It feels a little like fluffy set custard. Remove the pie from the oven and allow it to cool in the dish for 30 minutes.

6. Using a pastry brush, brush only the top of the fruit generously with fig leaf syrup, so that it pools in the crevices left by the stone. Dust with icing sugar, if you wish, and serve while it's still a little warm alongside scoops of the fig leaf parfait. (*end.*)

HOW TO SHIMMY WITH SPONGE

GLOSSARY

CANDIED CEDRO

Substitutes: any candied citrus fruit. Yuzu is the closest with the thick rind being very sisterly to the cedro. It is also hard to find, so I would suggest Meyer lemon as being the closest accessible substitute.

A large oblong shaped citrus fruit, ranging from neon lime to lemon yellow in colour, that has a bumpy, almost prehistoric appearance. Traditionally grown in Sicily. It has a very thick rind, smells like a highly perfumed lemon and has a small centre of segments that yield next to no juice. The main method of cooking is to candy it, rendering an otherwise useless citrus fruit edible. Once candied, it's sensational eaten as wafer-thin slices in salad or, as a raw ingredient, it can be chopped and cooked into marmalade.

CARTOUCHE

Substitute: a well-fitting lid. Although keep an eye on the heat as a really well-fitting lid will trap in all the heat and cause the liquid to boil too furiously as opposed to poaching.

A round piece of baking paper cut specifically to fit inside a saucepan perfectly in order to replace a lid. Usually for poaching fruit, it acts to keep the fruit submerged beneath the surface of the cooking liquid. Even if the fruit does pop above the surface there is steam in between the liquid and the cartouche that stops the fruit from drying out.

To me, spending the time to make a round cartouche that fits the saucepan perfectly is one of the last bastions of a professional chef.

CINNAMON MYRTLE

Substitute: cinnamon bark / quill and kaffir lime leaves combined.

Otherwise known as 'grey myrtle' it is a native Australian hardwood tree. Its leaves are scented like cinnamon and when crushed they small like kaffir lime. The flowers look like white fluffy stars and the birds and the bees love them for pollinating.

DAVIDSON PLUMS & POWDER

Substitute: queen garnet plums or any blood plum variety.

A Native Australian plum with a skin that is dark purple to red with black hues when they are really ripe. The flesh is bright ruby-red and has very sharp acidity and an almost sour flavour. I find the skins quite tough even when cooked and I tend to remove the skins afterwards so I am just left with the pulp of the fruit.

The powder is made by dehydrating the fruit and grinding it finely.

FENNEL BLOSSOM & POLLEN

Substitute: combine toasted and crushed fennel seeds or licorice root with honey.

Bright yellow flowers from the fennel plant, which is native to the shores of the Mediterranean. The pollen is harvested by drying the flowers and has the flavour of anise.

FLOUR

SUSTAINABLE WHEAT

With the incredible amount of flour available on the market now, I think it's important to tell you that by buying a bag of locally grown and milled wholegrain flour, you are impacting an economy that runs far deeper than you can imagine. Your purchase impacts an emerging grain economy that supports a whole system of growers, millers, bakers and brewers who are invested in creating a world where everyone's needs are met.

It's true it falls on the growers and their wisdom of more sustainable farming practices to sow grain that improves the health of the soil. But they need support from the consumer through their purchasing practices in order to continue to grow it. There are vast resources in education around this ecosystem that we are all a part of. I can recommend books such as Matthew Evans' *Soil* and pioneering movements like grAiNZ – a collective of local grain growers and users – that will reassure you there are people out there doing great things for our environment through education and by walking their own talk.

Through better farming practices this community is returning to old ways to regenerate our agroecology. In Australia, for instance, there is a library of wheats – modern, heritage and ancient – being grown under various conditions to determine which is most-suited to our climate. This has a trickle-down effect on farming when some of these wheats are cut a second time to bale for cattle.

So, the next time you find it a little bit harder to source a bag of flour, think about our future and the big influence you can have on improving it by choosing a more sustainable wheat.

All of the following flours, which are just the tip of the iceberg for sustainability, are available to purchase online.

EMMER WHEAT FLOUR

Substitute: a wholegrain, low-protein flour such as einkorn flour.

Along with einkorn wheat, emmer was one of the first domesticated crops to appear in the Middle East around 8800 BCE, and is often referred to as the mother of spelt. Unlike einkorn, which is plentiful throughout the northern hemisphere, emmer wheat is better suited to Australian conditions and produces far greater yield.

Emmer wheat is a very good source of manganese and dietary fibre. It is also low in protein, making it ideal for the sable pastries featured in my recipes. The flavour is quite nutty as it is high in bran and so the resting period is important in order to allow for hydration, which in turn, strengthens the gluten to achieve more structure.

If you are using it for bread, it's advisable to add a high protein bakers flour to give you the stretch that the structure of the bread requires.

ROSELLA WHEAT FLOUR

Rosella wheat is a modern grain developed by an Australian family on their NSW farm 'Woodstock' back in the '80s. I use it all the time for cakes, pastry and biscuits and I think my favourite thing about it is that it smells and tastes like honey. It can be used as a direct substitute for plain flour because of the soft, delicate crumb it imparts. Although, it also has the advantages of better flavour and higher nutritional value.

Woodstock is a quintessential example of many farms all over the world that are supporting the wellbeing of a community and landscape. In fact, it is believed that when we grow on the land we eat from, we are kin with country and that the world would be a better place if we all chose a species or place to protect.

SPELT

The spelt grain is an ancient variety of wheat that has been popularly grown in Europe due to its resistance to rain damage compared to other wheats. Thanks to the efforts and continued support of diverse food sovereignty movements, Australia now benefits from having original and genetically true spelt varieties. This is not always the case around the world, where spelt has been crossed with modern grains to improve yield. This cross-breeding has compromised genetic purity and provided some of the undesirable attributes of modern grain. The relationship with the miller and the grower is especially key here in order to maintain the integrity and quality of the flour we use.

JAPANESE CAKE FLOUR

Cake flour is from soft wheat (low in protein) and is finely milled to produce a very light texture. I believe Japanese cake flour is the best type of cake flour and it is used to make the light cotton sponges and chiffons. Certain varieties are bleached in order to break the proteins down further, resulting in a super fluffy cake crumb, so I would recommend looking for unbleached cake flour. The nutritional value of the cake will be compromised in either case and so, if you want to substitute for a more wholesome option, you can use plain flour with 15 per cent potato starch or cornflour. Cake flour can be substituted with emmer wheat as it is low in protein, although, you will still need to use 20 per cent potato starch or cornflour, otherwise you will have a dip in the middle of the cake due to the low protein. The starch will compensate by giving strength in the rise. A wholegrain flour, such as spelt or rosella, could be used, but with much heavier results. Sometimes asking for forgiveness and trying to do your best (most of the time) with the choice you have is what's called for here.

FREEZE-DRIED CITRUS POWDER

Substitute: zested citrus using a microplane.

A dried powder made by dehydrating citrus peel using a freeze drying method, then finely grinding it.

GRAPPA

Grape-based pomace brandy traditionally from Italy. Usually made by distilling the second pressing of the skins, pulp and seeds of the grapes.

HŌJICHA

Substitute: chai tea powder with a little green tea.

Japanese green tea that has been roasted over charcoal. It has a nutty, smoky cinnamon aroma. Finely ground hōjicha powder, which is made from grinding the tea leaves, is preferred for making cakes as it distributes through the crumb more effectively.

PISTACHIO PASTE

A paste made by grinding toasted pistachios so finely that the oils are extracted to form a nut butter. The best variety of pistachio paste is from Sicily, due to the quality of the pistachios that are grown in mineral-heavy, volcanic soil. It is not readily available in most parts of the world because of the cost. Iran is also a big producer of pistachios.

Alas the majority of pistachio paste is made by combining them with almonds and therefore decreasing the intensity of the flavour.

There is no substitute for pistachio paste regardless of the quality. If you absolutely can't find it for cakes, you can add very finely ground pistachios instead and sift them through the flour to distribute them.

QUANDONGS
Substitute: queen garnet plums.

A sacred peach tree indigenous to Australia. The fruit is only ever harvested by Indigenous people, usually women. It's a large-stoned fruit with thin ruby-coloured skin and very little flesh. It has sharp acidity with a flavour similar to blood plum.

STINGING NETTLES
Substitute: combine spinach and basil, although, nothing quite compares to the bright verdant nature of nettles.

A common weed native to Europe that has been eaten in Australia for tens of thousands of years. Nettles are one of the first to arrive in spring and usually grow around damp areas. Deep-green with serrated leaves and thousands of tiny stinging hairs. They need to be handled carefully with thick gloves and blanched in boiling water to remove the 'stings'.

TEMPERING CHOCOLATE

A method by which chocolate is heated and cooled at specific temperatures in order to re-arrange the molecules within, resulting in a desirable 'snap' to the texture and shine to the appearance.

TONKA BEAN
Substitute: combine vanilla seeds, freshly grated nutmeg and honey.

A dark and flat wrinkled seed more commonly referred to as a bean. Native to South America and highly fragrant with notes of marzipan, vanilla and cinnamon. Tonka been is grated finely into a hot liquid, such as cream, in order to infuse its flavour.

VANILLA

VANILLA INFUSION

When the seeds of a vanilla bean are scraped out using a paring knife and then placed in a heat infusion of cream or milk, along with the bean, there really is no more effective way to extract the full potential of that bean. You can rest assured – considering you've probably just given your right arm for one at the grocer, delivered from the far-flung regions of Madagascar – that this process allows the vanilla bean to live its best life through your baking.

If you aren't using a heat process to disperse the seeds, you may have an issue with them forming little clumps throughout the batter, consequently preventing them from realising their full and fragrant potential.

This is one of the reasons we use vanilla paste or it's faux version of essence. The other reason is because manufacturers have made it for us and we can use it quickly and easily. However, another way of using a vanilla bean efficiently in recipes that don't have a heat process is to make vanilla sugar. This method will also distribute the lovely seeds throughout your baking. It is very satisfying to see those dark flecks.

VANILLA SUGAR

Using the tip of a sharp paring knife, slice lengthways down the centre of the vanilla bean and open it up so it's flat on your chopping board. Now, using the middle part of the blade, scrape along the length of the bean to extract the seeds onto your board. Every seed is precious, so carefully push any seeds on the blade of the knife onto the board, along with any on your fingertips by using the blade and vice versa. Separate the bean from the seeds, placing the bean to one side for now. Sprinkle 1 tablespoon of caster sugar on top of the seeds directly on the chopping board, then using a little offset palette knife or a butter knife, rub the blade through the sugar and seeds. The abrasion of the sugar will separate the seeds and the little clumps will disappear.

(*cont.*)

Continue to work the sugar through the seeds, then once you are happy you have dispersed the seeds fully throughout the sugar, use a larger knife or palette knife to transfer the seeds and sugar to a bowl with the remaining amount of sugar the recipe requires. You can also mix it with 500 g of sugar to put in a jar to use later. Work on the ratio of 1 bean to 500 g sugar. If you're not using the bean to infuse, you can also pop it in the sugar jar for extra flavour. Remember, you can always use that bean at a later date to infuse into a custard or such, it's there waiting for you.

Once a vanilla bean is 'spent' by infusing it into heat, it can be removed from the application, boiled up in water for 5 minutes and then dried out in the open air and returned to the vanilla sugar jar.

YUZU
Substitute: meyer lemon.

A small, knobbly citrus fruit thought to have originated in China and commonly used in Japan. Yuzu is bright yellow and extremely sour, like combining a grapefruit and a lemon. It has a thick white rind with many, many seeds and tightly knit segments yielding very little juice. It is commonly considered to be quite an exotic fruit due to its rarity, although by magic, we seem to be able to source a small amount for marmalade and cake each year. We thank our lucky stars.

INDEX

A

A blessing for the seeds, 87–9
Agrarian apricots, 109–10
almonds
  Agrarian apricots, 109–10
  almond & cocoa nib praline crust
    (Cake for our wilderness), 27
  almond & praline paste
    (Enchanted almond tree), 35–6
  almond custard (Enchanted almond tree), 36
  almond rocher (Enchanted almond tree), 35–6
  almond sable (Agrarian apricots), 109–10
  Cake for our wilderness, 27–8
  Enchanted almond tree, 35–8
  Sakura, 157–9
  Under the quandong tree, 101–3
amaretti (Athena), 177–8
amaro, native
  amaro jelly, 80
  Autumn quince & amaro tart, 77–80
apples
  Apple & medlar Charlotte, 117–19
  Tree of life, 65–6
apricots
  Agrarian apricots, 109–10
Athena, 177–9
Autumn quince & amaro tart, 77–80

B

Ballymaloe trifle, 123–5
basil
  nettle & basil purée, 73
  Nettle ricotta cake, 73–4
bay leaves
  Cake for the angels, 181–2
berries
  berry compote, 172
  Love cake, 171–4
Between a thousand leaves of delight, 193–4
beurre noisette (Cake for the angels), 181
blackberries
  Ballymaloe trifle, 123–5
  blackberry compote (Mr & Mrs), 15
  Hansel & Gretel, 49–50
  Mr & Mrs, 15–18
blackcurrants
  blackcurrant compote, 132
  Exploring the landscape of my heart, 131–4
brambles
  Hansel & Gretel, 49–50
bread
  Workaday malt loaf, 25
brioche
  Apple & medlar Charlotte, 117–18
  Tropézienne, 205–6
brown butter breadcrumbs
  Hansel & Gretel, 49–50
butter
  beurre noisette (Cake for the angels), 181
  clarified (Apple & medlar Charlotte), 118
butter cake with meringue (Motherhood), 83
buttermilk sponge (Little Queenie), 91–2

C

cajeta, 150
  Takumi, 149–50
cakes
  Athena, 177–9
  butter cake with meringue (Motherhood), 83
  buttermilk sponge (Little Queenie), 91–2
  Cake for Jane & Jeremy Strode, 41–2
  Cake for joy, 217–18
  Cake for our wilderness, 27–8
  Cake for the angels, 181–2
  chamomile cake (Where the orchard meets the meadow), 168
  chiffon *SEE* chiffon cakes
  coconut cake (Mango extravaganza), 238–9
  cultured cream cake
    (Rockpools of figs & plums), 244
  Enchanted almond tree, 35–8
  Exploring the landscape of my heart, 131–4
  The fable of the wolves, 57–8
  French flourless chocolate sponge, 21–2, 36–7
  Gingerbread hug, 46–7
  Hansel & Gretel, 49–50
  Honeymoon cake, 225–8
  layer cake, 256
  Layers of memories, 189–91
  Little Queenie, 91–3
  Love cake, 171–4
  Lucky, 137–40
  Luna, 231–4
  Mango extravaganza, 237–9
  Mariù, 143
  Motherhood, 82–4
  Mr & Mrs, 15–18
  Nettle ricotta cake, 73–4
  Ode to John Olsen, 197–8
  Our friendship cake, 201–3
  ricotta cake (Citrus macadamia torte), 126–7
  Sakura, 157–9
  Savarin, 145–7
  Siren, 213–14
  sponges *SEE* sponges
  Takumi, 149–50
  Tropézienne, 205–7
  Truth-seeker, 95–8
  Under the quandong tree, 101–3
  The waltzing orange tree, 153–4
  Where the meadow meets the orchard, 166–9
  Your song for the sea, 221
calendula petals
  Lucky, 137–40
caramel mousse (Layers of memories), 190
cardamom
  Little Queenie, 91–3
  The waltzing orange tree, 153–4
cartouche, 259
cedro
  candied, 259
  Citrus macadamia torte, 126–7
chamomile
  Where the meadow meets the orchard, 166–9
Champagne
  Motherhood, 82–4
Charlotte
  Apple & medlar Charlotte, 117–19
cherries
  cherry compote (Sakura), 158
  Sakura, 157–9
  Siren, 213–14
chervil
  Your song for the sea, 221
chestnuts
  Chestnut torte, 31–2
  roasting, 32
chiffon cakes
  Our friendship cake, 201–3
  Truth-seeker, 96–7
chocolate
  Chestnut torte, 31–2
  chocolate ganache (Enchanted almond tree), 37–8
  chocolate mousse (Mr & Mrs), 15–16
  Enchanted almond tree, 35–8
  French flourless chocolate sponge, 21–2, 36–7
  gianduja ganache (Exploring the landscape of my heart), 133–4
  Mr & Mrs, 15–18
  My Christmas pudding, 52–3
  orange-scented ganache (The waltzing orange tree), 153
  Siren, 213–14
  tempering, 18, 261
Christmas pudding
  flaming the pudding, 53
  My Christmas pudding, 52–3
cinnamon
  Cake for our wilderness, 27–8
  Takumi, 149–50
cinnamon myrtle, 259
  Autumn quince & amaro tart, 77–80
  cinnamon myrtle custard, 78
citrus
  Citrus macadamia torte, 126–7
  freeze-dried powder, 260
  Love cake, 171–4
  Luna's citrus rosette, 232
  tutti frutti curd (Lucky), 138
clementines
  Savarin, 145–7
cocoa nibs
  almond & cocoa nib praline crust, 27
  Cake for our wilderness, 27–8
  First date tiramisu, 21–2
  Mr & Mrs, 15–18
coconut
  Cake for joy, 217–18
  coconut cake (Mango extravaganza), 238–9
  coconut meringue (Mango extravaganza), 239
  coconut sponge (Cake for joy), 217–18
  Honeymoon cake, 225–8
  Mango extravaganza, 237–9

toasted coconut cream (Honeymoon cake), 227
toasted coconut custard (Honeymoon cake), 226
coffee
  A blessing for the seeds, 87–9
  coffee cream (A blessing for the seeds), 89
  coffee pastry cream (A blessing for the seeds), 87–8
  First date tiramisu, 21–2
cream, cultured
  cultured cream cake, 244
  Rockpools of figs & plums, 241–4
  Tree of life, 65–6
crème Anglaise, 147
  Savarin, 145–7
crème fraîche frosting (Layers of memories), 191
crème madame (Tropézienne), 207
crusts
  almond & cocoa nib praline crust (Cake for our wilderness), 27
  pine nut crust (Eve), 113
  sunflower seed crust (Home), 70–1
curd
  lemon curd (Luna), 232–3
  lime curd (Honeymoon cake), 226
  lime curd (Mango extravaganza), 237–9
  passionfruit curd (Cake for joy), 217–18
  passionfruit curd (Layers of memories), 189–90
  tutti frutti curd (Lucky), 138
custard
  cinnamon myrtle custard (Autumn quince & amaro tart), 78
  ginger custard (Ode to John Olsen), 197
  honey custard (Where the orchard meets the meadow), 167–8
  lemon verbena custard (Under the quandong tree), 102
  mascarpone custard (First date tiramisu), 22
  thyme custard filling (Agrarian apricots), 110
  toasted coconut custard (Honeymoon cake), 226
  tonka bean custard (Love cake), 172
  whisky custard filling (Sakura), 157–8

D

dates
  Workaday malt loaf, 25
Davidson plums & powder, 259
  Love cake, 171–4
  Motherhood, 82–4
dill
  Gingerbread hug, 46–7
dulce de leche, 149
  Takumi, 149–50

E

eggs
  zabaglione (Motherhood), 83–4
emmer wheat
  Autumn quince & amaro tart, 77–80
  hazelnut & emmer sable, 78–9
  Workaday malt loaf, 25
Enchanted almond tree, 35–8
Eve, 113–15
Exploring the landscape of my heart, 131–4

F

The fable of the wolves, 57–8
fennel
  blossom & pollen, 259
  fennel & pine nut praline, 186
  Flora, 185–6
  Gingerbread hug, 46–7
figs
  Eve, 113–15
  fig leaf olive oil parfait (Rockpools of figs & plums), 242
  fig leaf syrup (Rockpools of figs & plums), 242
  Rockpools of figs & plums, 241–4
First date tiramisu, 21–2
Flora, 185–6
flour, 259
  types, 260
flourless baking
  Chestnut torte, 31–2
  Enchanted almond tree, 35–8
  French flourless chocolate sponge, 21–2, 36–7
  Mr & Mrs, 15–18
French flourless chocolate sponge, 21–2, 36–7
frostings
  Cake for joy, 217–18
  crème fraîche frosting (Layers of memories), 191
  quince frosting (Our friendship cake), 203
  Truth-seeker, 98
Full butter sourdough puff, 248–51

G

ganache
  chocolate ganache (Enchanted almond tree), 37–8
  ganache (Mr & Mrs), 18
  gianduja ganache (Exploring the landscape of my heart), 133–4
  lemon-scented ganache (Luna), 232
  Mr & Mrs, 18
  orange-scented ganache (The waltzing orange tree), 153
gianduja
  Exploring the landscape of my heart, 131–4
  gianduja ganache, 133–4
ginger
  The fable of the wolves, 57–8
  ginger custard (Ode to John Olsen), 197
  Gingerbread hug, 46–7
  Hansel & Gretel, 49–50
  Ode to John Olsen, 197–8
Gingerbread hug, 46–7
gooseberries
  Flora, 185–6
  gooseberry compote, 186
grapefruit
  Citrus macadamia torte, 126–7
  grapefruit confit (Citrus macadamia torte), 126, 138
  Your song for the sea, 221
grapes
  Mariù, 143
grappa, 179, 260
  Athena, 177–9
  raspberry, grappa & lime jam, 177

H

Hansel & Gretel, 49–50
hazelnuts
  A blessing for the seeds, 87–9
  hazelnut & emmer sable (Autumn quince & amaro tart), 78–9
  hazelnut dacquoise (Exploring the landscape of my heart), 132–3
  hazelnut dacquoise (Mr & Mrs), 15
  hazelnut praline (A blessing for the seeds), 87
  Mr & Mrs, 15–18
hemp seeds
  Your song for the sea, 221
hibiscus
  Little Queenie, 91–3
hōjicha, 260
  Takumi, 149–50
Home, 69–71
honey
  honey custard (Where the orchard meets the meadow), 167–8
  Under the quandong tree, 101–3
  Where the meadow meets the orchard, 166–9
Honeymoon cake, 225–8

J

jam
  tomato & passionfruit jam (Home), 69–70
jelly
  Ballymaloe trifle, 123–5
  Blood orange jelly slices (The waltzing orange tree), 153

K

kumquat
  Lucky, 137–40

L

lavender
  Your song for the sea, 221
Layers of memories, 189–91
lemon delicious pudding (Lucky), 139–40
lemon verbena
  lemon verbena custard, 102
  Under the quandong tree, 101–3
lemons
  lemon curd (Luna), 232
  lemon delicious pudding (Lucky), 139–40
  lemon-scented ganache (Luna), 232
  lemon sponge (Luna), 233
  Luna, 231–4
  Mariù, 143
lime
  Athena, 177–9
  Honeymoon cake, 225–8
  lime cream (Mango extravaganza), 238
  lime curd (Mango extravaganza), 226, 238
  Mango extravaganza, 237–9
  raspberry, grappa & lime jam (Athena), 177

lime, finger
    Cake for joy, 217–18
limoncello
    Luna, 231–4
Little Queenie, 91–3
Love cake, 171–4
Lucky, 137–40
Luna, 231–4

M

macadamia
    Citrus macadamia torte, 126–7
    Lucky, 137–40
    macadamia praline (Layers of memories), 190
    macadamia praline paste (Truth-seeker), 96
    macadamia rocher (Lucky), 139
    Truth-seeker, 95–8
malt
    Workaday malt loaf, 25
mandarin
    My Christmas pudding, 52–3
Mango extravaganza, 237–9
maple syrup
    Cake for Jane & Jeremy Strode, 41–2
Mariù, 143
marmalade
    yuzu marmalade (Truth-seeker), 95
mascarpone
    Athena, 177–9
    First date tiramisu, 21–2
    Luna, 231–4
    mascarpone cream heart (Athena), 178
    mascarpone custard (First date tiramisu), 22
    mascarpone filling (Little Queenie), 92
medlars, 119
    Apple & medlar Charlotte, 117–19
    medlar purée, 118
meringue
    butter cake with meringue (Motherhood), 83
    coconut meringue (Mango extravaganza), 239
    Where the meadow meets the orchard, 166–9
mille feuille
    Between a thousand leaves of delight, 193–4
    mille-feuille layers, 193–4
mint
    Little Queenie, 91–3
Motherhood, 82–4
mousse
    caramel mousse (Layers of memories), 190
    chocolate mousse (Mr & Mrs), 15–16
Mr & Mrs, 15–18
mulberries
    mulberry compote, 206
    Tropézienne, 205–7
My Christmas pudding, 52–3

N

nectarines
    roasted nectarines, 167–8
    Where the meadow meets the orchard, 166–9
nettles, 74
    nettle & basil purée, 73
    Nettle ricotta cake, 73–4

O

oatmeal
    The fable of the wolves, 57–8
Ode to John Olsen, 197–8
orange blossom
    orange-scented ganache (The waltzing orange tree), 153
    The waltzing orange tree, 153–4
oranges, blood
    Blood orange jelly slices, 153
    The waltzing orange tree, 153–4
Our friendship cake, 201–3

P

panna cotta
    Ballymaloe trifle, 123–5
parfaits
    fig leaf olive oil parfait (Rockpools of figs & plums), 242
    Flora, 185–6
passionfruit
    Cake for joy, 217–18
    passionfruit curd (Cake for joy), 217
    passionfruit curd (Layers of memories), 189–90
    tomato & passionfruit jam (Home), 69–70
pastry
    blossom pastry (Sakura), 157
    Cake for Jane & Jeremy Strode, 41–2
    Full butter sourdough puff, 248–51
    rough puff pastry (Rockpools of figs & plums), 243
    Tree of life, 65–6
pastry cream
    Between a thousand leaves of delight, 193
    coffee pastry cream (A blessing for the seeds), 87–8
    Tropézienne, 205
pavlova, 169
    Where the meadow meets the orchard, 166–9
peaches
    Ballymaloe trifle, 123–5
    Nettle ricotta cake, 73
    poached peaches (Ballymaloe trifle), 124
pears
    baked pears (Exploring the landscape of my heart), 132
    Cake for the angels, 181–2
    Exploring the landscape of my heart, 131–4
    poached pears (Cake for the angels), 181
Pedro Ximénez
    My Christmas pudding, 52–3
pepper, pink
    Little Queenie, 91–3
    pepper praline cream (Home), 71
pies
    Rockpools of figs & plums, 241–4
    Tree of life, 65–6
pine nuts
    Chestnut torte, 31–2
    Eve, 113–15
    fennel & pine nut praline (Flora), 186
    pine nut crust (Eve), 113

pineapple
    Honeymoon cake, 225–8
pistachios
    Ode to John Olsen, 197–8
    paste, 261
    pistachio sponge, 198
plums, Davidson
    baked plums (Takumi), 149
    Motherhood, 82–4
    plum compote (Motherhood), 83
    plums & powder, 259
    Rockpools of figs & plums, 241–4
    Takumi, 149–50
puddings
    Eve, 113–15
    My Christmas pudding, 52–3

Q

quandongs, 261
    quandong compote, 101
    Under the quandong tree, 101–3
quince
    Autumn quince & amaro tart, 77–80
    Our friendship cake, 201–3
    Poached quince (Autumn quince & amaro tart), 78
    quince frosting (Our friendship cake), 203

R

raisins
    Workaday malt loaf, 25
raspberries
    Athena, 177–9
    raspberry, grappa & lime jam, 177
rhubarb
    baked rhubarb (The fable of the wolves), 57–8
    baked rhubarb (Ode to John Olsen), 197
    Ode to John Olsen, 197–8
    The fable of the wolves, 57–8
rice
    Eve, 113–15
    tonka bean rice pudding (Eve), 115
ricotta
    Nettle ricotta cake, 73
    ricotta cake (Citrus macadamia torte), 126–7
    whipped ricotta (Exploring the landscape of my heart), 133
Rockpools of figs & plums, 241–4
rose
    Love cake, 171–4
    sugared rose petals (Our friendship cake), 201
    Your song for the sea, 221
rose geranium
    Ballymaloe trifle, 123–5
rosella wheat flour, 260
    Tree of life, 65–6
rosemary
    Mariù, 143
rye
    Cake for Jane & Jeremy Strode, 41–2

S

sage
  Cake for the angels, 181–2
Sakura, 157–9
Savarin, 145–7
sea salt
  Siren, 213–14
Siren, 213–14
sourdough
  Full butter sourdough puff, 248–51
  Sourdough starter, 254–5
speculaas
  Honeymoon cake, 225–8
  speculaas sponge, 227
sponges
  A blessing for the seeds, 88–9
  Ballymaloe trifle, 123–5
  buttermilk sponge (Little Queenie), 91–2
  coconut sponge (Cake for joy), 217–18
  French flourless chocolate sponge (Enchanted almond tree), 36–7
  French flourless chocolate sponge (First date tiramisu), 21–2
  how to shimmy with sponge, 256
  lemon sponge (Luna), 233
  Love crumble, 172–3
  pistachio sponge (Ode to John Olsen), 198
  speculaas sponge (Honeymoon cake), 227
  Takumi, 149–50
  Under the quandong tree, 102–3
strawberries
  Between a thousand leaves of delight, 193–4
  Home, 69–71
  Little Queenie, 91–3
  Motherhood, 82–4
  strawberry compote (Little Queenie), 92
stinging nettles, 261
  Nettle ricotta cake, 73–4
sunflower seeds
  sunflower seed crust (Home), 70–1

T

Takumi, 149–50
tangerine
  Lucky, 137–40
tarts
  Agrarian apricots, 109–10
  Autumn quince & amaro tart, 77–80
  Home, 69–71
techniques
  how to shimmy with sponge, 256
  Full butter sourdough puff, 248–51
  Sourdough starter, 254–5
thyme
  Agrarian apricots, 109–10
  thyme custard filling (Agrarian apricots), 110
tiramisu
  First date tiramisu, 21–2
toffee, 147
  Savarin, 145–7
tomatoes
  Home, 69–71
  tomato & passionfruit jam, 69–70
tonka bean, 261
  Eve, 113–15
  Love cake, 171–4
  tonka bean custard (Love cake), 172
  tonka bean rice pudding (Eve), 115
tortes
  Chestnut torte, 31–2
  Citrus macadamia torte, 126–7
treacle
  Workaday malt loaf, 25
Tree of life, 65–6
trifle
  Ballymaloe trifle, 123–5
Tropézienne, 205–7
Truth-seeker, 95–8
tutti frutti curd (Lucky), 138

V

vanilla
  Between a thousand leaves of delight, 193–4
  infusion, 261
  vanilla cream (Between a thousand leaves of delight), 194
  vanilla sugar (Where the orchard meets the meadow), 167, 261
vegan cake
  Cake for our wilderness, 27–8
verbena
  Your song for the sea, 221

W

walnuts
  Cake for Jane & Jeremy Strode, 41–2
The waltzing orange tree, 153–4
wattleseeds
  A blessing for the seeds, 87–9
Where the meadow meets the orchard, 166–9
whisky, Japanese
  Sakura, 157–9
  whisky custard filling (Sakura), 157–8
white chocolate
  Flora, 185–6
  lemon-scented ganache (Luna), 232
Workaday malt loaf, 25

Y

Yorkshire parkin (The fable of the wolves), 57–8
Your song for the sea, 221
Yuzu, 262
  Truth-seeker, 95–8
  yuzu marmalade, 95

Z

zabaglione (Motherhood), 83–4

ACKNOWLEDGEMENTS

Thank you, Julie Gibbs, for your encouragement and brilliance in selecting the best production team I could wish for to make *Love Crumbs*. Dan Ruffino and Simon & Schuster for giving me another opportunity to express myself through a book.

Evi O and Katherine Zhang for the feat of weaving all these layers together through your gorgeous design; Katrina O'Brien for your sensitivity in finessing my poetry during the challenging phases; Lara Picone for your acute attention to detail while editing to preserve the emotive way in which I like to write. Samantha Denmark, your illustrations give my narratives so much strength and transport me to the places where these cakes were born. Alan Benson, for shining light into all the dark places with your humour and kindness. Emma Knowles, for your inimitable styling that brings the soul to the photographs.

Annie Smithers your foreword is a gift, a perfect prelude to *Love Crumbs* and our reassurance to the reader of humankind's devotion to one another. Thank you.

Saskia Havekes for your intuitive sourcing of botanicals to articulate my narratives. Palisa Anderson for sharing a window into your world by opening up your garden and personally taking the time to cut clippings for me. Tania, Matt and Boris from Southern Wild Co for the cherry and plum branches, but more for the arduous task of keeping them attached to the branches during transit. Mark at Cedar Creek Orchard for driving me out to your orchard in your truck (secateurs in hand) to select the best peach and nectarine branches.

Kimberley Cruz for creating the gorgeous ceramics that would inspire unique shapes and forms in my baking and for cheering me on to push myself during the process. Jasmine Lethbridge for making me look and feel beautiful for my portrait with your hair wizardry. Margaret for giving me the confidence to challenge my doubting heart.

There is a band of poets whom I have stood on the shoulders of while writing this book. David Whyte, John O'Donohue, John Olsen (words and colour) and Eileen Chong, who held my hand while I searched for the right words to describe the nature of cake.

Team Flour and Stone for your unwavering support during the making and writing of *Love Crumbs*.

During the hardest parts of making this book, when I questioned if I could write even another word, you, my friends, were there with a listening ear and always with wisdom. I am eternally grateful for the love you bring to my life: Vicki Forbes, Silvia Forestieri, Cath Derksema, Amanda Webb, Anna Chipperfield, Michelle Crawford, Jane Grover, Sam Mackie, Amanda and Dave Teer.

Thank you, Jonathan (my long-suffering husband), for running around and calling all over Sydney and beyond to find the 'weird' ingredients. I couldn't have made this book without you. To my daughters, Poppy and Ruby, for inspiring me every day!

Love Crumbs
First published in Australia in 2024

A JULIE GIBBS BOOK

for

Simon & Schuster (Australia) Pty Limited
Suite 19A, Level 1, Building C, 450 Miller Street,
Cammeray, NSW 2062

10 9 8 7 6 5 4 3 2 1

Simon & Schuster: Celebrating 100 Years of Publishing in 2024
Sydney New York London Toronto New Delhi
Visit our website at www.simonandschuster.com.au

Text copyright © Nadine Ingram 2024
Photography copyright © Alan Benson 2024

All rights reserved. No part of this publication
may be reproduced, stored in a retrieval system,
or transmitted in any form or by any means, electronic,
mechanical, photocopying, recording or otherwise,
without prior permission of the publisher.

 A catalogue record for this book is available from the National Library of Australia

ISBN: 9781761422041

Publisher: Julie Gibbs
Design: Evi O Studio | Evi O, Katherine Zhang
Photographer: Alan Benson
Stylist: Emma Knowles
Illustration: Samantha Denmark
Project editor: Katrina O'Brien
Editor: Lara Picone
Printed and bound in China by RR Donnelley

The paper this book is printed on is certified against
the Forest Stewardship Council® Standards. RR Donnelley
(Guangdong) Printing Solutions Company Limited holds
chain of custody certification NC-COC-032126. FSC®
promotes environmentally responsible, socially beneficial and
economically viable management of the world's forests.